PERSPECTIVES IN SOCIOLOGY

PERSPECTIVES IN SOCIOLOGY

Herman R. Lantz, GENERAL EDITOR

ON THE

PENITENTIARY SYSTEM

IN THE UNITED STATES

AND ITS APPLICATION

IN FRANCE

Gustave de Beaumont & Alexis de Tocqueville

Introduction by THORSTEN SELLIN

Foreword by HERMAN R. LANTZ

SOUTHERN ILLINOIS UNIVERSITY PRESS

Carbondale and Edwardsville

TO WALTER C. RECKLESS

for his contribution to our understanding

of crime, delinquency and corrections

FOREWORD

THE PRESENT VOLUME is the first publication of the series "Perspectives in Sociology." The purpose of these works is to add depth to the understanding of human society. They are designed to bring together the richness from bordering disciplines in order to shed light on the social confrontations of man, in both time and space.

The work on the *Penitentiary System* is illustrative of our efforts in this series. It deals with the universal theme of the order and stability of human organization; and the efforts to deal with the inevitable problems of deviance which arise.

Although many of Tocqueville's writings have captured the imagination of scholars, much less interest has been aroused by the present work. In part, this may stem from the fact that the work on the *Penitentiary System* was shared with Beaumont. Indeed the writing, as Professor Sellin points out in his introduction, belongs largely to Beaumont. One would think that this alone would be sufficient to stir the imagination of Tocqueville scholars intrigued by the possibilities of reopening the question of Beaumont's contribution to other Tocqueville writings. Perhaps another reason for the lack of interest on the part of Tocqueville scholars stems from their historical literary and philosophical interests. As such, they have been less concerned with matters of a penitentiary system; considered by some only a technical report, and therefore less likely to be informative about Tocqueville as humanist or historian.

The present volume is significant, however, for several rea-

sons. It tells us much about Beaumont and Tocqueville since
the writing reveals those facets of social history and sociology to which the authors were sensitive. To describe an
agency of social control, in this instance the penitentiary
system, without revealing one's views about the broader fabric of social organization, and its main occupant — man
himself, would be impossible. The discerning reader will undoubtedly note the insightful observations on human nature,
as well as the political, social and economic variables which
influence social policy.

Moreover, the social views in the present volume have to
be seen at least in part as the products of the authors' aristocratic backgrounds, backgrounds implicated for several
centuries in the inequalities of a social system. Although the
questions that such liberals raised about matters of social
injustice were lodged primarily against the system that provided for their being, they felt no assurance that a new social
order would not produce its own excesses and abuses. Thus,
although the French Revolution was conceived in anticipation that the more constructive dimensions of man so long
repressed would flourish, the experiences of the Revolution
itself and the aftermath presented an image of man with unbridled passions and capacities for destructiveness. It is not,
therefore, surprising to learn in the present work that while
Beaumont and Tocqueville looked upon the prisoner as a
redeemable being, their basic attitude is one of marked res-
ervation about how much redemption is possible. There is
much to suggest that in many ways they were pessimistic
about reform. Although criminal behavior for the authors
is primarily the result of indolence and idleness, they see no
simple reformation of the criminal.

The present volume is significant for still another reason.
The sociological observations of the authors were extremely
astute and contemporary. Their remarks about the com-
plexity of measuring the results of remedial efforts, such as
a penitentiary system on the incidence of crime, dealing
with idleness in prisons, coping with the negative effects of
interaction between prisoners, and the problem associated
with mixing delinquents and hardened criminals, are much

with us today. The concern for all these problems can be found in any modern textbook on criminology. As such, the present volume reveals the range of the authors' perceptions and is at the same time some indication of the progress still to be made in these areas.

The sociological insights of the authors, however, have profound implications for human relationships quite apart from the penitentiary system. They were able to observe and report the effects of extreme social isolation on mind and body. In this sense, their efforts predate the findings of social psychological research in the area of social isolation and schizophrenia that appear about one hundred years later.

Beaumont and Tocqueville were also much aware of the significance of the mores of behavior long before the writings of William Graham Sumner although they did not identify the customs, practices and habits as such.

One can not help read this work without gaining some further appreciation of our indebtedness to the great minds of the past that were able to transcend the limitations of their own age and provide us with crucial insights about the nature of social organization. It is perhaps regrettable that we have been unable to profit more from their observations.

Francis Lieber, the translator of the present work, was a German liberal who was at odds with the prevailing political climate of the day. He was discouraged from studying in his own country, and traveled throughout Europe in the service of liberal causes. He came to America in 1827, lectured on history and politics, and was a scholar of wide ranging interests. He is perhaps best known for his several volumes of the "Encyclopedia Americana," and for his writings in political science.

Lieber's interest in the penitentiary system was part of his general concern for social reform, as well as the result of the first-hand experiences with the problems of prison life which he had encountered in Europe as a political prisoner. Moreover, he was widely read in the field of corrections and had been in contact with significant people in this field. Frank Freidel, in his work *Francis Lieber* (Baton Rouge: Louisiana State University Press, 1947) points out that when Lieber undertook the task of translating *On the Penitentiary System,* he was no longer willing to accept the role of translator. Instead, he became an editor, critic and commentator; this accentuated by his very special interest in the Pennsylvania penitentiary system. Thus Lieber argued considerably, through the use of copious footnotes, with the basic Beaumont-Tocqueville report. Although, in a sense interesting, these notes have been omitted from the present text because they are often digressive and not necessarily of central consideration.

Also deleted from the Lieber translation are the following sections from the Appendix: "On Penal Colonies"; "On Agricultural Colonies"; "Public Instruction in the United States"; "Pauperism in America"; "Imprisonment for Debt"; "Imprisonment of Witnesses"; "Temperance Societies"; "Inquiry Concerning the Penitentiary near Philadelphia"; "Letter of Mr. Barrett"; "Conversation with the Superintendent of Philadelphia House of Refuge"; "House of Reformation, South Boston"; "Some Statistical Notes on the States of New York, Maryland and Pennsylvania"; "Statistical and Comparative Observations on New York and Massachusetts"; "Some Comparisons between France and America"; "Finances"; "The Penitentiary System of Pennsylvania." These sections were omitted because they are of questionable relevance today; however relevant they may have been in the past. For persons interested, the original sources may still be obtained. The Pierson volume on Tocquevile and Beaumont in America is invaluable as a basic source for an initial search.

In addition to those changes mentioned above, spelling and punctuation, where it differed noticeably from presently accepted form, has been modernized. Sections of chapters which were distinctly separate from each other but which bore no distinguishing identification were given descriptive headings.

In all cases the changes were minor and the text allowed to remain in the words of the Lieber translation.

The editor wishes to express his deep appreciation to Dr. Ben Frank, Center for the Study of Crime, Delinquency and

Corrections at Southern Illinois University, for invaluable
suggestions regarding the wisdom of selecting the present
work as the first title in this series and for his time with numerous editorial tasks. The editor expresses his deep appreciation to Dr. John Anderson and the Research and Proj-
ects Committee of the Graduate School of Southern Illinois
University for their encouragement, wise counsel, and support of the series, "Perspectives in Sociology." Finally the
editor appreciates greatly the contribution of an index from
his wife, Judy.

The text has been introduced by Professor Thorsten Sellin, Professor of Sociology at the University of Pennsylvania, a specialist in the history of crime and penology, and
author of numerous works in the field. Professor Sellin has
taken as his task the presentation of the socio-historic back-
ground from which the Beaumont and Tocqueville report
may best be understood, the experiences of Beaumont and
Tocqueville in America, and the impact of their report on
the French prison system. His presentation is clear, concise,
and informative. It places the work in proper perspective
and adds enrichment for the reader.

Herman R. Lantz

Southern Illinois University
February, 1964

CONTENTS

TOCQUEVILLE AND BEAUMONT

AND PRISON REFORM

IN FRANCE

EARLY IN MAY, 1831, two young Frenchmen arrived in the United States. Alexis de Tocqueville was twenty-six and Gustave de Beaumont twenty-nine years old. Ostensibly they came — at their own expense — to study prison systems; they had requested a commission for that purpose from de Montalivet, Minister of Interior. But, their interest in prisons was peripheral. The mission would allow them to pursue a plan much closer to their hearts, namely a study on the spot of the social and political institutions of the young republic. Both were scions of old aristocratic families. Their friendship had begun several years earlier, when Tocqueville held an inferior judicial post at Versailles, where his father was prefect, and Beaumont was a substitute in the procurator's office of the King's Bench in Paris. They had together studied history, government and philosophy and had attended lectures at the Sorbonne, where after several years of suspension liberal savants like Guizot, Villemain and Cousin had been allowed to resume their teaching in 1828.

They had prepared for the voyage by a study of the available literature about America. Especially since the Revolution, which had driven many French aristocrats and other political dissenters into a more or less temporary exile, writings about American life and manners had multiplied.[1] Most of their authors had found much to admire in American institutions. Many of them had achieved high and influential positions upon their return to France, maintained contacts with friends in the United States, and offered hospitality to visiting Americans. Beaumont and Tocqueville had often shared that hospitality. Then there was La Fayette, whose love for the United States never wavered and whose home was a center of Franco-American cultural relations. Young Beaumont was a frequent visitor there. He was related to the family and later, in 1836, married a daughter of George Washington La Fayette, son of the Marquis. Through Beaumont Tocqueville was introduced into this circle. The effect of such personal relations was to heighten their interest in American affairs.

The offer to study American penitentiaries would probably not have been accepted had not such an inquiry appeared useful to the French government, which had just been urged by the Chamber of Deputies to hasten the reform of prisons. Even though most of the ten months the two travelers spent in the United States were devoted to other matters, they faithfully carried out their prison investigations. Several weeks in New York were spent in studying the House of Refuge for juvenile offenders, the penitentiary on Blackwell's Island, and the Bridewell of New York City, and lengthy visits were made to the penitentiaries of Sing Sing and Auburn. In Philadelphia, the Eastern Penitentiary was subjected to an equally detailed scrutiny; Tocqueville, for instance, speaking with every prisoner privately and making a record of these interviews. The Walnut Street prison and the House of Refuge were visited. The Connecticut state prison at Wethersfield, the House of Refuge and the state prison in Boston, and penal institutions in Baltimore and elsewhere were seen. Numerous documents in the form of official reports, pamphlets, etc. were collected for future reference. However, Tocqueville's notebooks, in which he recorded his experiences in America [2] contain little about prisons: a few pages about his interview with Elam Lynds, former warden of Sing Sing, in his hardware shop at Syracuse, New York; some pages on the labor program at Auburn prison; a brief note on a talk with Dr. Vaughan and Judge Coxe in Philadelphia about the Walnut Street prison; a brief memorandum of a page on that institution, the Philadelphia House of Refuge, and the Baltimore and Pittsburgh prisons; a few lines on the Louisiana prison system; and a page or two of observations on Sing Sing. His conversation with Roberts Vaux, the Pennsylvania prison reformer, appears to have dealt with political and economic affairs, and when he met Francis Lieber, who was to become the translator of the report the commissioners made on their return to France, prisons were apparently not mentioned. The notebooks are mostly filled with observations on political, social and economic matters that were later to furnish data for Tocqueville's great work on *Democracy in America*.

They were indefatigable travelers. The United States was crossed from Canada to Louisiana and from the East Coast to the midwestern frontier. Everywhere they were received with hospitality and given every assistance in their work, aided no doubt by the more than seventy letters of introduction from French dignitaries to correspondents and friends in the United States. Their official mission had been well-publicized in newspapers before they even arrived in New York, where they were lionized, much to their surprise and delight, considering their very subordinate status in the French bureaucracy. When they returned to France, in May of 1832, they had become ardent admirers of American institutions, by and large, and convinced that the American penitentiary system should be imitated in France.

Perhaps it was Tocqueville's preoccupation with his main concern — the structure and operation of democratic institutions in America — that filled his mind, for he found himself somehow unable to settle down to the composition of the report. According to Pierson:

> . . . he fell into a kind of stupor, a kind of mental numbness. He could neither work nor write. What Beaumont called the "steam engine" of his intelligence ran no longer . . . . Tocqueville . . . sat for weeks in front of some white sheets of paper and finally he left the entire task to his faithful companion and friend. In fact, his contribution was limited to a statistical appendix and to notes.[3]

The report was published in 1833 in Paris and the same year in Philadelphia, in Lieber's translation dedicated to Edward Livingston, Roberts Vaux and C. A. J. Mittermaier. [4]

Since Beaumont was Tocqueville's inseparable companion they shared, of course, their prison experiences in America. Beaumont, however, was not so much concerned with political and economic affairs as he was interested in American mores. This is evident from the only strictly personal writing which grew out of his trip — a novel [5] on slavery and race prejudice and especially on the plight of the mulatto in the United States. This work was issued in 1835, the same year that Tocqueville published the first two volumes of his *Democracy in America*. It was a social document of importance; half of the book consisted of appendices and notes elucidating incidents, references, or terms found in the novel. Its popularity was considerable and it ran to five editions. Rémond suggests that it may have been more read and commented upon than was Tocqueville's great work and that it must have had considerable influence judging from the number of allusions and references to it.[6]

Beaumont and Tocqueville were not the first foreigners to show an interest in the reforms made in the treatment of offenders in the United States since the American Revolution. Many had commented on them and some had actually visited prisons, but only incidentally as travelers do when they wish to see different aspects of life in a strange country. The two commissioners were the first of many official foreign delegations specifically appointed to investigate our penitentiaries. Consequently, their report has special significance. To analyze its findings and present the conclusions of its authors would seem superfluous, however, for they are fully displayed to the reader of this book. More profit might be gained from a look at attempts at prison reform in France since the Revolution of 1789 that made a personal study of the American penitentiary system seem desirable, and from a glance at what happened to the penal policy of France after the publication of the report on the American penitentiary system. In the formulation of that policy our two authors were to play an important role.

The Setting of Prison Reform

LEGAL EXPERTS in pre-revolutionary France claimed that imprisonment was not used there as punishment for crime but only for detention prior to trial or the execution of sentences. What they meant was, no doubt, that punishments which could be imposed by courts did not include imprisonment. Judges did impose sentences to hard labor in the galleys at the navy yards of Rochefort, Brest and Toulon, and this involved, of course, deprivation of liberty, incidental to the real penalty, for long terms of years and even for life. When women or children were sentenced to hard labor, the sentences were commuted to imprisonment. Wayward children were sometimes committed to prison at the request of parents or guardians, and some insane persons and beggars also found asylum there. The prisons were uniformly considered to be merely places of safekeeping, that might serve a deterrent purpose but had no concern for the rehabilitation or reformation of those confined. Indeed, capital and corporal punishments of a variety of kinds, publicly executed, were the common consequences of crime. Finally, imprisonment at the pleasure of the King, could be inflicted by executive *lettre de cachet;* the Bastille and the dungeons of Vincennes were common receptacles for persons who thus suffered Royal displeasure. Some of the prominent leaders of the Revolution experienced this fate, one of them being Mirabeau, who composed a famous tract on the subject.

Demands for reform of the law of crime and punishment were made effective by the Revolution. The groundwork had been laid by legal and political philosophers and publicists. Montesquieu had satirized French justice in his *Persian Letters*. Rousseau's *Social Contract* had challenged autocratic kingship, Voltaire had been a vigorous spokesman for reform, and the Encyclopedists generally had supported him. A tremendous influence was added by the publication in 1764 of the essay *On Crimes and Punishment* by the young Milanese Marquis of Beccaria — he was 26 years old — whose ideas were almost literally translated into the first penal code of France in 1791.

There were other foreign influences at work too, and they were to be reflected in various ways in the French reform movement. John Howard, for instance, had begun his great efforts to reform English prisons a couple of decades before the French Revolution. He had made three journeys to France before that event took place. His *State of Prisons* had not only undergone three revisions, but he had successfully, with William Blackstone and William Eden, secured the passage in 1779 of a bill establishing "penitentiaries" to replace the transportation system and provide for the housing of prisoners in individual cells at night and for employing them in labor of "the most servile and hard kind" under supervision that would prevent them fom communicating with one another. His book had been translated into French in 1788. Even though the realization of this plan in England was to be delayed for a long time, its features were not unknown to the revolutionary leaders concerned with penal reform. Furthermore, Howard had described penal or correctional institutions outside of England which had excited his admiration, such as the house of correction for boys in St. Michael's hospice in Rome, the Ghent house of correction organized by Count Vilain XIIII, and similiar institutions in various countries that he had visited on his foreign inspection trips. The germs of the "penitentiary system," both as to policies and architectural design were present in some of these establishments. Therefore, both a new philosophy of punishment and practical examples of its realization were at hand to spur the reforms of the revolutionary leaders after the fall of the Bastille.

The Constituent Assembly Acts

IN November, 1789, the Constituent Assembly selected a committee to make a report on the *lettres de cachet*. Mirabeau was appointed one of the rapporteurs for the committee, with the specific task of dealing with prisons, and his report was ready in the early part of 1790.[7] He deliberately excluded from consideration the "great criminals," who were entitled, he said, only to fresh air and healthful nourishment; the accused, who should be considered innocent until proven guilty and therefore should be treated with consideration; the debtors, who should not be subjected to imprisonment, and military prisoners. Only the loss of liberty should be imposed on these classes of persons. This left "ordinary crimes" and "ordinary prisons" for discussion.

These prisons, he said, should aim at something that almost all laws have neglected, namely the reformation of the offender.

One must hope to tame the most intractable character and the most ferocious minds by solitary confinement and continuous labor. It is necessary to establish asylums that defend the law by punishments proportioned to the crimes . . . , houses where time for repentance may follow upon the original mistakes, where a compulsory but always salutary meditation focuses thought on the cost of viciousness; houses where the guilty are not a charge on the society from which they are segregated and where they can support themselves by useful work; houses where there are graduated tests and the culprits pass from an habitual state of suffering to a supportable privation, from the horror of the solitary cell to reasonable labor, from shame to humiliation, arriving thus by stages to freedom, the reward for real repentance and a sincere change. To ensure this regeneration . . . we need a special kind of prison, for which humanity need not blush.[8]

He deplored the fact that existing French prisons were in such
a state that, in Europe, Turkey alone might profit from studying
them, since they lagged far behind the institutions of England,
Spain, Portugal, Italy, Switzerland, Denmark, Germany and
Holland.[9]

The remedy? There should be betterment houses (*maisons
d'amélioration*) one in each of the 83 *départements,* located at
at a riverside (Howard's suggestion) and not in city centers.
Each prisoner should have a cell, 10 by 8 feet and 9 feet high,
with a barred window at a height of 6 feet. There should be
12 to 15 acres of land, enclosed by a high wall, where certain
prisoners could work. There should be separate quarters for
males and females, each with its own workshops, infirmary,
cells, chapel, yards, gardens, and living quarters for the staff,
yet under one management. Warehouses, kitchen and a cemetery would be shared. No establishment should contain more
than 600 prisoners, 450 males and 150 females. The prisoner
should receive a pound and a half of bread daily and a weekly
ration of 3 pounds of meat and 3 of vegetables. Cells should
be furnished with an iron bedstead, two hempen sheets and
two woolen blankets and be darkened at 9 P.M. A surgeon,
an apothecary and two nurses would take care of sick prisoners
in the infirmary, and if a woman prisoner needed the help of
a midwife one should be available. A chaplain would visit inmates. Upon discharge, a prisoner should be given decent clothing and enough money to live on for a month, and attempts
should be made to find employers to give him work.

The management of each institution should be in the hands of
a board of three members, appointed by the assembly of the *département* for three years and not re-eligible. The board should
appoint a secretary to keep its records; it should appoint the
staff, purchase needed supplies, make regulations for the institution, and watch that these rules were obeyed and that prisoners
were not promoted to a higher class until they had proved themselves. The staff of each house should consist of a governor, two
chaplains, a doctor, an apothecary, a steward, and a work super-

intendent. Except for the first year their salaries and those of other employees should be paid from the profits of the house, because each house should be a factory. Prisoners should be engaged in maintenance work or turn mills, cut stone, polish marble, beat hemp, shred tobacco, rasp wood, cut straw, make ropes, or work the land; women would sew sacks, spin, make rugs, and make shirts and gaiters for the troops. Prisoners having no trade should be taught one. Some prisoners should be assigned to public works — repair roads, service docks, transport fuel, earth or stone, and when so doing they should wear some distinctive marking. Work should not exceed eight hours daily in winter and ten in summer, and accounts of the revenue from work should be faithfully kept.

Whether Mirabeau's report had any effect on those appointed in 1789 to produce a new penal code is difficult to say. He may well have expressed ideas that were in the minds of many members of the Assembly. In any case, in May, 1791, the Assembly's committees on the Constitution and on Criminal Legislation jointly presented their project of a penal code, Lepelletier de Saint-Fargeau acting as rapporteur. In public session he characterized the penal system of the day as something inherited from past ages.

> . . . innocent acts or minor faults blown up into serious crimes; the suspicion of crime often punished as severely as crime itself; atrocious tortures invented during barbarous times and conserved in times of enlightenment; no proportionality between crimes and their punishments; the wicked man driven by the law itself to extreme deeds, because even at his first offense he faces the supreme penalty; in other words, incoherent, unsystematic, inharmonious dispositions formulated at different epochs and mostly in view of momentary events, never assembled into a body of law but scattered in voluminous compilations and at times forgotten and at other times reactivated, and whose ferocious absurdity finds no remedy but in still another abuse — arbitrary interpretation and modification by judges.[10]

The penal code, said Lepelletier, should be different.

> Punishments should be humane, justly scaled, exactly
> proportionate to the nature of the offense, equal for all
> citizens, free from all judicial arbitrariness; they should
> not be diluted after sentence by the methods of their exe-
> cution; they should be repressive principally by imprison-
> ment and prolonged privations, by their publicity and
> their proximity to the place where the crime was commit-
> ted; they should correct the moral sentiments of the con-
> vict by habituation to labor; they should decrease in se-
> verity as they approach the end of the term fixed for their
> duration; and, finally, they should be temporary.[11]

The death penalty attached to 115 offenses, should be abolished, except for the leader of armed rebellion against the constituted authority. Beccaria's views were reflected in this as in the
other principles advocated by the committees. Lepelletier realized
that the Assembly might not wish to adopt such a radical view;
in that case, however, capital punishment should at least be re-
stricted to murder, arson and treason and, as in England, made
expeditious, i.e., deprive the offender of his life without torturing
accompaniments.

What, then, should be the dominant form of punishment?
Imprisonment. And, since all punishments should be temporary,
none should be sentenced for life. Each *département* should have
a "penal house" (*maison de peine*). Before sending a convict
there on sentence, he should be exposed to view in a public place,
attached to a post and fettered, a placard above his head giving
his name, crime and sentence. The length of his sentence and
the conditions governing it would depend on his offense, but it
was to be unalterably fixed in length by statute and not to be
changed by the Court or by an exercise of pardon.

The most serious form of imprisonment proposed was the
dungeon (*cachot*) reserved for murderers, arsonists and traitors.
It would be imposed for a term not less than twelve and not
more than twenty-four years. Next in severity was the *gêne,*
from four to fifteen years, and finally the *prison,* from two to

six years. A sentence to *cachot* was to be served in solitary confinement in a dark cell during two-thirds of the term. The re-
mainder would be served under conditions governing the *gêne*
and the *prison,* equally divided between the two and thus introducing a progressive amelioration of the penalty. During the
first third of his term, the prisoner would be allowed to work
two days and during the second third three days weekly, in solitude but in a light cell within the institution and free of fetters,
which otherwise had to be worn. A third of his income from
work would be retained by the institution and a part of the re-
mainder kept for him until his discharge. The rest he could use
to procure food beyond the bread and water diet which was to
be his daily fare. One day a month, the door of his cell would
be open and the public admitted to watch him in presence of the
jailer; his name, crime and sentence would be displayed on a
sign above his cell door. Female prisoners were not to wear fetters of any kind, but were otherwise to receive the same treatment.

The *gêne* was to be served in a light cell and without hand
and foot fetters. The prisoner would be allowed to work every
day in his cell, except two days a week when he was to work
with other prisoners on some common task but in complete silence. After work in common during one of these days weekly
he was to be allowed visitors in his cell in the presence of a
guard. As in the *cachot,* his bedding was straw; his income was
disposed of in the manner previously mentioned and he was subject to the monthly day of public viewing. After one year of
gêne he was promoted to the *prison* type of confinement.

The *prison* meant being housed in separate cells at night and
working with other prisoners in the daytime, men and women
being separated. Beds were to replace the straw. The basic diet,
the division of wages, the public viewing remained the same, as
did the rule governing visits.

The "penal house," which was to have three completely separate sections for the three types of prisoners mentioned, was to
be managed by the municipality where it was located, and re-

sponsibility for furnishing labor to the prisoners was to rest on the management. No prisoner would be allowed to receive gifts or funds from outside; this practice had resulted in much abuse at the galley prisons.

The proposed code also provided for a reduction of punishments for those under sixteen or over sixty years of age, decreed deportation for second offenders convicted of a crime punishable by any of the three types of imprisonment, and made it possible for a prisoner who had lived a blameless life for ten years after his prison term to be legally rehabilitated, i.e., have the legal consequences of his imprisonment cancelled.

Lepelletier's report was discussed at length by the Assembly and at his request, the question of capital punishment was placed first on the agenda. It provoked what is probably the first full-scale parliamentary debate on that issue in Europe, lasting four days. The code finally adopted retained the death penalty for murder, arson and treason. For crimes dealt with by trial courts, imprisonment of different types was decreed: irons (*fers*), reclusion, *gêne,* and *détention*. Males sentenced to "irons" were to have a chain with an iron ball attached to their legs, and be confined at hard labor for the profit of the State in security prisons (*maisons de force*), ports or arsenals, or at other public works. For female convicts, there was instead reclusion in a prison at hard labor, without fetters. For less serious crimes there was the *gêne*. The prisoner sentenced to this form of punishment was to serve his fixed term in a light cell, without fetters or bonds, and would not be allowed any communication with other prisoners or with people from outside. He would have to work but he could select his work. A third of his wage income would help to defray the costs of his maintenance; a part of the rest was to be held for his discharge and the balance he could use to buy supplementary food rations. *Détention* was chiefly for political prisoners and somewhat less harsh, since they could work in common or separately as they chose, cellular isolation being used only for disciplinary ends. Deportation was decreed for recidivists.

In the *gêne* we thus find solitary confinement with labor in-stituted by law in France. Jeremy Bentham promptly offered the plan for his "panopticon" to the Assembly and even offered to supervise its construction and management; he was duly thanked and made an honorary citizen. The times were not pro-pitious for reform, however. Institutions designed to house those sentenced to this punishment or to *détention* were never set up. Soon the Terror was to engulf the nation and the miseries brought by internal struggles and external wars occupied minds and drained public funds. In spite of the penal code, prisons remained, with minor improvements, much as they had been: re-pressive, congregate, places for safe keeping where reformation of the inmate was neither possible nor given much thought. The stimulus to reform was ultimately to come from the experiences of the New World and the first to convey it was a great nobleman.

La Rochefoucauld-Liancourt, Prison Reformer

FRANÇOIS, DUC DE LA ROCHEFOUCAULD-LIANCOURT had played an important role during the early period of the Revolution. His noble birth and his friendship with Louis XVI had not prevented him from embracing liberal ideas. He had a profound interest in social reform and was chairman of the Constituent Assem-bly's committee on mendicity, which tried to establish a system of public relief for all dependent classes. In the Assembly, of which he was elected president for a brief period immediately after the fall of the Bastille, he participated in the debate on the penal code, holding that one must pursue "the rehabilitation and the reintegration of convicted offenders." [12] In the autumn of 1792 he had to flee for his life to England, where he remained more than a year, during which he had contacts with Bentham among others and was the house guest of Horace Walpole. In 1794 he came to the United States and spent four years, mostly in extensive travels, including Canada. Many months were spent in Philadelphia, where he was well received as the friend of both Franklin and La Fayette, and enjoyed the company of Jefferson and his own countryman Talleyrand, also a refugee until called back to France in 1796. And it was in Philadelphia that he visited the Walnut Street prison and found its regime and its way of dealing with inmates so noteworthy that he wrote a small book about it. The book was issued in both a French and an English edition, in 1796, by another French temporary refugee, Moreau de Saint-Méry, who had a printing shop in the city.[13]

The Walnut Street prison had been constructed in 1776 to serve the county of Philadelphia, but during the Revolutionary War it had been used to house prisoners of war until 1784. The first state constitution of Pennsylvania, adopted in 1776, had urged reform of the criminal law to render it less harsh and make punishments in general more proportionate to crimes. Criminals not sentenced to death should be confined in houses where they would work for the benefit of the public or to indemnify victims, and citizens should be allowed admittance at proper times to watch them at work. The aim was to make deterrence more effective "by continued visible punishment of long duration."

Legislative action was delayed by the war. Conditions in the prison had become notorious, because of bad management and numerous abuses, and an experiment, begun in 1786, of using prisoners to clean the streets and privies of the city had failed. The following year, a group of citizens, many of them Quakers, organized a Society for Alleviating the Miseries of Public Prisons and began a campaign of prison reform, greatly influenced by John Howard's writings. As a result, several laws were enacted in subsequent years. In 1789, public labor was abolished and the criminal courts of the state given permission to commit to the Walnut Street institution prisoners with sentences to hard labor longer than one year.

In 1790 a separate cell house was ordered erected in the yard of the prison ". . . for the purpose of confining therein the more hardened and atrocious offenders . . . who have been sentenced to hard labour for a term of years [in the hope that] the addition of unremitted solitude to laborious employment, as far as it can be effected, will contribute as much to reform as to deter." The 1790 act also provided for the strict separation of the sexes and of different classes of prisoners. Those sentenced to hard labor would, upon their arrival, be temporarily kept in quarantine, washed, cleaned and seen by a physician before allowed to mingle with other prisoners. Convicts were to wear a plain uniform, work at tasks of "the hardest and most servile kind" and "kept separate and apart from each other" at work, if possible. Those with longer sentences than six months were to be charged the cost of their food, clothing, and materials for work; they were to be credited with their work income and separate accounts were to be set up for them. If this account showed a profit when a prisoner was ready for his discharge, half of this was to be given to him or used to buy him decent clothing.

The act of 1794 marked the last step in the reform. This act removed the death penalty for all crimes except murder in the first degree and provided that prisoners who arrived with sentences to hard labor for crimes previously capital were to be ". . . kept in the solitary cells . . . on low and coarse diet, for such part . . . of his or her imprisonment as the court, in their sentence, shall direct and appoint," not less than one twelfth or more than one half of the term imposed. The board of inspectors, created by the act of 1790 to manage the institution, were given the power to permit the prisoner to serve the solitary part of the term in installments and to determine arbitrarily the length of time such solitary confinement might be imposed, if the prisoner was a recidivist sentenced to life or twenty-five years.

The cell house, which came to be called the "penitentiary house" had been finished in 1791. It had sixteen cells; each was 8 × 6 feet and 10 feet high, with a barred and louvered window near the ceiling and a toilet. These cells became the means to effectuate the first use of solitary confinement that marked the primitive phase of what came to be known as the Pennsylvania system of prison discipline.

This was the institution that La Rochefoucauld-Liancourt so greatly admired. He was fortunate in that he saw it in a period when it was enjoying its best years.

> The inspectors were highminded men, the labor program was varied and profitable both to the institution and the prisoners, who, under private contracts with citizens, received wages almost equal to those of free workers. The discipline was good . . . and elementary and religious education was provided.[14]

The report of his visit, also printed in Paris, was the first notice in France of an American system of prison discipline that aimed at the reformation of the prisoner and was not a great burden on the public treasury, a system that, according to its administrators, was a very effective instrument in reducing criminality.

Although La Rochefoucauld-Liancourt returned to Europe late in 1797 his name was not removed from the list of émigrés until 1800, permitting him to return to Paris. In the meanwhile he divided his time between Hamburg, where the organization of public assistance was an object of study, and Amsterdam, where he pursued his study of prison reform. In Paris he devoted himself to various charitable enterprises; for the next quarter of a century there was no important organization in this field which did not count him a member, a director or a founder, but until the fall of the Empire, his deep concern for prison reform apparently gave him little opportunity for action.

Groping for Solutions

THE FAMOUS penal code of 1810 had not evoked the support of liberal thinkers. It was a very severe and repressive code, which paid little attention to the criminal as a human being.

Punishments were to protect society by the fear they engendered. The Restoration of 1814 brought into power a group of men who were aware of the need for improvements in the penal system and who recognized La Rochefoucauld-Liancourt's worth. He promptly wrote to Decazes, Minister of Police: ". . . if you think that I can be useful in the inspection or direction of hospitals or prisons, I am disposed to consecrate my life to this work, which, as you know, has been my life's occupation." [15] Shortly afterwards, Louis XVIII signed an ordinance creating a pilot prison (*prison d'essai*) in Paris for youthful offenders, where the Philadelphia system of treatment was to be applied and later extended to all prisons of the kingdom. Nothing came of it, because in May, 1815, Napoleon returned from Elba, and after the "Hundred Days" the government was more occupied with settling its account with the rebels than with the reform of its prisons. The regulations governing the pilot prison, prepared by La Rochefoucauld-Liancourt, who was to have been its director, were never issued; but they envisaged a regime that would aim at the moral regeneration of the prisoner, by every possible means.[16] Ideally, the prisoners should have individual cells to sleep in, but cellular isolation should only be used as a disciplinary punishment. Six to eight prisoners could be housed together under constant surveillance. Custodians were to treat them with justice and never use insulting language or physical violence toward them. A chaplain would not only minister to their spiritual needs but also teach them to read and write, since education is a powerful way of raising a person's self-esteem. Six inspectors, chosen from among benevolent citizens should, in rotation, visit the prison daily. When the prisoner arrived in the institution, a document giving an account of his offense, family situation, previous residence, etc., should accompany him and be placed in a dossier into which there would be later entries concerning his conduct in the institutions.

The pilot prison was to be a workhouse. Each shop should have up to ten workers and be in charge of a person responsible for tools, materials, and labor. Free craftsmen would teach trades to begin with. The work introduced should not require too long an apprenticeship before becoming productive. It should be of a kind that the prisoner could engage in when released. Preferably, it would be provided under a contract system by which entrepreneurs in the city would furnish materials and the price of the product set. It was hoped that this would result in enough profit above the cost of maintenance charged to the prisoner-worker to leave a sum which could be paid him in part at the time of release and the rest three months later, if his conduct until then had been satisfactory. While serving his sentence, a well-behaved prisoner should also be allowed to use a third of his work income for aiding his family or other close relatives. He would not be able to spend it in a commissary (*cantine*) for none would be permitted in the institution, thus obviating the notorious abuses common in other prisons. The director and the supervisory board would help the prisoner to find employment on discharge, receive reports on his conduct and give him counsel if needed.

It is a pity that circumstances prevented La Rochefoucauld-Liancourt to make his experiment with the system of correction he had found in the Walnut Street prison. In 1832, several years after his death, the Paris institution for juvenile delinquents, La Petite Roquette, was to embody many of his ideas in its system of treatment.

The belief that imprisonment must also serve a reformative purpose, which was coming to be accepted by the leading circles in the government, led Decazes to secure the King's approval for the creation, in 1819, of the Royal Society of Prisons. From its members, among whom we find La Fayette, twenty-four were appointed to form a General Prison Council. Among its first members were La Rochefoucauld-Liancourt, who had just issued the final edition of his book on the Philadelphia prisons, de Broglie, and Guizot, to mention but a few.

The Society was charged with several tasks. It was to make an inspection of all the prisons of the country, gather information about prison administration, prepare a plan for reform, and draw up rules for the management of prisons. Supervisory boards of from three to seven members were set up in every *département* to see that the regulations were followed, and a special Council was to deal with the prisons of Paris. A dozen important reports were produced by the Council members, among them one by La Rochefoucauld-Liancourt, who had drafted the report on regulations, incorporating most of the rules he had hoped to institute in the pilot prison. Some improvements resulted, but the Society soon lost the battle. With the accession of Charles X to the throne in 1824, its influence declined. La Rochefoucauld-Liancourt was not only forced to resign but was deprived of other official functions. Prior to that event, he had assisted, in 1821, in founding the Society of Christian Morality, serving as its first president until 1825. Penal reform was naturally one of its many concerns. In 1822, Guizot, who was one of the editors of the *Journal* of the Society, published his work demanding the abolition of the death penalty for political offenses and in 1826 the Society awarded a prize to Charles Lucas, a youthful Paris lawyer for a work that extended that demand to all crimes. Tocqueville and Dufaure, who were to be closely associated in politics and prison reform decades, later published their first essays in the *Journal*.[17]

The condition of the prisons continued to be the object of criticism by publicists. Religion was relied upon to furnish the stimulus to reformation of prisoners, but it had formidable competition. Says Mossé:

> it is the epoch when the commissaries [i.e., the stores in the prisons, usually run by the contractor of prison labor, where inmates could buy merchandise] were liberally provided, the prisoners' wages high, contacts with the outside grossly tolerated, money-lending and the use of tobacco permitted, etc. It has been referred to as the golden age of prisoners. The discipline of the prisons became so relaxed that it at times created scandals.[18]

In the meanwhile, recidivism appeared to increase, adding an additional argument in favor of reform.

American Stimuli

THE MODELS for this reform were in the United States. The solitary confinement system in Philadelphia, described by La Rochefoucauld-Liancourt, was one such model, albeit he did not defend it, and the New York State prisons at Auburn and Sing Sing, built in the early 1820s, furnished the other. The New York prisons provided individual sleeping cells for the prisoners, who worked in shops during the day under a strict rule of silence, designed to isolate the inmate from his fellow-prisoners. The Auburn prison soon became known in France, as did the writings of Americans, who debated the relative merits of the penal philosophy of the Philadelphians and that underlying the Auburn system.

Among these, Edward Livingston came to have an important place. His remarkable Code of Reform and Prison Discipline was part of a set of codes dealing with crime and punishment, commissioned by the legislature of Louisiana in 1821. It was translated, together with the introductory essay, in which Livingston presented his views on penal reform, by Charles Lucas in 1828.[19] His plan provided for a house of detention for the accused and unsentenced, a penitentiary, a school of reform for offenders under eighteen years of age, and a house of refuge for ". . . all such discharged convicts as may be desirous of gaining a subsistence by labor, . . ." until they could secure employment. Livingston's penitentiary was to be a cellular prison where murderers would suffer solitary confinement for life, but allowed to work most of the time; other prisoners were also to be confined to individual cells, at first in solitude, but as they showed perseverance in labor, obedience, moral conduct and a desire to reform they would gradually be granted various privileges: a better diet, a partial relief from solitude, and the means of education by the visits and lessons of a teacher, permission to read instructive books, occasional visits from relatives or friends, admission to a class for instruction, and finally, after a long probationary period, work in common with other prisoners. Work would be secured for the prisoner under contract with private "mechanics"; he would receive a portion of his wage income when discharged and a ". . . certificate of good conduct, industry, and skill, in the trade he has learned, which may enable him to gain the confidence of society." Livingston considered the Auburn system unacceptable because he did not believe that it could be truly reformative, nor did he approve of solitary confinement in idleness. Solitude and labor, combined and gradually modified when the prisoner was responsive to efforts to aid him, were the main ingredients of his system.

When Lucas published his second work, already mentioned,[20] he was able to refer not only to Livingston's code but to survey — on the basis of official American reports, pamphlets, and the early reports of the Boston Prison Discipline Society — all the prisons of the United States and even the Houses of Refuge for juvenile delinquents recently established in New York and Philadelphia; he also described the prisons of five European countries. In a petition to the Chambers, which he included in his book, he pleaded for the introduction of the penitentiary system in France by putting into effect the plan for the pilot prison, which had been decreed in 1814.

Little else of any consequence was known about the penitentiaries of the United States, when Beaumont and Tocqueville undertook their journey. The July Revolution which brought the liberal minded Louis Philippe, Duke of Orleans, son of Philippe-Égalité, to the throne, also introduced a period when prison reform was to be a matter which engaged the attention of a large number of authors, especially after the appearance of Beaumont's and Tocqueville's report. Their book permitted the advocates of reform to examine American prison administration and policies as viewed by objective observers. The newly constructed Eastern State Penitentiary in Philadelphia, which was in full operation in 1831, epitomized the Pennsylvania system of "solitude and labor." The Auburn prison in New York was the chief representative of the system of cellular isolation at night and congregate labor under a strict rule of silence. The American supporters of these competing systems extolled their respective merits, led by Roberts Vaux of Philadelphia and Louis Dwight of Boston. Beaumont and Tocqueville had taken a neutral stand, seeing certain virtues and deficiencies in both systems. Now the war of the "systems" was to be fought in France as well. The debate continued during the next two decades. It engaged men of letters, politicians, physicians, lawyers, architects, philanthropists, prison wardens, and government inspectors of prisons.

In 1836, a second official commission was sent to the United States, composed of F. A. Demetz, a magistrate, and A. Blouet, an architect. Their report [21] favored the Pennsylvania system. Surveys were made by others of prisons in various European countries. The government took steps to cause the *départements* to construct cellular detention jails, but no full-fledged plan for reform took shape until 1840, the year Beaumont and Tocqueville were elected to the Chamber of Deputies. Since their report on their American journey they had been occupied in writing and in travels in England and Ireland. Tocqueville had just published the last two volumes of the *Democracy in America* and Beaumont his finest work, a book on Ireland.

The Chamber of Deputies Finally Moves

EARLY IN May, 1840, de Rémusat, Minister of Interior, submitted a project of prison reform to the Chamber of Deputies. It was proposed to suppress the galleys and gradually substitute constant cellular isolation, with hard labor, make all local detention jails cellular, and, gradually, as experience dictated, introduce the Pennsylvania system in the central prisons to be constructed.[22] Six weeks later, the committee of the Chamber appointed to examine the bill made its report.[23] Beaumont was a member of the committee and Tocqueville its rapporteur. Many parts of the project were commended, but after presenting the relative merits of the Auburn and Pennsylvania systems, the rapporteur argued at length in favor of the latter, not because one could be certain that it produced the moral regeneration of the prisoner, but because it was least likely to make him worse and most likely to have a deterrent effect. The project was then withdrawn by the Government, to be revised in conformity with the committee's views.

Three years later, Count Duchâtel, then Minister of the Interior, brought in the revised project.[24] Now the government suggested that the Pennsylvania system be applied to all prisoners, young and old, except that prisoners serving very long terms should after twelve years be allowed to congregate during the day as would those over seventy years of age. The new committee, of which Tocqueville was again the rapporteur,[25] accepted the project in general, and in 1844, seventeen days were given by the Chamber to a debate in which over seventy members took part.[26] Among the defenders of the project, besides Tocqueville and Duchâtel, were Beaumont and Taillandier, who twenty years earlier had published a translation of Livingston's penal code. One of the leading opponents was the Marquis de La Rochefoucauld-Liancourt, son of the Duke, who had died in 1827.

In a long speech during the debate, Beaumont made a résumé of the views of prominent French writers for and against the Pennsylvania system. He noted only three worthy opponents: the Marquis de La Rochefoucauld-Liancourt, Charles Lucas, inspector general of prisons, and Léon Faucher, a distinguished publicist. Among the proponents, on the other hand, he listed Moreau-Christophe, inspector general of prisons; Bérenger, member of the Chamber of Peers and of the Institute; F. A. Demetz, magistrate; Victor Foucher, advocate general; Aylies, judge; Lelut, physician and member of the Institute; and several others, not forgetting fifty-five of the departmental prison councils, and most of the inspectors general of prisons of the kingdom, who had pronounced their preference for the Pennsylvania system. When chided for his and Tocqueville's lukewarm attitude a decade earlier, he said that they had tried to be so impartial and objective in their report that their friends had often told them that they could not discern any preference for the one or the other system.

It is very true, [said Beaumont] that . . . when we published our work, I would not have hesitated to prefer even the Auburn system, with its deficiencies, to the bad prison regime then found in France . . . Since then twelve years have passed. In face of facts revealed, in face of manifest truths, both scientific and those established by experience . . . these new facts have, since our impartial report, made us finally adopt the view which seemed to us most in conformity with the data of science and experience.[27]

The Chamber enacted the bill with slight changes. The most important was a substitution of deportation after ten years of cellular confinement. But events again intervened. The Chamber of Peers had also taken up the project. Four years were spent by its committee, aided by an extra-parliamentary committee, in an elaborate study of its provisions, but when the time for decision arrived the February Revolution, 1848, occurred. Had the committee report been adopted, the Pennsylvania system would have won a complete victory. As it was, the government of the Second Republic continued, by executive order of August 20, 1849, the policy of constructing cellular prisons.[28] The order was issued by Tocqueville's and Beaumont's friend Dufaure, who had joined Odilon Barrot's cabinet, as Minister of Interior two months earlier. Tocqueville had at the same time assumed the post of foreign minister and was to hold it for five months, during which time he sent Beaumont to Vienna as ambassador, Beaumont having earlier served in that capacity briefly in London.

The Aftermath

WHEN Louis Napoleon, the prince-president, ended the Second Republic by his *coup d'état* of December 2, 1851, Beaumont and

Tocqueville participated in a protest meeting and were arrested and imprisoned during a few days. Sincere believers in a republican form of government, they could not support the man who was soon to proclaim himself emperor. Their political careers were finished.

Their hopes for a basic reform of the prison system were not to be fulfilled during their lifetimes. The construction of cellular prisons was ordered stopped in 1853 and in some prisons the cellblocks already built were ordered razed. The following year, the transportation of convicts to penal colonies was introduced. Two decades were to pass before the movement for prison reform again received an impetus after the Franco-Prussian war.[29]

Tocqueville devoted the remaining years of his life to a study of the French Revolution and its causes and published a volume on the subject in 1856.[30] It was received with great acclaim. Three years later he died after a lingering illness. Before Beaumont died in 1866, he had edited and published eight volumes of his friend's papers and correspondence, a final tribute to one who had been his inseparable companion.

*

In the preface to a book by Nassau William Senior, long time friend and correspondent of both Beaumont and Tocqueville, we find the following vignette of the latter:

> . . . his voice . . . sweet, low, and varied in its tones, added . . . much to the charm of his conversation. In person he was small and delicate. He had very thick and rather long black hair, soft yet brilliant dark eyes and a finely marked brow. The upper lip was long and the mouth wide, but sensitive and expressive. His manner was full of kindness and playfulness, and his fellow-countrymen used to say of him that he was a perfect specimen of the *"gentilhomme de l'ancien régime."* [31]

Member of the intellectual elite and well fitted for a life of scholarship, he nevertheless found the arena of politics attractive. According to Beaumont, his friend's speeches in the legislative assemblies were composed with the greatest care but delivered like a professorial lecture. Senior claims that he was, in fact, the leader of his party and would have been so in title, except that his health did not permit him to take such active part; furthermore ". . . he is intolerant of mediocrity. He will not court, or talk over, or even listen to the commonplace men who form the rank and file of every Assembly; he scarcely knows their names." [32]

Beaumont was a man of larger mold physically. According to Senior he was not a completely fluent speaker in the Chamber, but had occasionally spoken well.

His diplomatic absences have put him out of practice, but his talent and knowledge must force him on, and they are aided by his popularity. Never was there a more agreeable companion. He must have astonished, however, his colleagues in London and Vienna. His vehemence, his *brusquerie*, his *abandon* are charming but not quite diplomatic.[33]

Thorsten Sellin

ON THE

PENITENTIARY SYSTEM

IN

THE UNITED STATES,

AND

ITS APPLICATION IN FRANCE;

WITH AN APPENDIX

ON PENAL COLONIES,

AND ALSO,

STATISTICAL NOTES.

BY

G. DE BEAUMONT AND **A. DE TOQUEVILLE,**
COUNSELLORS IN THE ROYAL COURT OF PARIS, AND MEMBERS OF THE HISTORI-
CAL SOCIETY OF PENNSYLVANIA.

TRANSLATED FROM THE FRENCH,

WITH AN INTRODUCTION, NOTES AND ADDITIONS.

By FRANCIS LIEBER.

PHILADELPHIA:
CAREY, LEA & BLANCHARD.
1833.

TRANSLATOR'S PREFACE

MM. DE BEAUMONT AND DE TOCQUEVILLE had the kindness to send me, a few months ago, their work on the *Penitentiary System in the United States*, before it had issued from the press in Paris, requesting me, at the same time, to translate it, if possible, for the American public. My time was, at that period, and is still so much occupied by previous engagements, that I doubted at first whether I should be able to comply with the wishes of my friends, though my personal regard for them would not have allowed me to hesitate for a moment. The great importance of the subject, however, soon induced me to undertake the task, trusting that the public would excuse, in a work of this kind, the value of which essentially depends upon statements of facts, and upon statistical numbers, a want of that accuracy and precision of language, without which, in the ordinary course, no work ought to appear before its reader. The authors themselves seem to have considered the facts and observations which they had to communicate, of an importance greatly superior to the manner of conveying them to the public. May I not hope for the reader's indulgence for yet another reason? A man may adopt a foreign country as his own, and be devoted to its institutions with his whole soul, because they are what he always wished and strove for; he may physically and morally acclimatize himself, yet his language will prove the most difficult in accommodating itself to the change. In my case I feel it sensibly. The heart is much more willing than the tongue. If the reader, however, will excuse some peculiarities, and a want of ease and pliability of style, my translation will be found, I hope, at least clear and intelligible. I know it to be faithful.

In most cases the reader will find that they investigated the subject, for the inquiry of which they were sent by their government to this country, with faithful zeal, intelligence, and that readiness to see and state the truth, which we do not find too often in visiters of our country. It is always of great service to hear the observations upon one's own country, made by a foreigner who has a discerning eye and an honest heart. What intelligent German has not read with profit some parts of Madame de Staël's work on his country? Even if such observers are mistaken, which they cannot possibly always avoid being, provided they are intelligent and sincere, their remarks will always be useful and welcome to those who truly love their country. But sickened as the Americans naturally are by the smattering observations of hasty travellers, whose arrogance generally is in an inverse ratio to the length of time which they spent in this country, the chief interest of which consists in the beauty of its nature, and the character of its institutions, it will be a peculiar satisfaction to the reader to find in the following pages an important institution of his country once carefully inquired into. Institutions must be studied, their history as well as their operation cannot be understood by a superficial glance, and hence there is good reason why we find so little of them in the descriptions of a six weeks', three months', eight months' residence, or at most in that of a year and a half in the United States. In the work of which I offer a translation, the authors give the results of their minute inquiry into an institution, which, besides its importance to all mankind, has for Americans the additional interest of having originated with them, and been brought to a high degree of perfection. Whether they praise or censure, is in itself of little interest, compared with the fact that they studied their subject earnestly, and state their result frankly. Truth appears to have been their sole object, and no pains were spared to arrive at this noble end, or to give an accurate statement of the various investigations — a care which shows itself even in the correct writing and printing of the many names of persons and places occurring in the work, which, though apparently an insignificant matter, will appear in a different light to all who are acquainted with the general and great neglect of the orthography of foreign names in French works.

Prisons have been called hospitals for patients laboring under moral diseases, but until recently, they have been in all countries where any existed, and unfortunately continue still to be in most countries, of a kind that they ought to be compared rather to the plague-houses in the East, in which every person afflicted with that mortal disorder is sure to perish, and he who is sent there without yet being attacked, is sure to have it. The awful inscription which the mighty bard of Florence tells us he read over the gates of the infernal regions, would have found a fit place over the entrance of these moral lazarettos, intended for punishment and for the prevention of crime, but in reality, generating it and effecting the total ruin and corruption of their unhappy inmates.

> Through me you pass into the city of wo:
> Through me you pass into eternal pain:
> Through me among the people lost for aye.
> All hope abandon ye who enter here.

In some countries no prisons have been erected as yet. Thus we learn from Mr. Burkhardt's report on houses of correction and punishment in Switzerland, Zurich, 1827, that in the canton of Uri, no prison for punishment exists. Corporal punishment, the pillory, branding and placing the culprit in foreign military service, are used as substitutes. In Appencell-Outer-Road, imprisonment is inflicted for lighter offenses only.

The progress of mankind from physical force to the substitution of moral power in the art and science of government in general, is but very slow, but in none of its branches has this progress, which alone affords the standard by which we can judge of the civil development of a society, been more retarded than in the organization and discipline of prisons, probably for the simple reason that those for whom the prisons are established, are at the mercy of society, and therefore no mutual effort at amelioration, or struggle of different parties, can take place. At length the beginning has been made, and it is a matter of pride to every American, that the new penitentiary system has been first established and successfully practiced in his country. That community which first conceived the idea of abandoning the principle of mere physical force even in respect to prisons, and of treating their inmates as redeemable beings, who are subject to the same principles of action with the rest of mankind, though impelled by vitiated appetites and perverted desires; that community, which after a variety of unsuccessful trials, would nevertheless not give up the principle, but persevered in this novel experiment, until success has crowned its perseverance, must occupy an elevated place in the scale of political or social civilization. The American penitentiary system must be regarded as a new victory of mind over matter — the great and constant task of man. Though of more vital interest to the whole civilized world, it exhibits the same progress of society, which is indicated by the abolition of the *laths* [1] in the Prussian army, and of corporal punishment for most offenses in the army of Great Britain. At least it is fervently hoped, that the house of lords will not thwart the endeavors of the commons to remedy an evil, in respect of which the discipline of English troops has remained so long behind that of the land forces of the most civilized nations on the European continent.

Though the penitentiaries are monuments of a charitable disposition of the honest members of society toward their fallen and unfortunate brethren, and of a penetrating practical sense, we must not forget that little more than the mere beginning has as yet been accomplished, and it cannot be impressed too much upon the mind of the public how necessary is a reformation of all prisons, how impossible it is to think of a *penitentiary system*, without its principle being carried through in all branches. It is praiseworthy, indeed, that the state prisons have been changed into penitentiaries, and that houses of refuge for juvenile offenders have been established; but there remain yet, almost every where in our country, all the other prisons to be refashioned in the same spirit. As long as this is not done, as long as there shall not exist *houses of detention*, in which persons arrested under the presumption of guilt, indicted individuals and witnesses, as urgent circumstances sometimes require their detention, are separated from each other, as well as from prisoners who have been convicted and sentenced, our system will be like the calling for medical assistance after all the gradual stages of the disease have been neglected, when aid would have been easy and cheap, and the disorder shows itself with alarming violence, or has become a settled and incurable disease; or like paying attention only to dikes and embankments when the flood rushes in, after having looked with indolence upon the injury when it was time yet for efficient repair. He who neglects repeated colds, must not be surprised when consumption shows its first and fearful symptoms; he who does not diligently inspect his dikes, and quickly repair whatever injury he finds, must be prepared for disastrous inundations. But it is not only unwise that we have, in most cases, confined our attention to the state prisons. It is contrary to justice and religion, — the first, because we expose those who have not yet been tried, and others who have been found guilty of slight offenses only, to the poisonous infection of aggravated and confirmed crime; the latter, because we occupy ourselves with the convict, who suffers for grave crimes, while we neglect him whose first offenses are perhaps but the fruits of bad seeds, which a vicious education laid deeply in his soul, or the effects of weakness, rashness, or oppressive want. Our vanity is flattered more by our exertions to redeem a hardened criminal, than by kindly preventing many from becoming such, but a gardener who loves his garden, roots out the weeds as early as he can, and does not allow them to shoot up and scatter their destroying seeds before he concludes to rid his beds of them. If it is noble to reclaim fallen virtue; it is much better still to prevent the fall.

So many gifted authors have spoken upon this important point, that I fear I should trespass on the reader's patience, were I to dwell any longer upon it. I shall only point out one of them, who has exhibited the magnitude of its importance in his accustomed lucid manner — Mr. Edward Livingston.

The erection of the Blackwell's Island penitentiary, and the appointment of a committee by the legislature of Massachusetts, to inspect all prisons, and report on a general plan, which shall embrace the prison system of the whole state, show that this want of a general penitentiary system is felt in the community at large and begins to have its practical effects.[2] But the necessity for reforming all prisons in a state according to the same principle, is not any more urgent than that for the erection of houses of arrest or detention, as I have indicated above, destined for the reception of detained but not yet imprisoned persons. Humanity; justice, even a spirit of decency require it.

There is one point, however, connected with this special topic, to which I should invite the reader's attention for a few moments longer — the imprisonment of women. It is a branch of administration of penal justice, much and unfortunately neglected in our country.

In all countries women commit less crimes than men, but in none is the disproportion of criminals of the two sexes so great as in ours. The authors of the present work have given some interesting comparative tables on this subject, and I have stated my views on some of the causes of this fact. Unhappily, the small number of crimes committed in our country by women, has caused a comparative neglect of female criminals. Public attention has hardly turned itself toward this subject, and yet none claims it in a higher degree.[3]

The influence of women, as wives and mothers, upon their family, and also, if they stand single in society, upon those who are in some connection with them, is, generally speaking, greater than that of men, as husbands, fathers, or single, upon the morals of those who surround or are connected with them. The influence of woman upon manners in society, is not greater than that which she may exercise on morals, and even upon crimes, in those classes whose wants expose them more to commit offences than others. A prudent and moral mother, may, in a great degree, counteract in her family the unhappy consequences of her husband's intemperate or dissolute life, much more than it is possible for an honest and industrious husband to counteract the melancholy effects of the bad conduct of an immoral wife. The wife's sphere is supremely that of domestic life; there is the circle of activity for which she is destined, and there, consequently, she has the greatest influence; and the lower we descend in the scale of society, the greater the influence of woman in her family. If she is unprincipled, the whole house is lost, while, if she walks on the path of virtue and religion, she is the safest support of a son, thrown upon the agitated sea of life, or of a husband, oppressed by misfortune or misery, and beset by a thousand temptations. That tender age, in which the very seeds of morality must be sown and fostered in the youthful soul, is much more dependent upon the mother's care, than upon that of the father — in all working classes it is almost solely dependant upon the former. A woman given to intemperance, and, what is generally connected with it, to violence and immoral conduct in most other respects, is sure to bring up as many vagabonds and prostitutes as she has male and female children. I believe I am right in stating, that the injury done to society by a criminal woman, is in most cases much greater than that suffered from a male criminal. Around one female criminal flock a number of the other sex, and ask any police officer what incalculable mischief is done by a single woman who harbors thieves and receives stolen goods, called in the slang of criminals *a fence*. I have taken pains to ascertain the history of a number of convicts, and though my inquiry has been but limited, yet, as far as it goes, it shows me that there is, almost without an exception, some unprincipled or abandoned woman, who plays a prominent part in the life of every convict, be it a worthless mother, who poisons by her corrupt example the soul of her children, or a slothful and intemperate wife, who disgusts her husband with his home, a prostitute, whose wants must be satisfied by theft, or a receiver of plunder and spy of opportunities for robberies. It might be said, that man and woman being destined for each other's company, some woman will be found to play a prominent part in the life of every man, and nothing more natural, therefore, than that we find the same to be the case with criminals. This is true, and would only corroborate what I say, that the influence of woman is great. But in addition, I maintain that I found that most criminals have been led on to crime, in a considerable degree, by the unhappy influence of some corrupted female.

To all this must be added the fact, known to all criminalists, that a woman once renouncing honesty and virtue, passes over to the most hideous crimes which women commit, with greater ease than a man proceeds from his first offense to the blackest crimes committed by his sex. There is a shorter distance between a theft committed by a woman and her readiness to commit murder by poison, or arson, from jealousy or hatred, than between forgery or theft committed by a man, and murder or piracy. A male criminal may be a thief for a long series of years, and yet as unwilling to steep his hands in the blood of a fellow man, as many honest men. A person may commit depredation upon public property for his whole life, and yet shudder at the idea of highway robbery. With women this is not often the case. It seems, moreover, that the majority of those characters in the annals of crimes at which we shudder most, have been females. That crime, the most revolting to human nature — poisoning, has found its blackest and foulest adepts among the women. I only need remind the reader of the society of female poisoners under the direction of Hieronyma Spara, of the Marchioness de Brinvilliers, and of the woman Gottfried,[4] who, in 1831, was executed in Bremen for having poisoned more than thirty persons, among whom were her parents, children, husbands, lovers, friends, and servants.[5]

This rapid and precipitous moral fall of women, can be sufficiently accounted for. The two sexes have been destined by the Creator for different spheres of activity, and have received different powers to fulfil their destiny. The woman destined for domestic life, and that sphere in which attachment and affection are the most active agents, has been endowed with more lively feeling and acuter sensibility: she feels ; man reasons. Her morality has its roots more in her feelings than in her understanding or reasoning faculty, and if she has once lost that delicate bloom of moral bashfulness, if she has lost the acuteness of her moral feelings, if she has stepped further and committed an offense against the laws, the almost only ground on which her moral actions depended is shaken ; if she once gives up the retired activity of her domestic sphere, she is led into an element for which she is but rarely calculated. This seems to be also the reason why, with all nations and at all times, the loss of chastity has been considered with women so much more grave and dangerous an offense than with men. They felt that the former lose more of their moral nature by it than the latter.[6]

It is otherwise with man. The Creator destined him for an agitated life. He has to make his way, to break new paths; he must, as Schiller says, "win and dare," and has to decide between opposed interests, and, not infrequently, between conflicting duties. He, therefore, has been endowed with feelings less acute and prompt, stronger reasoning powers, and calmer judgment. If he loses the delicacy of his feelings, great as the loss may be, his judgment will yet supplant it in a degree; his moral guide does not yet, for this reason, entirely fail him. Hence it often happens that men, committing acts which are considered by all others immoral, perhaps criminal, make themselves what the French call *des raisons,* false excuses indeed, yet they prevent them not infrequently from going further. The manifold scenes of life, politics, the varieties of business make him acquainted with many impure actions, with which a woman is not brought into contact. It accustoms his mind to see acts which do not agree with the strict laws of morality, and if he himself commits a similar one, he need not have sunk so deep as a woman if she commits the same, and he retains yet a considerable part of that power which always regulated his moral conduct. Besides, crimes which, according to the state of our civil society, may be easily committed by women, are mostly of a kind requiring great baseness.

It appears, then, from the preceding observations, that a woman, when she commits a crime, acts more in contradiction to her whole moral organization, i. e. must be more depraved, must have sunk already deeper than a man. She abandons shame as much as a man, who commits the same, but shame is of still greater moral importance to her than to him.

I have thought I found in these arguments also, the reasons why, in all countries, girls, in houses of refuge for juvenile offenders, are so much more difficult to be reclaimed than boys; and that it is almost impossible to reclaim them, if they have been prostitutes, as the reader will find in a note added to the chapter on houses of refuge.

We should be wrong in concluding from the small number of crimes committed by women, compared with those com-

mitted by men, that there is a greater moral capacity in
women in general; and therefore, that penitentiaries for females are comparatively unimportant. Women commit fewer
crimes from three causes chiefly: (1) because they are,
according to their destiny and the consequent place they occupy in civil society, less exposed to temptation or to induce-
ment to crime; their ambition is not so much excited, and
they are naturally more satisfied with a dependant situation; [7] (2) they have not the courage or strength necessary
to commit a number of crimes which largely swell the lists of
male convicts, such as burglary, robbery, and forcible murder; (3) according to their position in society they cannot
easily commit certain crimes, such as bigamy, forgery, false
arrest, abuse of official power, revolt, etc. There are some
crimes they cannot commit at all, such as rape; but there are
on the other hand, crimes which men cannot commit, as abor-
tion; or to which they are not so easily induced, as infanti-
cide. According to the *Compte général de l'Administration
de la Justice criminelle* (in France) for 1826 and 1827, we
find that in 1826, 5712 men, and 1276 women were accused
of crimes, and 126,089 men, and 33,651 women of offenses
judged by "correctional tribunals." In 1827, 5657 men, and
1272 women were accused of crimes, and 133,936 men, and
37,210 women of offenses. In 1827 there were accused for
killing, eleven women and 277 men; for murder, 32 women
and 236 men; for maiming, 22 women and 353 men; for highway robbery, 10 women and 183 men.

But this proportion, so favorable to the female sex,
changes immediately in respect to parricide and poisoning.
Of 23 parricides, sixteen were men and seven women; 12
women and 22 men were accused of poisoning; 25 women and
61 men of arson. In 1826, twelve women and fourteen men
had been accused of poisoning. So in 1826, there were 427
women and 745 men accused of domestic theft; in 1827, 343
women and 554 men, while for common theft, 2563 men and
531 women were accused.

Are we then justifiable, after all these considerations, in
not providing more effectually for the correction of female
convicts? The only remaining question can be; are separate
penitentiaries for females required? I believe they are, if the

Pennsylvania penitentiary system is not adopted, and with that system a matron at least will be necessary for the special superintendence of the female prisoners; she is quite indispensable if the Auburn system is applied to women as well as men; she alone can enforce the order of this system, while it is nearly impossible for male keepers. The whole spirit of opposition in womankind is raised against him. Besides, the moral management of female convicts must differ from that of male criminals, and even their labor requires a total separation. Separate houses might be easily built, and proper committees appointed to superintend them. In Wethersfield and Auburn, women are subjected to the penitentiary system, which takes its name from the latter; matrons superintend them. If it should be found impossible to make the labor of female convicts as profitable as that of men, we must not allow ourselves to be retarded by a financial consideration in providing for them, since we have seen how important their proper treatment is.

The penitentiary system has not escaped the common fate of all questions of vital interest to society. Many of its opponents as well as its advocates, have run into extremes; the former, judging by vague impressions derived from superficial knowledge, both of the character of convicts and the penitentiary system, assert not unfrequently, with a kind of levity, that criminals ought to suffer severely for their crimes, and should not be treated with tenderness; the latter, carried away by a pious zeal, often believe that an individual who has from early childhood received bad impressions, imbibed vicious principles, and has allowed himself to be governed during his whole life by unchecked desires and unbridled appetites, who has, in fact, contracted bad habits deeply rooted in his whole character, may be influenced by the same religious means which affect honest persons, and suddenly become a contrite sinner, and, soon after, change into a saint.

It ought always to be born in mind, that a convict is neither a brute nor a saint, and to treat him as either, is equally injurious to himself and to society.

Though opposition to the penitentiary system has greatly abated, and entirely ceased to take an active part in many states of our union, there are, nevertheless, many individuals who believe that too much pains are taken with convicts; and, as I have heard it myself not infrequently expressed, say that "they ought to be punished." Were they to inquire but slightly into the matter, they would soon find that as long as a convict remains unchanged in mind, a penitentiary with its constant labor and strict order, its silence, its solitude during night, or, if we speak of the Pennsylvania system, its uninterrupted solitude day and night, is a punishment to him whose element has been disorder and idleness (as is the case with most criminals) a hundred times greater than a prison, the inmates of which, though loaded with chains and oppressed with filth, and unhealthy diet, yet can freely communicate with each other. It is a fact that criminals fear penitentiaries much more than prisons on the old plan; yet they know that they live, physically, much better in the former, and are aware of the torturing misery of the latter. But what they are afraid of is, the order, obedience, and silence imposed upon them; they shun, consciously, or instinctively, that moral character which pervades the whole system, so odious to criminal people. They shun, by a vague presentiment, perhaps, the being corrected and reformed in spite of themselves, and the contemplation of their unhappy life, spent and lost in evil deeds. It is this, the same instinct which causes so often the wicked to fear moral society, the same feeling which makes a criminal so afraid of his own lucid intervals, and leads him on to new perverted activity, to quiet, for the moment, his unhappy soul.

Were those opponents but to inquire into prisons, the statistics of crimes, and the history of criminals, they soon would find that charity, our own interest, and justice, equally require their most active support of the penitentiary system — charity requires it, because, though crime necessarily must be punished, yet the history of by far the greatest majority of criminals, shows the afflicting fact, that they were led to crime by the bad example of their parents, loose education, hard masters, or a gradual progress in vice, for which society often offers but too many temptations. Ask those conversant with the lives of criminals, how many of them are led to the prison by the lottery alone! Interest requires it, be-

cause the old prisons were an enormous burden to society,
while the penitentiaries cost little, and often yield a revenue.
Even Sing Sing, which had to contend with many unusual
and great difficulties, will, as I have been assured from the
best authority, defray all its expenses during the next year.
Justice requires it, because society has a right to punish, but
not to brutalize, to deprive of liberty, but not to expose to
filth and corruption; and if it is obstinately insisted upon
that government, as such, has no obligation to correct the
morals of convicts, it is, at all events, its sacred duty not to
lead them to certain ruin, and society takes upon itself an
awful responsibility, by exposing a criminal to such moral
contagion, that, according to the necessary course of things,
he cannot escape its effects. Besides, is it not the interest of
society to try all means at its disposal to reclaim a criminal?

However, we are happy to say, that, in this country, there
are few, if any, who pretend that the question of morality
should not enter at all into the discussion of this topic.

Those, on the other hand, who try to attract great attention to a few cases, in which, according to their opinion,
criminals have become most pious men, ought to remember
that there is no greater contradiction in itself, than noisy
piety or showy devotion, especially with a convict. If an individual, who has greatly sinned against divine and human
laws, make a sincere effort to return to the path of virtue,
what honest man would not rejoice at it with all his heart?
But direct not public attention to such cases, because nothing but long experience can show the truth or deception of
the case; and, if in truth a convict have morally recovered,
he must sincerely wish to remain in quiet and unobserved
communion with his Maker, and not to attract public attention now by his devotion, as formerly by his crime. If the success of the penitentiary system depended upon these few
cases, it would be founded upon no firm ground; they always
must remain but few in number; and have those few cases
answered the pious expectation of those who directed public
attention to them? Many former convicts are now honestly
gaining their livelihood, but among them are few of those who
gave surprising signs of sudden conversion. If those convicts
who suddenly became devout, were sincere at the time they

showed those symptoms of piety, it must have been an excitement of feeling, which has subsided as soon as the exciting
causes ceased, and which is not sufficient to prevent a relapse
into former vices, when former temptations re-appear. To
correct a criminal radically, more is required than an excitement of feeling; his habits must be broken: his mind must be
trained. Society cannot be expected, and has not even the
right to do any thing, except it is directly or indirectly for
the general interest. Penitentiaries cannot be erected, in
order to bring out of many thousand criminals, a few to a
state of great and therefore uncommon piety, but it is its interest to establish them, if according to the organization of
the human soul, and the principles of our actions, it can be
fairly supposed that many of these convicts will contract
better habits, more correct views of society, and of themselves, and come to a better knowledge of their obligations
toward God, and society; and especially if experience shows
the success of these praiseworthy endeavours. All who are
well acquainted with the penitentiary system, know that recommittals decrease, and, probably, would become rare, if
released convicts could be prevented from returning to large
cities. The recommittals of those convicts, who go into the
country after the expiration of their imprisonment, are comparatively few.[8] In all countries, the population of large
cities produces proportionally more crimes than the rest of
the nation, and again the cities and towns more than the villages, etc. It is so in France, in all states of Germany, in
England; it is so with ourselves. There is in large cities a
greater and more variegated activity, and, therefore, more
opportunity for crimes than elsewhere; wants are greater,
temptations more frequent and powerful, inducements to
pleasure and idleness more alluring and diversified; life is
more unobserved, and as the concourse of people in general
is greater, so also that of criminals, who soon meet with each
other in corrupting company, which, for a former convict,
is peculiarly dangerous. In several countries, therefore, the
government has thought it necessary to prevent released convicts from going to the capital and its vicinity, for a series
of years, after the expiration of their imprisonment. A
French galley slave, leaving the bagne, is not allowed to go

to Paris. Our large cities are, if not equally dangerous to released convicts, sufficiently so to authorize us to adopt some similar measures, but none in so high a degree as New York, owing to its peculiar situation, and unequalled activity, the many emigrants who resort to it, and several other reasons, unnecessary to be mentioned here, but which, if I remember right, cause the greater number of convicts, released from Auburn or Sing Sing, soon to be recommitted, if they go to the city of New York. The legislature of the state of New York, therefore, ought to consider the propriety of passing a law, which would make the prohibition of going to the city of New York, for a number of years, proportionate to the duration of imprisonment, after its expiration, inherent in each sentence. The justice of such a law cannot be doubted; its expediency would be evident. If the penitentiary system is a truly salutary one, if it attempts the moral, or at least the civil restoration of an individual, nothing can be more natural than to prohibit a person, whom the law considers convalescent, to expose himself to an atmosphere dangerous to his feeble state. On general grounds, such a measure could not possibly be found unjust, provided the prohibition is included in the sentence; and the objection that it would be assuming arbitrary power over citizens restored to all their rights, would be sufficiently refuted by the consideration, that, in case such measure should be adopted, the law would not consider the individual as yet entirely restored to all the rights of a citizen. Such a law would have no characteristic trait of a police measure. The prohibition would be legally awarded as a sentence. There are, moreover, in several of our states, New York included, laws which disqualify a former convict for certain civil functions. It remains only to inquire whether the advantage of a greater opportunity which a released convict finds in New York, for the practice of the trade which he has learned in Sing Sing or Auburn, and consequently the greater chance of leading an honest life, does not overbalance the disadvantage of moral exposure. This question of mere expediency can be decided only by the examination of facts. If most convicts, proceeding to New York after the expiration of their sentence, are recommitted, and most of those who go into the country do not return, or if a proportionately greater number of the former are recommitted, it is of course expedient to pass the law.[9] The inhabitants of New York could not, in such case, be considered as favored at the expense of the other citizens, for two reasons; (1) Even after such a law should be passed, they will remain nevertheless more exposed to the depredations of foreign criminals, and those brought up in our country, attracted as they all are by the largest city in the country, which everywhere operates as a kind of drain of bad subjects. The whole state of New York profits by the activity of the city of New York, but the people are not proportionately as exposed to criminals as the inhabitants of the city; (2) Most of the released convicts are supposed to lead an honest life if they go into the country, or the law would not be passed.

It is with such a law, that, in my opinion, the penitentiary system would show itself to its greatest advantage, because it would rapidly decrease that criminal population which forms a kind of society for itself. And though it never can prevent crime, because desires, temptations, and opportunities, do not lie in its reach, it would lead back to honest life many individuals, by teaching them how to support themselves honestly, and by guarding them, during the time of imprisonment, against further corruption, and thus prevent the propagation of crime by the released convicts, who, it is well known, are the most dangerous and most numerous members of that criminal community, just alluded to. If the penitentiary system have once succeeded in breaking up or greatly diminishing this corrupted and rapidly corrupting community, for which the Pennsylvania system is so eminently qualified; if it have once succeeded in reducing most crimes to individual acts, produced by degenerated appetites, or want of principles, indeed, but not by long confirmed corruption, which makes a profession of crime — its greatest and surest victory will be gained. Most criminals then will enter the prison less hardened, they will be more susceptible to the influence of the penitentiary system, and, after the expiration of their imprisonment, it will be easier for them to live honestly, because they have not become the initiated members of a corrupted society, which now entangles those who sincerely resolve to reform with a thousand difficulties.

There are few men, indeed, who having been imprisoned for the first time, and suffered a severe but not brutalizing, infamous, or still more corrupting punishment, are not disposed to attempt a life more congenial to the laws of their country. They find out, if no better reason influences them, that an honest life is after all more comfortable than a dishonest one, and every person, after he has attained his thirtieth year, wishes more or less some kind of solid comfort. The roving disposition loses much of its activity after this period, and it is well known that most crimes are committed between the ages of twenty and thirty. Let a former convict but acquire habits of honesty, and he will also gradually acquire honest views and feelings. Let him obey the just laws of our country, and he will soon love them.

From the recommittals of convicts who go to live in the country, and small towns, and not in the most populous cities, after the expiration of their punishment, it would, perhaps, be the fairest to judge of the efficacy of the penitentiary system, because it ought to be supported and assisted by all necessary laws which justice permits, and because in several countries, perhaps in most, in which the old prison system exists, such laws are actually existing. We would then only make the comparison on even ground. But even if the criminals recommitted from the largest cities must be taken into account, it is by the recommittals, not by the sum total of criminals, that we must judge of the efficacy of a prison discipline. Yet not even by the recommittals alone can we be guided.

The prevention of first crimes depends much more upon the certainty of punishment, and, therefore, upon the excellence of laws and the administration of justice, than upon the manner of punishment. As long as we see an overwhelming number of commitments and indictments compared to convictions, we may safely conclude either that the law is deficient, in allowing, by not being sufficiently accurate, too easily of accusation or acquittal, or in the prescribed procedure and form of trial. There are some exceptions to this rule, for instance, in our times, the numerous accusations in France for offenses of the press against government, and the almost universal acquittals. I only speak of common crimes, and a state of society not excited by some peculiar causes. The opposite, that few acquittals always indicate sound laws, and a wise administration of justice, is by no means equally true. The Turkish cadis acquit rarely; and in many countries, (e. g. in most, I believe in all states of Germany) exists the absolving *ab instantia*, which neither finds guilty nor acquits, but leaves the trial suspended — a measure which is in most cases extremely hard, and altogether repulsive to our ideas of justice. We find in the years 1826–27 that 3594 persons were tried in the kingdom of Bavaria, for crimes and offenses; of these, 644 were found guilty of crimes, 1141 were found guilty of offenses, 396 were absolved *ab instantia* for crimes, 609 were absolved *ab instantia* for offenses, 328 absolved for crimes, 453 absolved for offenses, 7 declared innocent of crimes, and 16 declared innocent of offenses.

I hope that what the authors and myself have said on the insufficiency of judging of the efficacy of the penitentiary system by the increase or decrease of crimes in general, will contribute to dissipate so great and injurious an error. The number of crimes, or to speak more accurately, of trials and convictions, because they are the only known crimes, proves, without further consideration, actually nothing. So much so, that in some cases the increase of trials and convictions may indicate the decrease of crimes. If the *compte général* of criminal justice in France, shows that in 1825 there were only thirty-three criminal trials for adultery, in 1827 only fifty-seven trials of this kind, are we to conclude that the thirty-one millions of people with whom so few trials for adultery occur, are uncommonly chaste, or that on the contrary, if domestic manners should improve with them, adultery would be more often punished? I believe the latter. There are several nations, for instance the Spanish and Portuguese, with whom murder is very often but negligently prosecuted, because the people do not feel the same indignation or horror at a murder committed under certain circumstances, which the crime produces with other nations. In Italy every one of the lower classes assists a criminal in escaping the arms of justice. With us every citizen assists government as much as it is in his power, and a comparison between murders and other violent crimes tried in Italy, and those tried in this country, without making allowance for this difference, would lead to erroneous results.

A minute knowledge of all co-operating circumstances is nowhere more indispensable, in order to arrive at just conclusions, than in the statistics of crimes. There are certain laws which experience teaches us, and if we disregard them we shall continually be liable to draw false conclusions. For instance, that certain causes, as an unusually cold winter, famine, stagnation of business, and poverty, caused by war, etc., never fail to effect a rapid increase of crimes, while the ceasing of these causes by no means effects a proportionally rapid decrease of crime. These considerations respecting the increase or decrease of crime, are not only important in regard to prison discipline, but also as to the progress of morality, or the demoralization of mankind in general.

Civilization certainly increases the number of tried crimes and offenses, for two very simple reasons: (1) because it increases the opportunity of crime, since it increases the variety of pursuits and mutual relations between men; every progress in industry offers naturally to the wicked a new opportunity for abusing this industry, or the new relations which it creates between men; civilization, moreover, increases our wants and our ambition; (2) because it increases at the same time the means and opportunities for prosecutions of crime. It sounds paradoxical, when Pangloss, shipwrecked on the coast of Portugal, drew the inference from seeing men in chains that he was in a civilized country; yet he was right considering his time, and it may be safely said, that a community of any magnitude, within which no crime is committed, cannot be far advanced in civilization. There is a latent criminality in such communities, which shows itself whenever opportunity offers. If the wants of men are reduced to the simplest food which the field offers, and to clothing which is provided by their own flocks, they are easily satisfied, and hardly an opportunity exists for the numerous crimes and offenses committed against property in a civilized and active society. There is or may be an absence of crime, but between this and positive morality there is yet a vast difference. Mankind are destined for civilization, and the great problem is to arrive through civilization at morality. I have spoken here of mankind only as it has shown itself so far. That same power which operated such great changes in the dispositions of men — which has taught them that there is greater security in living close together, in towns and villages, than isolated in fastnesses, depending on mere physical security; that taught them that free labor is more productive than the labor of compelled serfs; that governments, supported by moral power, stand firmer than states founded on brutal strength; that nations may serve their own interest much more efficiently by treating their neighbors liberally, than by injuring or paralyzing them; that diplomatic frauds lead to no good in their mutual intercourse; or which has already rendered the more brutal crimes rarer, that same power may also, at some future period, diminish the number of crimes in general. Mankind may not grow better, but a more correct knowledge of their true interest may become diffused among them, and may by degrees largely influence their general feeling, as in fact has been the case already in some other respects. Some more remarks on this subject may be found in a note of mine added to a passage of this work, in which the authors speak of the influence of knowledge on crimes.

In respect to the moral state of a nation, I would not attach so much importance to the fact, that crimes against persons decrease in proportion to crimes against property, with the progress of civilization, as of late several writers, and particularly Mr. Lucas, have been inclined to do.

It is impossible for me to enter here into a discussion on the question, so often put, whether civilization renders nations more moral or not.[10] It would be necessary previously to agree upon the accurate meaning of a number of expressions, generally as freely used as they are indistinctly applied; my wish is merely to show here that this division of crimes alone, though very interesting and useful for various inquiries, does not authorize us as yet to draw any definite conclusion respecting the moral state of nations. First, the line dividing crimes against persons from those against property, is not so distinct as it may appear at first glance. False testimony, perjury, escape of prisoners, are enumerated

among the crimes against persons, but a witness who gives
false testimony, actuated so to do by compassion for the
prisoner, does not necessarily injure the rights of persons,
though he acts contrary to his duty as a citizen. Even rebellion, ranked among crimes against persons, is not necessarily
such, and at all events it indicates very often a less degree of
demoralization than a number of crimes against property.
On the other hand, a number of crimes against property partake much of the character of crimes against persons, for
instance, arson from vengeance, or exchanging of infants.
Secondly, I do not believe that this division separates at the
same time the more heinous crimes from the less immoral
ones. Society punishes, in general, crimes against persons
with greater severity than those against property, because
they are more dangerous to the general peace, and more injurious to the suffering party. But if we wish to judge of the
degree of demoralization requisite for committing this species
of crime, we ought not to forget that the greater part of
crimes against persons are acts committed in rashness, while
those committed against property are nearly all premeditated crimes, and often require a baseness not necessarily to
be supposed in the authors of crimes against persons. It is
this consideration which explains, why the laws of ancient
Germanic tribes punished theft with death, while they required *compositio* (fine) only for killing and maiming. Whoever is acquainted with criminal justice, will remember
numerous crimes which have been committed rashly, and
necessarily punished by the law with a heavy penalty, but
which nevertheless left no doubt but that their authors were
morally better than numerous convicts, again and again
recommitted for petty larceny. How often is the very principle of honor, or the feeling of being unworthily treated, the
cause of a passion which leads an individual to crime — feelings which never disturb the baseness of others, who commit
crimes against property.

Moreover, the moral state of a society cannot be judged
merely by the number of committed crimes, cognizable by
the law, perhaps not even chiefly. To do this, we must inquire
into a number of other subjects. Suppose we apply the rule
by which Mr. Lucas judges, to the various classes of society.

There was never, perhaps, a more demoralized class of men than the highest classes in France, under the regency of the Duke of Orleans, or Louis XV, or the court of Charles II; yet, were we in possession of statistical accounts of those times, we should in all probability find that most crimes, of which the law takes cognizance, were committed among the lowest and middling classes, that, nevertheless, had not arrived at that state of demoralization in which their fellow subjects of the highest nobility revelled. The comparison of the immorality of man to a state of disease, is applicable also to the point in question. The climate of some places renders the greater number of their inhabitants more or less sickly, though violent diseases affecting a great number at the same time may be there rare, and other places may now and then suffer much from disorders of this kind, and yet be on the whole more generally healthy.

I trust the reader does not misunderstand me; I am far from intimating that those countries in which few crimes against property are committed, and many against persons, are probably more moral than those countries in which the contrary takes place. My previous remarks must show that I am no admirer of that state of ignorance which guards a whole nation against many crimes, only by leaving it without wants, but which nourishes revenge, and leaves passions unbridled. My object is to show, that so far, this division of crimes allows us only to conclude, that civilization renders people calmer, i. e. more civilized.

Among many other considerations, which ought to guide us, if we are desirous of drawing conclusions respecting the morality of a people from the list of crimes, a division into premeditated and unpremeditated crimes, will be found necessary. Still more we ought to judge from the motives, to which the admirable and already often quoted *Comptes généraux de l'Administration de la Justice criminelle*, annually published by the keeper of the seals of France, assign a separate table. And having mentioned these important and instructive documents, I cannot refrain from expressing my belief, that few more important services could be rendered to the well-being of our people, than the passing of laws which should enjoin the proper authorities, the clerks of the courts, and agents of the penitentiaries, in particular, to keep accurate and complete statistical tables, according to prescribed forms, to be laid annually before the legislatures. We have an excellent model in the above *comptes généraux*, which already have led to several inquiries of vital interest to the French nation, and the influence of which, if continued as we hope, must be incalculable. Statistical accounts, if judiciously used, are the very charts of legislators; legislation without them, is, in most cases, but a groping in the dark. They often dispel prejudices, though for centuries cherished, by irresistible facts, and again direct our attention to points, where we least expected the roots of a long known evil. At the same time, the trouble of collecting those at least of which I speak here in particular, is very little compared with the magnitude of their importance. The clerks of the courts, and the agents of the penitentiaries, have but faithfully to fill the blanks of prescribed schedules, from which a competent committee may make its annual reports. The politician, the moralist, the public economist, the criminalist, the divine, the promoter of prison discipline — all who have the welfare of their nation at heart, are equally interested in this measure. What important consequences would result from such accurate and extensive statistical accounts, if but Maryland, Pennsylvania, New York, Connecticut, Massachusetts, etc. would resolve to keep them, especially if they were so kept, that they should agree in their chief features, which, by an easy understanding, might be effected without any difficulty. I am well aware that much has been done already by the annual reports of the agents of several penitentiaries, but the statistical part of them may yet be much improved.

It is among other things important to know the sex, age, and education of the convict; whether the latter was bad, common, good, or polite; his trade, color, the trade of his parents, whether he lost them and at what age; in what month the crime was committed; whether it is a first, second, third, etc. crime; from what motive (from want, revenge, dissipation, etc.); whether the crime was premeditated or not; the causes of the convict's bad habits (intemperance, lottery, women, gambling, etc. bad example of parents or masters); if the convict is a female, whether a prostitute (which is generally the case); if they are emigrants, how long in this country; whether married or not, whether he or she has children, how many; when and where convicted, nature of the crime, sentence, how long imprisoned before the trial; how long after the crime was committed the trial took place, etc.; general state of health; what religion, or, at least, in which educated; whether the term expired, or was abbreviated by pardon or death, behavior in prison, etc. It is farther of the greatest importance to know how many indictments, and for what offenses, took place; how many acquittals, and for what the indictment was; how many recommendations by the court, or court and jury to mercy; how many crimes were committed by a single individual or more; how many pleaded guilty; how many criminal cases were finished by the court during one term, etc. I believe that a single glance at the tables of which the French *comptes-généraux* consist, will satisfy every body of their great utility. That similar statistical accounts of civil cases would be of great importance to the legislator, I have no doubt, but it does not fall within the province of this work to treat of them.

I have now come to the last topic of my preface, with which I have, perhaps, detained the reader already too long — the power of pardoning. So much has been written on this point, so urgently has been the abolition of the abuse of pardon, asked for by writers full of eloquence and energy, that it might appear to many of my readers superfluous to touch again upon this subject, especially in this place, since the work itself exposes the abuse in strong colors; but the defect appears to me of such magnitude, and of so vital an interest to our society, that I may be allowed to add a few general observations.

Two things seem very certain: (1) That as long as the pardoning power shall be abused in the way that now but too frequently happens, the effect of penitentiaries, as well as of criminal justice, can be but limited. It is the certainty of the punishment, not its cruelty, which prevents crime. The criminal, yet at large, calculates on pardon as one of his chances of impunity, and the imprisoned convict, having a chance of being pardoned any day, is deprived of that calm resignation, which the certainty of his punishment alone can produce, and which must precede any salutary reflection on his past life, and earnest resolution to become a better member of society. (2) That as long as one individual in a state is invested with the pardoning power, it will be often abused to the injury of society.

It seems to me, that wherever the pardoning power is intrusted to a single person, this person does not withstand, in many cases, the vehement solicitations and personal prayers which have the opportunity of reaching him. But the difference is, that, in monarchies, few individuals of those personally interested in the fate of convicts, have an opportunity to accost the monarch, or, if so, to state their whole case; while the governor of a republican state, as our commonwealths are, is, and by right ought to be, accessible to the people. He therefore will yield sometimes to the urgent prayers of the distressed, or to the recommendations of people well disposed but weak, when, according to justice, he ought not to make use of that privilege which the constitutions of most of our states bestow upon the chief magistrates. Yet does this comport with the spirit which pervades our whole political government? We boast, that the law is our only master, and here an individual defeats their effect at his pleasure. The constitution, indeed, bestows this privilege upon him. But can a constitution, which emanated from one moral person only, and is no compromise between conflicting parties, possibly contain any provision which intentionally defeats the operation of other provisions of the law? Can such a constitution contain any other provision but such as was at least supposed would give effect to the law, and promote the welfare of the people? Certainly not; and the only interpretation which can be given to the provision investing the governor with the privilege of pardoning, is, that he shall use it for the still more effective operation of the law. If a law, owing to the imperfection of human language, foresight, or any other deficiency, operates against its own spirit, its own intention, as cases of this kind will happen, a governor may conscientiously make use of his privilege. If the innocence of a convicted person is proved, or rendered highly probable, the laws of the land which established the trial, court, and the law by which sentence was passed, operated against their spirit, which is to protect innocence, and a governor ought to pardon. If a number of peculiar circumstances, which the law, owing to its generality, without which it would not be a law, could not contemplate, contribute to excuse an individual who, nevertheless, according to its strict letter is guilty, the governor may, or ought to use his privilege. Such a peculiar case happened quite recently in one of the Atlantic states. But the case of a mother of many children, suffering great poverty, because the arm of stern justice took their protector away from them, to be punished in a prison: or a respectable family, known in the best society, distressed by the shame brought upon them by the crime of a worthless son, and a number of other cases, hard and cruel as they are for the sufferers, do not entitle the individual in question to a pardon, because the legislators well knew, when they passed the law, that it would strike fathers of poor families, and sons of respected parents, as well as other individuals; and, if its free course is interrupted, the sway of the law has ceased. What would be thought of a society who erected, with great expense, dikes against the inroads of the hostile element, but invested one individual with the peculiar privilege of boring holes in these dikes at his own pleasure, and allowing the flood to rush in and to destroy their property? It would be a strange privilege, and yet nothing more than the privilege of pardoning, as it is now abused by some chief magistrates of our states. We make laws with great expense; we enforce them at great expense, by paying judges, juries, witnesses, the police, etc.; and by rewards for arresting criminals, and a single individual, after all, defeats their operation. Are those who thus return a convict upon society, before the expiration of the time of imprisonment which it has thought proper to fix for a given crime, prepared to be resonsible for the new injuries inflicted upon society, by these imperfectly punished criminals, and, before all, for the injury done by themselves, by thus rendering the operation of the law still more uncertain than it unfortunately always must be, according to the imperfection of human institutions? Yet, who will say, that, placed in the same situation, besieged by the same prayers, and importuned by the same recommendations, and endowed with the same power to grant the relief so pressingly asked for, he would never yield? Now and then, an individual may be placed at the head of our state governments, who, gifted with peculiar energy, may resist with the calm conviction of duty. But, according to the common character of man, this can be but rarely the case; and, as it is in general one of the noblest tasks of man to make reason triumph over chance, it is peculiarly so in the province of law and justice. Besides, the pardoning power, where it is vested in a single individual, has come to us somewhat in a traditional form, and probably not been established by unbiased reflection. In European monarchies, the pardoning privilege rose out of the power, not legally bestowed, but physically exercised, to interfere with justice, and, at the same time, from a vague feeling of the necessity that somewhere a power ought to exist, which might sometimes modify the literal application of the law, particularly when the latter is cruel. Having originated in times in which all the branches and operations of government were but illy defined, this power gradually rose into a distinct privilege, cherished by as many rulers, probably, for its great political importance, as for its merciful character, so grateful to a paternal monarch. It agreed well with the religious-political character, given to the exalted station of the crowned and anointed sovereign. Poetry compared it to divine mercy. The privilege existed when we separated from our mother country; it was necessary to invest somebody with it, or to abrogate it. It was, naturally enough, given to the chief magistrates. But it is time to inquire whether it agrees with our institutions, which are rendered as little as possible dependant upon the individuality of a single person. In monarchies, one of the fundamental principles of which is to reconcile abstract law with the individuality of a single person, this interference of an individual with the free and unchecked operation of the law, has nothing contrary to their characteristic spirit. With us, it is out of place. Let us then try to remedy the evil.

It is evident, that the privilege of pardoning, or as it would be called with much more propriety, the *responsibility*, ought to be vested in a body of men, not in an individual. If you divide the responsibility for any act, it is much easier to bear it. Some of our states have conferred the power of pardoning on the legislature. I think they ought not to be imitated. Legislatures are chosen for political purposes, are too much occupied with legislative business, and above all, are much too numerous to be able to investigate a petition for pardon with that patience, care, and nicety which a question, the very character of which is, to deviate from the law, necessarily requires. The most advisable, therefore, would seem to be, to establish a committee or chamber of pardon, consisting of seven or nine members, some of whom ought to be judges, perhaps under the presidency of the chief justice, which might convene twice a year to recommend for pardon those prisoners to the governor, who have been judged by them to be fit subjects for it, after hearing a deliberate report on each case by one of their members; because it would be improper to leave this important act dependent upon indefinite and vague feelings. But as it is injurious to leave in matters of law any thing indefinite which need not be so, and as it would operate injuriously upon the penitentiary system, to allow the hope of pardon to be any longer the cause of excitement to the prisoners, it would be proper perhaps to adopt a law similar to that of the republic of Geneva, where the penitentiary system has been introduced; i. e. that every prisoner has a right to petition the *commission de recours* — a committee consisting of nine members for judging of the fitness for pardon — after two-thirds of the imprisonment, for which he has been sentenced, have elapsed. Sentence for life is considered in this case equal to thirty years. The court and jury alone, who have felt themselves bound by facts and law to award a certain judgment, but feel, nevertheless, that it is a case in which the law falls too hard upon the convict, should have the right to recommend a case to the consideration of the committee of pardon, previously to the lapse of two-thirds of the imprisonment. And the governor, or any other authority, yet definitely invested with this privilege, might have the power to charge the committee to consider a case at any time, and to report thereon respecting the propriety of making use of the pardoning power. But in no case ought the governor or any other authority to have the right of pardoning without a previous investigation of the case by the committee of pardon. It may be objected that a rogue, in order to obtain pardon after the expiration of two-thirds of his term, to which a similar law would give him a kind of right, may behave apparently well, without truly reforming. But let a man who has been sentenced for ten years, behave apparently well for six years and a half, and nine times out of ten it will have a salutary influence. Besides, is hypocrisy not much more excited at present when pardon may be granted at any time?

Mr. Dumont is so convinced of the necessity of eliminating uncertainty from all matters of law and punishment as much as possible, that he uses the following words in his report to the representative council of Geneva, January 5, 1825, in consequence of which the above-mentioned law of that republic was adopted:

It may be laid down as an incontestable principle, that in matters of penal justice, I was going to say, in penal pharmacy, every thing which diminishes the certainty of punishment is an evil; every punishment which is not fixed, which floats between fear and hope, is a punishment badly contrived. The causes of uncertainty between the law and its operation, are already but too numerous; if this is an inevitable evil, it ought to be reduced to its narrowest limits; but what shall we think of a law, the object of which is to render the punishment uncertain! and this is nevertheless the result of a tribunal of pardon, open to the petitions of the prisoner during the whole term of his imprisonment. We should know man very imperfectly were we not aware of the readiness with which he takes his wishes for hopes, and his hopes for probabilities. I agree, that a convict wishing for pardon, will take care not to create himself difficulties by acts of insubordination or violence; I allow that he will pay attention to his words and behaviour: but it is a fact, that this idea, always present to his mind, causing a disturbed feeling of anxiety and expectation, will absorb and prevent him from being resigned to his situation, and following his labor with reflection and calmness. He feels like an indigent person, who having taken a lottery ticket, has his imagination absorbed by dreams of success, and fears of misfortune. It has been observed that prisoners, after having been unsuccessful in their petitions for pardon, became more calm and resigned to their situation and duties as soon as their fate was fixed. I owe this interesting observation to our jailor. Thus far the double end of increasing the certainty of punishment and of making it more subservient to moral correction, this indefinite recourse to pardon ought to be abolished, and a fixed character be given to it.[11]

The committee of pardon of Geneva consists of nine members, most of whom are judges.

Such, or a similar limitation of the pardoning power, would require in some states, the modification of certain laws, which seem to continue in their severity only, because it is understood that the governor shortens the imprisonment of all those, whose sentence (by the law) seems to be hard according to our present views. It is peculiar, but it is nevertheless true, that, comparatively speaking, criminal law has been little attended to in England, or in the United States, while in two countries, in which the citizen is by far less protected in his rights — Germany and Italy — criminal law has been made the subject of the deepest study by many of their first jurists. Beccaria, Filangieri, Feuerbach, Mittermaier, may be mentioned out of a host. The reason may be, that in a free and well regulated country, the criminal trial forms but a very limited part of that whole system which guaranties to the citizen his rights and privileges, so that little interest is attached to it by the nation at large, while in absolute monarchies the penal trial is one of the very few cases in which the individual and the government meet as parties, and, as it were, on even ground, (which at least is the case where the court does not accuse, inquire, try, defend, and sentence). The criminal trial in many countries, is the only case in which the citizen, or rather the subject, appears under the aegis of distinct and acknowledged rights and privileges. It cannot surprise us therefore, if we find some authors treating criminal law as if they were treating of constitutional law. However this may be, it is very desirable that criminal law should be made in our country a subject of more general and deeper study; because this is the only preparation for such laws which finally will entirely accord with the penitentiary system. A chair for criminal law is indispensable, and let us never forget that the Germans and Italians have attended most to criminal law, the French and English least. To the literature of the former, particularly to the first, we must direct our attention.

In France, pardon is reduced in some degree to certainty, by Article 463 of the *Code Pénal,* according to which the judges have the right to award in certain cases, a punishment under the minimum of punishment mentioned by the code. In the year 1827, use was made of this provision in 10,493 cases. But it must be remembered that this provision has reference to correctional cases only, in which no jury exists. Of late a law was issued in France, according to which pardon was held out as a reward for good behavior in prison. At first it had an admirable effect, but soon it created the reverse, by disappointing some prisoners, exciting others, etc.

The authors have only treated of our prisons and those of France. I intended at first, to extend my notes to the consideration of prisons in all other countries of the civilized world, as far as the materials in my possession would enable me, but I soon found, that this vast subject could not conveniently be treated in the form of notes or an appendix. It would be an ample subject for a work of itself.[12]

Francis Lieber

Manhattanville, City of New York
May, 1833

AUTHORS' PREFACE

Society, in our days, is in a state of disquiet, owing, in our opinion, to two causes:

The first is of an entirely moral character; there is in the minds of men an activity which knows not where to find an object; an energy deprived of its proper element; and which consumes society for want of other prey.

The other is of an entirely material character; it is the unhappy condition of the working classes who are in want of labor and bread; and whose corruption, beginning in misery, is completed in the prison.

The first evil is owing to the progress of intellectual improvement; the second, to the misery of the poor.

How is the first of these evils to be obviated? Its remedy seems to depend more upon circumstances, than upon human provisions. As to the second, more than one effort has already been made to free mankind from it; but it is not yet known whether success is possible.

Such is the insufficiency of human institutions, that we see melancholy effects resulting from establishments which in theory promise none but happy results.

In England it has been believed that the springs of crime and misery may be dried up by giving work and money to the unfortunate. But we see the number of paupers and criminals every day increasing in that country.

There is not one philanthropic institution, the abuse of which does not border closely on its usefulness.

Alms, however well distributed, tend to produce poverty,

and assistance afforded to a forsaken child causes others to be abandoned. The more we contemplate the melancholy spectacle presented by public benevolence, struggling without success against human sufferings, the more we are obliged to acknowledge, that there exist evils, against which it is generous to strive, but of which our old societies seem incapable to rid themselves.

Yet the wound exists, open to every eye. There are in France two millions of paupers, and forty thousand liberated convicts, who have gone forth from the bagnes or other prisons.

Alarmed by so formidable an evil, public opinion asks a remedy from government, which does not cure it, perhaps, because it considers it incurable.

But notwithstanding it may be true that this vicious state of society cannot be cured altogether, it seems equally certain that there are circumstances which tend to aggravate it, and institutions whose influence renders it less fatal.

Various voices are raised in our time to indicate to government the path which is best to be pursued.

Some ask for the establishment of agricultural colonies in those parts of the French soil which have as yet been left uncultivated, and where the labor of convicts and paupers might be made useful and productive.

This system, which has met with great success in Belgium and Holland, is worthy of the particular attention of statesmen.

Others are particularly struck with the danger to which society is exposed from liberated convicts, whose corruption has been increased in prison. These believe that the evil would be remedied in a great degree, if the criminals were subjected during the time of their imprisonment to a penitentiary system, which, instead of further depraving them, made them better.

Some writers (one of whom has just received a prize from the French academy) being persuaded that the moral reformation of the criminal is impossible, and that his restoration to society cannot take place without imminent danger, think that it would be better if all convicts were transported out of France.[1]

In the midst of these clashing opinions, some of which however are not irreconcilable, it appeared to us that it would be of use to introduce into this discussion some authentic documents on one of the important points in dispute.

Such has been the origin of the travels we have undertaken under the auspices of the French government.

Having been commissioned to examine into the theory and practice of the penitentiary system in the United States, we have accomplished this task; government has received our report; and we now owe it to our country to give an account of our labors.[2]

If the results of our investigations shall be deemed valuable, it is chiefly owing to the generous hospitality with which we were received in the United States. Every where in that country, establishments of all kinds were thrown open to us, and all necessary materials were furnished with a readiness which awakened in us the liveliest feeling of gratitude.

The importance of our mission was understood in America, and the public functionaries of the highest order, as well as private gentlemen, vied with each other in facilitating its execution.

We have had no means of manifesting our sense of so much kindness. But if this book should find its way to America, we are happy to think that the inhabitants of the United States will find here a feeble expression of our heartfelt gratitude.

CHAPTER ONE

AN HISTORICAL OUTLINE

OF

THE PENITENTIARY SYSTEM

Though the penitentiary system in the United States is a new institution, its origin must be traced back to times already long gone by. The first idea of a reform in the American prisons, belongs to a religious sect in Pennsylvania. The Quakers, who abhor all shedding of blood, had always protested against the barbarous laws which the colonies inherited from their mother country. In 1786, their voice succeeded in finding due attention, and from this period, punishment of death, mutilation and the whip were successively abolished in almost all cases by the Legislature of Pennsylvania. A less cruel fate awaited the convicts from this period. The punishment of imprisonment was substituted for corporal punishment, and the law authorized the courts to inflict solitary confinement in a cell during day and night, upon those guilty of capital crimes. It was then that the Walnut Street prison was established in Philadelphia. Here the convicts were classed according to the nature of their crimes, and separate cells were constructed for those whom the courts of justice had sentenced to absolute isolation. These cells also served to curb the resistance of individuals, unwilling to submit to the discipline of the prison. The solitary prisoners did not work.[1]

This innovation was good but incomplete.

The impossibility of subjecting criminals to a useful classification, has since been acknowledged, and solitary confinement without labor has been condemned by experience. It is nevertheless just to say, that the trial of this theory has not been made long enough to be decisive. The authority given to the judges of Pennsylvania, by the law of April 5, 1790, and of March 22, to send criminals to the prison in Walnut Street, who formerly would have been sent to the different county jails, soon produced in this prison such a crowd of convicts, that the difficulty of classification increased in the same degree as the cells became insufficient.[2]

To say the truth there did not yet exist a penitentiary system in the United States.

If it be asked why this name was given to the system of imprisonment which had been established, we would answer, that then as well as now, the abolition of the punishment of death was confounded in America, with the penitentiary system. People said — *instead of killing the guilty, our laws put them in prison; hence we have a penitentiary system.*

The conclusion was not correct. It is very true that the punishment of death applied to the greater part of crimes, is irreconcilable with a system of imprisonment; but this punishment abolished, the penitentiary system does not yet necessarily exist; it is further necessary, that the criminal whose life has been spared, be placed in a prison, whose discipline renders him better. Because, if the system, instead of reforming, should only tend to corrupt him still more, this would not be any longer a penitentiary system, but only a bad system of imprisonment.

This mistake of the Americans has for a long time been shared in France. In 1794, the Duke de la Rochefoucauld-Liancourt, published an interesting notice on the prison of Philadelphia: he declared that this city had an excellent prison system, and all the world repeated it.[3]

However, the Walnut Street prison could produce none of the effects which are expected from this system. It had two principal faults: it corrupted by contamination those who worked together. It corrupted by indolence, the individuals who were plunged into solitude.

The true merit of its founders was the abolition of the sanguinary laws of Pennsylvania, and by introducing a new system of imprisonment, the direction of public attention to this important point. Unfortunately that which in this innovation deserved praise, was not immediately distinguished from that which was untenable.

Solitude applied to the criminal, in order to conduct him to reformation by reflection, rests upon a philosophical and true conception. But the authors of this theory had not yet founded its application upon those means which alone could render it practical and salutary. Yet their mistake was not immediately perceived, and the success of Walnut Street prison boasted of in the United States still more than in Europe, biased public opinion in favor of its faults, as well as its advantages.

The first state which showed itself zealous to imitate Pennsylvania, was that of New York, which in 1797, adopted both new penal laws and a new prison system.

Solitary confinement without labor, was admitted here as in Philadelphia, but, as in Walnut Street, it was reserved for those who especially were sentenced to undergo it by the courts of justice, and for those who opposed the established order of the prison. Solitary confinement, therefore, was not the ordinary system of the establishment; it awaited only those great criminals who, before the reform of the penal laws, would have been condemned to death. Those who were guilty of less offenses were put indiscriminately together in the prison. They, different from the inmates of the solitary cells, had to work during the day, and the only disciplinary punishment which their keeper had a right to inflict, in case of breach of the order of the prison, was solitary confinement, with bread and water.

The Walnut Street prison was imitated by others: Maryland, Massachusetts, Maine, New Jersey, Virginia, etc., adopted successively, the principle of solitary confinement, applied only to a certain class of criminals in each of these states. The reform of criminal laws preceded that of the prisons.[4]

Nowhere was this system of imprisonment crowned with

the hoped-for success.[5] In general it was ruinous to the public treasury; it never effected the reformation of the prisoners. Every year the legislature of each state voted considerable funds towards the support of the penitentiaries, and the continued return of the same individuals into the prisons, proved the inefficiency of the system to which they were submitted.

Such results seem to prove the insufficiency of the whole system; however instead of accusing the theory itself, its execution was attacked. It was believed that the whole evil resulted from the paucity of cells, and the crowding of the prisoners; and that the system, such as it was established, would be fertile in happy results, if some new buildings were added to the prisons already existing. New expenses therefore, and new efforts were made.

Such was the origin of the Auburn prison [1816].

This prison, which has become so celebrated since, was at first founded upon a plan essentially erroneous. It limited itself to some classifications, and each of these cells was destined to receive two convicts: [6] it was of all combinations the most unfortunate; it would have been better to throw together fifty criminals in the same room, than to separate them two by two. This inconvenience was soon felt, and in 1819 the Legislature of the State of New York, ordered the erection of a new building at Auburn (the northern wing) in order to increase the number of solitary cells. However, it must be observed, that no idea as yet existed of the system which has prevailed since. It was not intended to subject all the convicts to the system of cells, but its application was only to be made to a greater number. At the same time the same theories produced the same trials in Philadelphia, where the little success of the Walnut Street prison would have convinced the inhabitants of Pennsylvania of its inefficiency, if the latter, like the citizens of the State of New York, had not been led to seek in the faults of execution, a motive for allowing the principle to be correct.

In 1817, the Legislature of Pennsylvania decreed the erection of the penitentiary at Pittsburgh, for the western counties, and in 1821, that of the penitentiary of Cherry Hill, for the city of Philadelphia and the eastern counties.[7]

The principles to be followed in the construction of these

two establishments were, however, not entirely the same as those on which the Walnut Street prison had been erected. In the latter, classification formed the predominant system, to which solitary confinement was but secondary. In the new prisons the classifications were abandoned, and a solitary cell was to be prepared for each convict. The criminal was not to leave his cell day or night, and all labor was denied to him in his solitude. Thus absolute solitary confinement, which in Walnut Street was but accidental, was now to become the foundation of the system adopted for Pittsburgh and Cherry Hill.

The experiment which was to be made, promised to be decisive; no expense was spared to construct these new establishments worthy of their object, and the edifices which were elevated, resembled prisons less than palaces.

In the meantime, before even the laws which ordered their erection, were executed, the Auburn prison had been tried in the State of New York. Lively debates ensued on this occasion, in the legislature, and the public was impatient to know the result of the new trials, which had just been made.

The northern wing having been nearly finished in 1821, eighty prisoners were placed there, and a separate cell was given to each. This trial, from which so happy a result had been anticipated, was fatal to the greater part of the convicts. In order to reform them, they had been submitted to complete isolation; but this absolute solitude, if nothing interrupts it, is beyond the strength of man; it destroys the criminal without intermission and without pity; it does not reform, it kills.[8]

The unfortunates, on whom this experiment was made, fell into a state of depression, so manifest, that their keepers were struck with it; their lives seemed in danger, if they remained longer in this situation; five of them, had already succumbed during a single year;[9] their moral state was not less alarming; one of them had become insane; another, in a fit of despair, had embraced the opportunity when the keeper brought him something, to precipitate himself from his cell, running the almost certain chance of a mortal fall.

Upon similar effects the system was finally judged. The Governor of the State of New York pardoned twenty-six of those in solitary confinement; the others to whom this favor was not extended, were allowed to leave the cells during day, and to work in the common workshops of the prison. From this period, (1823) the system of unmodified isolation ceased entirely to be practiced at Auburn. Proofs were soon afforded that this system, fatal to the health of the criminals, was likewise inefficient in producing their reform. Of twenty-six convicts, pardoned by the governor, fourteen returned a short time after into the prison, in consequence of new offenses.

This experiment, so fatal to those who were selected to undergo it, was of a nature to endanger the success of the penitentiary system altogether. After the melancholy effects of isolation, it was to be feared that the whole principle would be rejected : it would have been a natural reaction. The Americans were wiser : the idea was not given up, that the solitude, which causes the criminal to reflect, exercises a beneficial influence ; and the problem was, to find the means by which the evil effect of total solitude could be avoided without giving up its advantages. It was believed that this end could be attained, by leaving the convicts in their cells during night, and by making them work during the day, in the common workshops, obliging them at the same time to observe absolute silence.

Messrs. Allen, Hopkins, and Tibbits, who, in 1824, were directed by the Legislature of New York to inspect the Auburn prison, found this new discipline established in that prison. They praised it much in their report, and the Legislature sanctioned this new system by its formal approbation.

Here an obscurity exists which it has not been in our power to dissipate. We see the renowned Auburn system suddenly spring up, and proceed from the ingenious combination of two elements, which seem at first glance incompatible, isolation and reunion. But that which we do not clearly see, is the creator of this system, of which nevertheless some one must necessarily have formed the first idea.

Does the State of New York owe it to Governor Clinton, whose name in the United States is connected with so many useful and beneficial enterprises?

Does the honor belong to Mr. Cray, one of the directors of Auburn, to whom Judge Powers, who himself was at the head of that establishment, seems to attribute the merit?

Lastly, Mr. Elam Lynds, who has contributed so much to put the new system into practice, does the glory also of the invention belong to him? [10]

We shall not attempt to solve this question, interesting to the persons whom we have mentioned, and the country to which they belong, but of little importance to us.

In fine, does not experience teach us that there are innovations, the honor of which belongs to nobody in particular, because they are the effects of simultaneous efforts, and of the progress of time?

The establishment of Auburn has, since its commencement, obtained extraordinary success. It soon excited public attention in the highest degree. A remarkable revolution took place at that time in the opinions of many. The direction of a prison, formerly confided to obscure keepers, was now sought for by persons of high standing, and Mr. Elam Lynds, formerly a captain in the army of the United States, and Judge Powers, a magistrate of rare merit, were seen, with honor to themselves, filling the office of directors of Auburn.

However, the adoption of the system of cells for all convicts in the state of New York, rendered the Auburn prison insufficient, as it contained but 550 cells after all the successive additions which it had received.[11] The want of a new prison, therefore, was felt. It was then that the plan of Sing Sing was resolved upon by the legislature (1825) and the way in which it was executed is of a kind that deserves to be reported.

Mr. Elam Lynds, who had made his trials at Auburn, of which he was the superintendent, left this establishment; took one hundred convicts, accustomed to obey, with him, led them to the place where the projected prison was to be erected; there, encamped on the bank of the Hudson, without a place to receive, and without walls to lock up his dangerous companions; he sets them to work, making of every one a mason or a carpenter, and having no other means to keep them in obedience, than the firmness of his character and the energy of his will.

During several years, the convicts, whose number was gradually increased, were at work in building their own prison, and at present the penitentiary of Sing Sing contains one thousand cells, all of which have been built by their criminal inmates.[12] At the same time (1825) an establishment of another nature was reared in the city of New York, but which occupies not a less important place among the improvements, the history of which we attempt to trace. We mean the house of refuge, founded for juvenile offenders.

There exists no establishment, the usefulness of which, experience has warranted in a higher degree. It is well known that most of those individuals on whom the criminal law inflicts punishments, have been unfortunate before they became guilty. Misfortune is particularly dangerous for those whom it befalls in a tender age; and it is very rare that an orphan without inheritance and without friends, or a child abandoned by its parents, avoids the snares laid for his inexperience, and does not pass within a short time from misery to crime. Affected by the fate of juvenile delinquents, several charitable individuals of the city of New York [13] conceived the plan of a house of refuge, destined to serve as an asylum, and to procure for them an education and the means of existence, which fortune had refused. Thirty thousand dollars were the produce of a first subscription. Thus by the sole power of a charitable association, an establishment eminently useful, was founded, which, perhaps, is still more important than the penitentiaries, because the latter punish crime, while the house of refuge tends to prevent it.

The experiment made at Auburn in the state of New York (the fatal effects of isolation without labor) did not prevent Pennsylvania from continuing the trial of solitary confinement, and in the year 1827, the penitentiary of Pittsburgh began to receive prisoners. Each one was shut up, day and night, in a cell, in which no labor was allowed to him. This solitude, which in principle was to be absolute, was not such in fact. The construction of this penitentiary is so defective, that it is very easy to hear in one cell what is going on in another; so that each prisoner found in the communication with his neighbor a daily recreation, i.e. an opportunity of inevitable corruption. As these criminals did not work, we may say that their sole occupation consisted in mutual corruption. This prison, therefore, was worse than even that of Walnut street, because, owing to the communication with each other, the prisoners at Pittsburgh were as little occupied with their reformation, as those at Walnut Street. And while the latter indemnified society in a degree by the produce of their labor, the others spent their whole time in idleness, injurious to themselves, and burdensome to the public treasury.[14]

The bad success of this establishment proved nothing against the system which had called it into existence, because defects in the construction of the prison, rendered the execution of the system impossible. Nevertheless, the advocates of the theories on which it was founded, began to grow cool. This impression became still more general in Pennsylvania, when the melancholy effects caused by solitude without labor in the Auburn prison, became known, as well as the happy success of the new discipline, founded on isolation by night, with common labor during the day.[15]

Warned by such striking results, Pennsylvania was fearful she had pursued a dangerous course. She felt the necessity of submitting to a new investigation the question of solitary imprisonment without labor, practiced at Pittsburgh and introduced into the penitentiary of Cherry Hill, the construction of which was already much advanced.

The legislature of this state, therefore, appointed a committee in order to examine which was the better system of imprisonment. Messrs. Charles Shaler, Edward King, and T. I. Wharton, commissioners charged with this mission, have exhibited, in a very remarkable report, the different systems then in practice (December 20, 1827), and they conclude the discussion by recommending the new Auburn discipline, which they pronounce the best.

The authority of this inquiry had a powerful effect on public opinion. It however met with powerful opposition: Roberts Vaux, in Pennsylvania and Edward Livingston, in Louisiana, continued to support the system of complete solitude for criminals. The latter, whose writings are imbued with so elevated a philosophy, had prepared a criminal code, and a code of Prison Discipline for Louisiana, his native state. His profound theories, little understood by those for whom they were destined, had more success in Pennsylvania, for which they had not been intended. In this superior work, Mr. Livingston admitted, for most cases, the principle of *labor of the convicts.* Altogether, he showed himself less the advocate of the Pittsburgh prison, than the adversary of the Auburn system. He acknowledged the good discipline of the latter, but powerfully opposed himself to corporal punishment used to maintain it. Mr. Livingston, and those who supported the same doctrines, had to combat a powerful fact: this was the uncertainty of their theories, not yet tested, and the proven success of the system they attacked. Auburn went on prospering: everywhere its wonderful effects were praised, and they were found traced each year with great spirit, in a work justly celebrated in America, and which has essentially co-operated to bring public opinion in the United States, on the penitentiary system, to that point where it now is. We mean the annual publications of the Prison Discipline Society at Boston. These annual reports — the work of Mr. Louis Dwight, give a decided preference to the Auburn system.[16]

All the states of the Union were attentive witnesses of the controversy respecting the two systems.

In this fortunate country, which has neither troublesome neighbors, who disturb it from without, nor internal dissensions which distract it within, nothing more is necessary, in order to excite public attention in the highest degree, than an essay on some principle of social economy. As the existence of society is not put in jeopardy, the question is now how to live, but how to improve.

Pennsylvania was, perhaps, more than any other state, interested in the controversy. The rival of New York, it was natural she should show herself jealous to retain, in every respect, the rank to which her advanced civilization entitles her among the most enlightened states of the Union.

She adopted a system which at once agreed with the austerity of her manners, and her philanthropical sensibility. She rejected solitude without labor, the fatal effects of which experience had proved everywhere, and she retained the absolute separation of the prisoners — a severe punishment, which, in order to be inflicted, needs not the support of corporal chastisement.

The penitentiary of Cherry Hill, founded on these principles, is therefore a combination of Pittsburgh and Auburn. Isolation during night and day, has been retained from the Pittsburgh system: and, into the solitary cell, the labor of Auburn has been introduced.[17]

This revolution in the prison discipline of Pennsylvania, was immediately followed by a general reform of her criminal laws. All punishments were made milder; the severity of solitary imprisonment permitted an abridgment of its duration; capital punishment was abolished in all cases, except that of premeditated murder.[18]

While the states of New York and Pennsylvania made important reforms in their laws, and each adopted a different system of imprisonment, the other states of the Union did not remain inactive, in presence of the grand spectacle before them.

Since the year 1825, the plan of a new prison on the Auburn model, has been adopted by the legislature of Connecticut; and the penitentiary at Wethersfield has succeeded the old prison of Newgate.

In spite of the weight which Pennsylvania threw into the balance, in favor of absolute solitude with labor, the Auburn system, i. e. common labor during the day, with isolation during night, continued to obtain a preference. Massachusetts, Maryland, Tennessee, Kentucky, Maine, and Vermont, have gradually adopted the Auburn plan, and have taken the Auburn prison as a model for those which they have caused to be erected.[19]

Several states have not stopped here, but have also founded houses of refuge for juvenile offenders, as an addition, in some measure, to the penitentiary system, in imitation of New York. These latter establishments have been founded in Boston in 1826, and in Philadelphia in 1828. There is every indication that Baltimore also, will soon have its house of refuge.

It is easy to foresee, that the impulse of reform given by New York and Pennsylvania, will not remain confined to the states mentioned above.

From the happy rivalship which exists among all the states of the Union, each state follows the reforms which have been effected by the others, and shows itself impatient to imitate them.

It would be wrong to judge all the United States by the picture which we have presented of the improvements adopted by some of them.

Accustomed as we are to see our central government attract everything, and propel in the various provinces all the parts of the administration in a uniform direction, we sometimes suppose that the same is the case in other countries; and comparing the centralization of government at Washington with that at Paris, the different states of the Union to our departments, we are tempted to believe that innovations made in one state, take, of necessity, place in the others.[20] There is, however, nothing like in the United States.

These states, united by the federal tie into one family, are in respect to everything which concerns their common interests, subjected to one single authority. But besides these general interests, they preserve their entire individual independence, and each of them is sovereign master to rule itself according to its own pleasure. We have spoken of nine states which have adopted a new system of prisons; there are fifteen more which have as yet made no change.[21]

In these latter, the ancient system prevails in its whole force; the crowding of prisoners, confusion of crimes, ages, and sometimes sexes, mixture of indicted and convicted prisoners, of criminals and debtors, guilty persons and witnesses; considerable mortality; frequent escapes; absence of all discipline, no silence which leads the criminals to reflection; no labor which accustoms them to an honest mode of subsistence; insalubrity of the place which destroys health; ignism of the conversations which corrupt; idleness that depraves; the assemblage, in one word, of all vices and all immoralities — such is the picture offered by the prisons which have not yet entered into the way of reform.

By the side of one state, the penitentiaries of which might serve as a model, we find another, whose jails present the example of everything which ought to be avoided. Thus the State of New York is without contradiction one of the most advanced in the path of reform, while New Jersey, which is separated from it but by a river, has retained all the vices of the ancient system.

Ohio, which possesses a penal code remarkable for the mildness and humanity of its provisions, has barbarous prisons. We have deeply sighed when at Cincinnati, visiting the prison. We found half of the imprisoned charged with irons, and the rest plunged into an infected dungeon; and are unable to describe the painful impression which we experienced, when, examining the prison of New Orleans, we found men together with hogs, in the midst of all odors and nuisances.[22] In locking up the criminals, nobody thinks of rendering them better, but only of taming their malice; they are put in chains like ferocious beasts; and instead of being corrected, they are rendered brutal.[23]

If it is true that the penitentiary system is entirely unknown in that part which we mentioned, it is equally true that this system is incomplete in those states even where it is in vigor.[24] Thus at New York, at Philadelphia, and Boston, there are new prisons for convicts, whose punishment exceeds one or two years' imprisonment; but establishments of a similar nature do not exist to receive individuals who are sentenced for a shorter time, or who are indicted only.[25] In respect to the latter, nothing has been changed; disorder, confusion, mixture of different ages and moral characters, all vices of the old system still exist for them: we have seen in the house of arrest in New York (Bridewell) more than fifty indicted persons in one room. These arrested persons are precisely those for whom well-regulated prisons ought to have been built. It is easy in fact to conceive, that he who has not yet been pronounced guilty, and he who has committed but a crime or misdemeanor comparatively slight, ought to be surrounded by much greater protection than such as are more advanced in crime, and whose guilt has been acknowledged.

Arrested persons are sometimes innocent and always supposed to be so. How is it that we should suffer them to find in the prison a corruption which they did not bring with them?

If they are guilty, why place them first in a house of arrest, fitted to corrupt them still more, except to reform them afterwards in a penitentiary, to which they will be sent after their conviction? [26]

There is evidently a deficiency in a prison system which offers anomalies of this kind.

These shocking contradictions proceed chiefly from the want of unison in the various parts of government in the United States.

The larger prisons (state prisons) corresponding to our *maisons centrales*, belong to the state, which directs them; after these follow the county jails, directed by the county; and at last the prisons of the city, superintended by the city itself.

The various branches of government in the United States being almost as independent of each other, as the states themselves, it results that they hardly ever act uniformly and simultaneously. While one makes a useful reform in the circle of its powers, the other remains inactive, and attached to ancient abuses.

We shall see below, how this independence of the individual parts, which is injurious to the uniform action of all their powers, has nevertheless a beneficial influence, by giving to each a more prompt and energetic progress in the direction which it follows freely and uncompelled.

We shall say nothing more of the defective parts in the prison system in the United States. If at some future period France shall imitate the penitentiaries of America, the most important thing for her will be to know those which may serve as models. The new establishments then, will form the only object of our further inquiry.

We have seen, in the preceding remarks, that few states have as yet changed entirely their system of imprisonment; the number of those which have modified their penal laws is still less. Several among them yet possess part of the barbarous laws which they have received from England.

We shall not speak of the Southern states, where slavery still exists. In every place where one-half of the community is cruelly oppressed by the other, we must expect to find in the law of the oppressor, a weapon always ready to strike nature which revolts or humanity that complains. Punishment of death and stripes — these form the whole penal code for the slaves.[27] But if we throw a glance at those states even which have abolished slavery, and which are most advanced in civilization, we shall see this civilization uniting itself, in some, with penal laws full of mildness, and in others, with all the rigor of a code of Draco.

Let us but compare the laws of Pennsylvania with those of New England, which is, perhaps, the most enlightened part of the American Union. In Massachusetts, there are ten different crimes punished by death — among others, rape and burglary.[28] Maine, Rhode Island, and Connecticut, count the same number of capital crimes.[29] Among these laws, some contain the most degrading punishments, such as the pillory; others revolting cruelties, as branding and mutilation.[30] There are also some which order fines equal to confiscations.[31]

While we find the remains of barbarism in some states, with an old population, there are others, which, risen since yesterday, have banished from their laws all cruel punishments not called for by the interest of society. Thus, Ohio, which certainly is not as enlightened as New England, has a penal code much more humane than those of Massachusetts or Connecticut.

Close by a state where the reform of the penal laws seems to have arrived at its summit, we find another, the criminal laws of which are stamped with all the brutalities of the ancient system. It is thus that the States of Delaware and New Jersey, so far behind in the path of improvement, border on Pennsylvania, which, in this respect, marches at the head of all others.[32]

We should forget the object of our report were we to dwell any longer on this point. We were obliged to present a sketch of the penal legislation of the United States, because it exercises a necessary influence on the question before us.

In fact it is easy to conceive to what point the punishments which degrade the guilty, are incompatible with a penitentiary system, the object of which is to reform them. How can we hope to awaken the moral sense of an individual who carries on his body the indelible sign of infamy, when the mutilation of his limbs reminds others incessantly of his crime, or the sign imprinted on his forehead, perpetuates its memory?[33]

Must we not ardently wish, that the last traces of such barbarism should disappear from all the United States, and particularly from those which have adopted the penitentiary system, with which they are irreconcilable, and whose existence renders them still more shocking?[34]

Besides, let us not blame these people for advancing slowly on the path of innovation. Ought not similar changes to be the work of time, and of public opinion? There are in the

United States a certain number of philosophical minds, who, full of theories and systems, are impatient to put them into practice; and if they had the power themselves to make the law of the land, they would efface with one dash, all the old customs, and supplant them by the creations of their genius, and the decrees of their wisdom. Whether right or wrong the people do not move so quickly. They consent to changes, but they wish to see them progressive and partial.[35] This prudent and reserved reform, effected by a whole nation, all of whose customs are practical, is, perhaps, more beneficial than the precipitated trials which would result, had the enthusiasm of ardent minds and enticing theories free play.[36]

Whatever may be the difficulties yet to be overcome, we do not hesitate to declare that the cause of reform and of progress in the United States, seem to us certain and safe.

Slavery, the shame of a free nation, is expelled every day from some districts over which it held its sway; and those persons themselves who possess most slaves, are convinced that slavery will not last much longer.

Every day punishments which wound humanity, become supplanted by milder ones; and in the most civilized states of the north, where these punishments continue in the written laws, their application has become so rare that they are to be considered as fallen into disuse.

The impulse of improvement is given. Those states which have as yet done nothing, are conscious of their deficiency; they envy those which have preceded them in this career, and are impatient to imitate them.

Finally, it is a fact worth remarking, that the modification of the penal laws and that of prison discipline, are two reforms intimately associated with each other, and never separated in the United States.

Our special task is not to enlarge on the first; the second alone shall fix our attention.

The various states in which we have found a penitentiary system, pursue all the same end: the amelioration of the prison discipline. But they employ different means to arrive at their object. These different means have formed the subject of our inquiry.

CHAPTER TWO

OBJECTIVES

OF PENITENTIARY SYSTEMS

T HE PENITENTIARY SYSTEM in the proper acceptation of the word, relates only to individuals condemned and subjected to the punishment of imprisonment for the expiation of their crime.

In a less confined sense, it may be extended to all arrested persons, whether their arrest precedes or follows the judgment: that is to say, whether these persons are arrested as suspected or indicted for a crime, or as condemned for having committed it. In this wider acceptation, the penitentiary system comprehends prisons of all kinds, state and other prisons, houses of arrest and refuge, etc.

In this latter sense we shall use it.

We have already said that in the United States those prisons which correspond to our houses of arrest, (*maisons d'arrêt*) that is to say, those which are destined for persons provisionally arrested, and for individuals sentenced to a short imprisonment, have undergone no reform as yet. Consequently, we shall not speak of them. We should be able to present in this respect but a theory, and it is practical observations with which we have, above all, to occupy ourselves.

We shall therefore, immediately direct our attention to the penitentiaries, properly so called, which contain in the United States, those convicts, who, according to our laws, would be sent to the "central houses of correction," of "detention," and to the "bagnes."

The punishment of imprisonment in the different states in which it is pronounced, is not varied as by our laws. With us a distinction is made between simple imprisonment, *reclusion*, detention, and hard labor; each of these punishments has certain traits which are peculiar to it. Imprisonment in the United States has a uniform character; it differs only in its duration.

It is divided into two principal classes: (1) imprisonment from one month to one or two years, applied to breaches of the laws of the police, and to lighter offenses (*délits*); (2) imprisonment from two years to twenty or for life, which serves to punish crimes of a graver character. It is for the convicts suffering the second class of punishment, that in the United States a penitentiary system exists:

1. In what consists this system, and what are its fundamental principles?
2. How is it put into practice?
3. By what disciplinary means is it maintained?
4. What results have been obtained in respect to reformation of the prisoners?
5. What have been its effect in a financial respect?
6. What information can we obtain from this system for the amelioration of our prisoners?

These are the principal questions respecting which we shall give a summary of our observations and inquiries.

Having accomplished this task, we shall conclude our report by an examination of the houses of refuge for juvenile offenders. These establishments are rather schools than prisons, but they form, nevertheless, an essential part of the penitentiary system, since the regulations to which these young prisoners are subjected, have for their object, to punish those who have been declared guilty, and aim at the reformation of all.

A Comparison of Two Systems

WE FIND in the United States two distinctly separate systems: the system of Auburn and that of Philadelphia.

Sing Sing, in the State of New York; Wethersfield, in

Connecticut; Boston, in Massachusetts; Baltimore, in Maryland; have followed the model of Auburn.[1]

On the other side, Pennsylvania stands quite alone.

The two systems opposed to each other on important points, have, however, a common basis, without which no penitentiary system is possible; this basis is the *isolation* of the prisoners.[2]

Whoever has studied the interior of prisons and the moral state of their inmates, has become convinced that communication between these persons renders their moral reformation impossible, and becomes even for them the inevitable cause of an alarming corruption. This observation, justified by the experience of every day, has become in the United States an almost popular truth; and the publicists who disagree most respecting the way of putting the penitentiary system into practice, fully agree upon this point, that no salutary system can possibly exist without the separation of criminals.

For a long time it was believed that, in order to remedy the evil caused by the intercourse of prisoners with each other, it would be sufficient to establish in the prison, a certain number of classifications. But after having tried this plan, its insufficiency has been acknowledged. There are similar punishments and crimes called by the same name, but there are no two beings equal in regard to their morals; and every time that convicts are put together, there exists necessarily a fatal influence of some upon others, because, in the association of the wicked, it is not the less guilty who act upon the more criminal, but the more depraved who influence those who are less so.

We must therefore, impossible as it is to classify prisoners, come to a separation of all.[3]

This separation, which prevents the wicked from injuring others, is also favorable to himself.

Thrown into solitude he reflects. Placed alone, in view of his crime, he learns to hate it; and if his soul be not yet surfeited with crime, and thus have lost all taste for anything better, it is in solitude, where remorse will come to assail him.

Solitude is a severe punishment, but such a punishment is merited by the guilty. Mr. Livingston justly remarks, that a prison, destined to punish, would soon cease to be a fearful object, if the convicts in it could entertain at their pleasure those social relations in which they delighted, before their entry into the prison.

Yet, whatever may be the crime of the guilty prisoner, no one has the right to take life from him, if society decree merely to deprive him of his liberty. Such, however, would be the result of absolute solitude, if no alleviation of its rigors were offered.

This is the reason why labor is introduced into the prison. Far from being an aggravation of the punishment, it is a real benefit to the prisoner.

But even if the criminal did not find in it a relief from his sufferings, it nevertheless would be necessary to force him to it. It is idleness which has led him to crime; with employment he will learn how to live honestly.

Labor of the criminals is necessary still under another point of view: their detention, expensive for society if they remain idle, becomes less burdensome if they labor.

The prisons of Auburn, Sing Sing, Wethersfield, Boston, and Philadelphia, rest then upon these two united principles, solitude and labor. These principles, in order to be salutary, ought not to be separated: the one is inefficient without the other.

In the ancient prison of Auburn, isolation without labor has been tried, and those prisoners who have not become insane or did not die of despair, have returned to society only to commit new crimes.

In Baltimore, the system of labor without isolation is trying at this moment, and seems not to promise happy results.

Though admitting one-half of the principle of solitude, the other half is rejected. The penitentiary of this city contains a number of cells equal to that of the prisoners who are locked up at night, but during day, they are permitted to communicate freely with each other. Certainly separation during night is the most important; but it is not sufficient. The intercourse of criminals is necessarily of a corrupting nature, and this intercourse must be prevented if we wish to protect the prisoners from mutual contagion.[4]

Thoroughly convinced of these truths, the founders of the new penitentiary at Philadelphia, thought it necessary that each prisoner should be secluded in a separate cell during day as well as night.

They have thought that absolute separation of the criminals can alone protect them from mutual pollution, and they have adopted the principle of separation in all its rigor. According to this system, the convict, once thrown into his cell, remains there without interruption, until the expiration of his punishment. He is separated from the whole world; and the penitentiaries, full of malefactors like himself, but every one of them entirely isolated, do not present to him even a society in the prison. If it is true that in establishments of this nature, all evil originates from the intercourse of the prisoners among themselves, we are obliged to acknowledge that nowhere is this vice avoided with greater safety than at Philadelphia, where the prisoners find themselves utterly unable to communicate with each other; and it is incontestable that this perfect isolation secures the prisoner from all fatal contamination.

As solitude is in no other prison more complete than in Philadelphia, nowhere, also, is the necessity of labor more urgent. At the same time, it would be inaccurate to say, that in the Philadelphia penitentiary labor is imposed; we may say with more justice that the favor of labor is granted. When we visited this penitentiary, we successively conversed with all its inmates.[5] There was not a single one among them who did not speak of labor with a kind of gratitude, and who did not express the idea that without the relief of constant occupation, life would be insufferable.[6]

What would become, during the long hours of solitude, without this relief, of the prisoner, given up to himself, a prey to the remorses of his soul and the terrors of his imagination? Labor gives to the solitary cell an interest; it fatigues the body and relieves the soul.

It is highly remarkable, that these men, the greater part of whom have been led to crime by indolence and idleness, should be constrained by the torments of solitude, to find in labor their only comfort. By detesting idleness, they accustom themselves to hate the primary cause of their misfortune; and labor, by comforting them, makes them love the only means, which when again free, will enable them to gain honestly their livelihood.

The founders of the Auburn prison acknowledged also the necessity of separating the prisoners, to prevent all inter-

course among themselves, and to subject them to the obligation of labor; but they follow a different course in order to
arrive at the same end.

In this prison, as well as in those founded upon the same
model, the prisoners are locked up in their solitary cells at
night only. During day they work together in common workshops, and as they are subjected to the law of rigorous
silence, though united, they are yet in fact isolated. Labor
in common and in silence forms then the characteristic trait
which distinguishes the Auburn system from that of Philadelphia.

Owing to the silence to which the prisoners are condemned,
this union of the prisoners, it is asserted, offers no inconvenience, and presents many advantages.

They are united, but no moral connection exists among
them. They see without knowing each other. They are in
society without any intercourse; there exists among them
neither aversion nor sympathy. The criminal, who contem-
plates a project of escape, or an attempt against the life of
his keepers, does not know in which of his companions he may
expect to find assistance. Their union is strictly material, or,
to speak more exactly, their bodies are together, but their
souls are separated; and it is not the solitude of the body
which is important, but that of the mind. At Pittsburgh, the
prisoners, though separated, are not alone, since there exist
moral communications among them. At Auburn, they are
really isolated, though no wall separates them.

Their union in the workshops has, therefore, nothing dangerous: it has, on the contrary, it is said, an advantage
peculiar to it, that of accustoming the prisoners to obedience.

What is the principal object of punishment in relation to
him who suffers it? It is to give him the habits of society, and
first to teach him to obey. The Auburn prison has, on this
point, its advocates say, a manifest advantage over that of
Philadelphia.

Perpetual seclusion in a cell, is an irresistible fact which
curbs the prisoner without a struggle, and thus deprives
altogether his submission of a moral character; locked up in
this narrow space, he has not, properly speaking, to observe
a discipline; if he works, it is in order to escape the weari-

ness which overwhelms him: in short, he obeys much less the established discipline than the physical impossibility of acting otherwise.

At Auburn, on the contrary, labor instead of being a comfort to the prisoners, is, in their eyes, a painful task, which they would be glad to get rid of. In observing silence, they are incessantly tempted to violate its law. They have some merit in obeying, because their obedience is no actual necessity. It is thus that the Auburn discipline gives to the prisoners the habits of society which they do not obtain in the prisons of Philadelphia.[7]

We see that silence is the principal basis of the Auburn system; it is this silence which establishes that moral separation between all prisoners, that deprives them of all dangerous communications, and only leaves to them those social relations which are inoffensive.

But here we meet with another grave objection against this system; the advocates of the Philadelphia system say, that to pretend to reduce a great number of collected malefactors to absolute silence, is a real chimera; and that this impossibility ruins from its basis, the system of which silence is the only foundation.[8]

We believe that this reproach is much exaggerated. Certainly we cannot admit the existence of a discipline carried to such a degree of perfection, that it guaranties rigorous observation of silence among a great number of assembled individuals, whom their interest and their passions excite to communicate with each other. We may say, however, that if in the prisons of Auburn, Sing Sing, Boston, and Wethersfield, silence is not always strictly observed, the cases of infraction are so rare that they are of little danger. Admitted as we have been into the interior of these various establishments, and going there at every hour of the day, without being accompanied by anybody, visiting by turns the cells, the workshops, the chapel and the yards, we have never been able to surprise a prisoner uttering a single word, and yet we have sometimes spent whole weeks in observing the same prison.

In Auburn, the building facilitates in a peculiar way the discovery of all contraventions of discipline. Each workshop where the prisoners work, is surrounded by a gallery, from which they may be observed, though the observer remains unseen. We have often espied from this gallery the conduct of the prisoners, whom we did not detect a single time in a breach of discipline. There is moreover a fact which proves better than any other, how strictly silence is observed in these establishments; it is that which takes place at Sing Sing. The prisoners are there occupied in breaking stones from the quarries, situated without the penitentiary; so that nine hundred criminals, watched by thirty keepers, work free in the midst of an open field, without a chain fettering their feet or hands. It is evident that the life of the keepers would be at the mercy of the prisoners, if material force were sufficient for the latter; but they want moral force. And why are these nine hundred collected malefactors less strong than the thirty individuals who command them? Because the keepers communicate freely with each other, act in concert, and have all the power of association; while the convicts separated from each other, by silence, have, in spite of their numerical force, all the weakness of isolation. Suppose for an instant, that the prisoners obtain the least facility of communication; the order is immediately the reverse; the union of their intellects effected by the spoken word, has taught them the secret of their strength; and the first infraction of the law of silence, destroys the whole discipline. The admirable order which prevails at Sing Sing, and which silence alone is capable of maintaining, proves then that silence there is preserved.[9]

We have thus shown the general principle upon which the systems of Auburn and of Philadelphia rest: how are these principles put into action? How and by whom are the penitentiary establishments administered? What is the order of the interior, and what is the regulation of each day? This shall form the subject of the following section.

Administration of Penitentiary Systems

THE ADMINISTRATION of the prison is intrusted everywhere to a superintendent,[10] whose authority is more or less extensive. He employs a clerk, charged with the financial business of the establishment.

Superior to the superintendent, are three inspectors, charged with the general direction and moral surveillance of the prison,[11] and under him is a number more or less considerable of inferior jailors.

At Auburn, Sing Sing, Philadelphia, and Wethersfield, the superintendent is appointed by the inspectors; in Boston, the governor appoints him; in Connecticut, the inspectors are chosen by the legislature; in Massachusetts, by the governor, and in Pennsylvania, by the supreme court. Everywhere the power which appoints the superintendent, has the right to discharge him at pleasure.

The reader sees that the election of those persons who direct the penitentiary establishments, belongs to important authorities.

The nomination of the jailors belongs, in the prisons of Sing Sing, Wethersfield, Boston, and Philadelphia, to the superintendent himself; at Auburn they are chosen by the inspectors. The superintendents of all the prisons, with the single exception of that of Philadelphia, are bound to give sufficient security for their good behavior.[12] At Philadelphia and at Wethersfield, the office of inspector is without any compensation, and in the other prisons it is very trifling. The sum which they receive in Massachusetts is hardly equal to the expense incurred by visiting the prison.[13] They are always chosen from among the inhabitants of the place.[14] Persons distinguished by their standing in society, are desirous of filling this place; it is thus that we see in Philadelphia, among the inspectors of the penitentiary, Mr. Richards, mayor of the city, and in Boston, Mr. Grey, senator of Massachusetts.

Though the inspectors are not the immediate agents of the administration, they nevertheless direct it. They make the regulations, which the superintendent is charged to execute, and they constantly watch over this execution; they have even the power to modify them at their pleasure, according to the exigency of circumstances. In no case do they take part in the acts of the actual administration of the prison; the superintendent alone directs it; because he alone is answerable for it. They have everywhere the same legal authority; yet they do not exercise it in the same way, in all the prisons of which we treat. Thus at Sing Sing, the superintendence of the inspectors appeared to us superficial, while at Auburn and at Wethersfield they took a much more active part in the affairs of the prison.

On the whole we may say, that the privileges of the inspectors are much more extended in law than in reality; while the superintendent, whose written authority is not very great, is yet the soul of the administration.

The most important place then in the prison, is without a doubt, that of the superintendent. Generally it is intrusted in the penitentiaries of the United States, to honorable men, entitled by their talent to functions of this nature. It is thus that the Auburn prison has had for directors men like Mr. Elam Lynds, a former captain of the army; and Mr. Gershom Powers, a Judge of the State of New York. At Wethersfield, Mr. Pillsbury; at Sing Sing, Mr. Robert Wiltze; at Boston, Mr. Austin, a captain in the navy, are all men distinguished by their knowledge and their capacity. To great probity and a deep sense of their duty they add much experience, and that perfect knowledge of men so necessary in their position. Among the superintendents of the American penitentiaries, we have especially to mention Mr. Samuel Wood, director of the new Philadelphia prison — a man of superior mind, who, influenced by religious sentiments, has abandoned his former career, in order to devote himself entirely to the success of an establishment so useful to his community.

The inferior agents, the under-wardens, are not so distinguished either for their standing in society or for talent. They are, however, in general, intelligent and honest men. Charged with superintending the labor in the workshops, they have almost always a special and technical knowledge of the mechanical arts with which the prisoners occupy themselves.

The salary of the various officers, without being exorbitant, is nevertheless sufficient to furnish an honorable support to the superintendents, and to the others, all the necessaries of life.[15]

Besides, we must not judge of the merit of the prison officers by the amount of their salary. In Virginia, the superintendent of the Richmond prison receives annually $2000.
Yet he is the director of one of the bad prisons in the United
States; while the superintendent of Wethersfield, which is
one of the good prisons, if it is not the best, receives but
$1200. We may make the same observation by comparing the
good prisons among each other; thus in Connecticut, the
whole sum paid for the various salaries of the officers at
Wethersfield, does not amount to more than $3713.33 for
174 prisoners; while in that of Boston, the corresponding
expenditure for 276 prisoners, amounts to $13,171.55. So
that at Boston, where the number of the prisoners is not
double those at Wethersfield, the expenses of the officers
amount to three and one-half times more than in the latter
prison.

In investigating the organization of the new establishments, we have been struck with the importance which is
attached to the choice of the individuals who direct them.
As soon as the penitentiary system was adopted in the United
States, the *personnel* changed in nature. For jailor of a
prison, vulgar people only could be found; the most distinguished persons offered themselves to administer a *penitentiary* where a moral direction exists.

We have seen how the superintendents, however elevated
their character and position may be, are subject to the control of a superior authority — the inspectors of the penitentiary. But above both, there is an authority stronger than
all others, not written in the laws, but all-powerful in a free
country; that of public opinion. The improvements in these
matters having excited general attention, public opinion
directed itself entirely toward this point, and it exercises
without obstruction its vast influence.

There are countries in which public establishments are considered by the government as its own personal affair, so that
it admits persons to them only according to its pleasure, just
as a proprietor refuses at his pleasure admission into his
house; they are a sort of administrative sanctuaries, into
which no profane person can penetrate. These establishments, on the contrary, in the United States, are considered

as belonging to all. The prisons are open to everyone who chooses to inspect them and every visiter may inform himself of the order which regulates the interior. There is no exception to this liberty but in the penitentiary at Philadelphia. Yet, if one wish, he may see the buildings and the interior of the establishment. It is only not permitted to see the prisoners, because the visits of the public would be in direct contradiction to the principle of absolute solitude, which forms the foundation of the system.

Instead of avoiding the inspection of the public, the superintendents and inspectors of the prisons ask for the examination and attention of all. Each year the inspectors give an account, either to the legislature or to the governor, of the financial situation of the prison, as well as of its moral state; they indicate existing abuses and improvements to be made. Their reports, printed by order of the legislatures, are immediately handed over to publicity and controversy; the papers, the number of which in that country is immense, republish them faithfully. Thus there is not a citizen of the United States who does not know how the prisons of his country are governed, and who is not able to contribute to their improvement, either by his opinion or by his fortune. The general interest being thus excited, in each town, particular societies form themselves for the progress of prison discipline: all public establishments are carefully examined; all abuses are discovered and pointed out. If it is necessary to construct new prisons, individuals add their contributions to the funds furnished by the state, to meet the expenses. This general attention, a source of perpetual vigilance, produces with the officers of the prisons, an extraordinary zeal and extreme circumspection, which they would not be possessed of, were they placed in the shade. This surveillance of public opinion which constrains them in some respects, produces also its compensation, because it is this public opinion which elevates their functions, and makes them honorable, low and obscure as they formerly were.

We have seen the elements of which the prison is composed. Let us now examine how its organization operates. When the convict arrives in the prison, a physician verifies the state of his health. He is washed; his hair is cut, and new dress, according to the uniform of the prison is given to him. In Philadelphia, he is conducted to his solitary cell, which he never leaves; there he works, eats, and rests; and the construction of this cell is so complete, that there is no necessity whatever to leave it.[16]

At Auburn, at Wethersfield, and in the other prisons of the same nature, the prisoner is first plunged into the same solitude, but it is only for a few days, after which he leaves it, in order to occupy himself in the workshops.[17] With daybreak, a bell gives the sign of rising; the jailors open the doors. The prisoners range themselves in a line, under the command of their respective jailors, and go first into the yard, where they wash their hands and faces, and from thence into the workshops, where they go directly to work. Their labor is not interrupted until the hour of taking food. There is not a single instant given to recreation.[18]

At Auburn, when the hours of breakfast or of dinner have arrived, labor is suspended, and all the convicts meet in the large refectory. At Sing Sing, and in all other penitentiaries, they retire into their cells, and take their meals separately. This latter regulation appeared to us preferable to that at Auburn. It is not without inconvenience and even danger, that so large a number of criminals can be collected in the same room; their union renders the discipline much more difficult.

In the evening, at the setting of the sun, labor ceases, and the convicts leave the workshops to retire into their cells. Upon rising, going to sleep, eating, leaving the cells and going back to them, everything passes in the most profound silence, and nothing is heard in the whole prison but the steps of those who march, or sounds proceeding from the workshops. But when the day is finished, and the prisoners have retired to their cells, the silence within these vast walls, which contain so many prisoners, is that of death. We have often trod during night those monotonous and dumb galleries, where a lamp is always burning: we felt as if we traversed catacombs; there were a thousand living beings, and yet it was a desert solitude.

The order of one day is that of the whole year. Thus one hour of the convict follows with overwhelming uniformity the other, from the moment of his entry into the prison to the expiration of his punishment. Labor fills the whole day. The whole night is given to rest. As the labor is hard, long hours of rest are necessary; it is not denied to the prisoner between the moment of going to rest and that of rising. And before his sleep as after it, he has time to think of his solitude, his crime and his misery.

All penitentiaries it is true have not the same regulations, but all the convicts of a prison are treated in the same way. There is even more equality in the prison than in society.

All have the same dress, and eat the same bread. All work; there exists in this respect, no other distinction than that which results from a greater natural skill for one art than for another. On no condition is labor to be interrupted. The inconvenience of giving a task, after which the prisoner is at liberty to do nothing, has been ackowledged. It is essential for the convict as for the order of the prison, that he should labor without interruption; for him, because idleness is fatal to him; for the prison, because according to the observation of Judge Powers, fifty individuals who work, are more easily watched than ten convicts doing nothing.

Their food is wholesome, abundant, but coarse; it has to support their strength, but ought not to afford them any of those gratifications of the appetite, which are agreeable merely.

None can follow a diet different from that of the prison. Every kind of fermented liquor is prohibited; water alone is drunk here. The convict who might be possessed of treasures, would nevertheless live like the poorest among them; and we do not find in the American prisons, those eating houses which are found in ours, and in which the convict may buy everything to gratify his appetite. The abuse of wine is there unknown, because the use of it is interdicted.

This discipline is at the same time moral and just. The place which society has assigned for repentance, ought to present no scenes of pleasure and debauch. And it is iniquitous to allow the opulent criminal, whose very riches increase his criminality, to enjoy himself in his prison by the side of the poor wretch whose misery extenuates his fault.[19]

Application to labor and good conduct in prison, do not

procure the prisoner any alleviation. Experience shows that the criminal who, while in society, has committed the most expert and audacious crimes, is often the least refractory in prison. He is more docile than the others, because he is more intelligent ; and he knows how to submit to necessity when he finds himself without power to revolt. Generally he is more skilful and more active, particularly if an enjoyment, at no great distance, awaits him as the reward of his efforts ; so that if we accord to the prisoners privileges resulting from their conduct in the prison, we run the risk of alleviating the rigor of imprisonment to that criminal who most deserves them, and of depriving of all favors those who merit them most.

Perhaps it would be impossible, in the actual state of our prisons, to manage them without the assistance of rewards granted for the zeal, activity, and talent of the prisoners. But in America, where prison discipline operates supported by the fear of chastisement, a moral influence can be dispensed with in respect to their management.

The interest of the prisoner requires that he should never be idle ; that of society demands that he should labor in the most useful way. In the new penitentiaries none of those machines are found, which, in England, the prisoners set in motion without intelligence, and which occupy them merely in a mechanical way.

Labor is not only salutary because it is the opposite of idleness ; but it is also contemplated that the convict, while he is at work, shall learn a business which may support him when he leaves the prison.

The prisoners therefore, are taught useful trades only ; and among these, care is taken to choose such as are the most profitable, and the produce of which finds the easiest sale.[20]

The Philadelphia system has often been reproached with rendering labor by the prisoners impossible. It is certainly more economical and advantageous to make a certain number of workmen labor together in a common workshop, than to give each of them employment in a separate place. It is moreover true, that a great many arts cannot be pursued with advantage by a single workman in a narrow place ; yet the penitentiary of Philadelphia shows that the various

occupations which can be pursued by isolated men, are sufficiently numerous to occupy them usefully.[21] The same difficulty is not met with in those prisons in which the convicts
work in company. At Auburn and at Baltimore, a very great
variety of arts is pursued. These two prisons offer the sight
of vast manufactories which combine all useful occupations.
At Boston and Sing Sing the occupation of the convicts has,
so far, been more uniform. In these two prisons, the greater
part of the criminals are employed in cutting stones. Wethersfield offers, on a small scale, the same spectacle as Auburn.

In general, the labor of the prisoners is hired to a contractor, who gives a certain price for each day, and receives
everything manufactured by the convict.

There is an essential difference between this system and
that which is practised in our prisons. With us the same person contracts for the food, clothing, labor, and sanitary department of the convicts — a system equally injurious to the
convict and the discipline of the prison,[22] to the convict, because the contractor, who sees nothing but a money affair in
such a bargain, speculates upon the victuals as he does on
the labor. If he loses upon the clothing, he indemnifies himself
upon the food, and if the labor is less productive than he
calculated upon, he tries to balance his loss by spending less
for the support of the convicts, with which he is equally
charged. This system is alike fatal to the good order of the
prison. The contractor, regarding the convict as a laboring
machine, thinks only how he can use him to the greatest advantage for himself; everything appears allowable, in order
to excite the zeal of the prisoner; and he cares little if the
expenses of the convict are made to the injury of good order.
The extent of his privileges, moreover, gives him an importance in the prison, which he ought not to have; it is therefore advisable to separate him as much as possible from the
penitentiary, and to counteract his influence, if it cannot be
neutralized entirely.[23]

It appeared to us, that the evil which we have thus pointed
out, has been generally avoided in the new penitentiaries in
the United States. In these establishments, neither the system of entire domestic management, nor that by contract,
have been exclusively adopted.

The clothing and bedding of the convicts are generally furnished by the superintendent, who himself makes all the contracts relative to these subjects; he avoids many purchases, by causing the prisoners themselves to make the materials necessary for their clothing. At Auburn, Sing Sing, and Boston, the prisoners are fed by contract, but this contract is not allowed to be made for more than one year. At Wethersfield, the prison itself provides this article. The contractor who, at Auburn, is charged with the food of the prisoners, is not the same who makes them work.

There exists also a different contractor for each branch of industry; the contracts thus being multiplied, the contractor cannot obtain in the prison more than a limited and passing influence. At Wethersfield, the government of the prison not only nourishes and maintains the convicts without the assistance of contract, but it also realizes the value of the greater part of the labor.[24]

In all these establishments, the contractor cannot, under any pretext, interfere with the internal discipline of the prison, nor influence in the least degree its regulations. He cannot hold any conversation with the prisoners, except in order to teach them that art, with which he is charged to instruct them; and can only do this in the presence and with the consent of one of the jailors.

In spite of these precautions, the presence of the contractor or his agents in the prisons has been found to be not without its inconvenience. Formerly the Auburn prison managed itself all its affairs, and when the principle of contract was introduced, Mr. Elam Lynds, then its superintendent, did not allow the contractor to approach the convicts. The contractor engaged to give the stipulated price for the articles manufactured by the prisoners, and these articles were delivered to him, without his having directed their manufacture. Much was gained in point of discipline by this order of things. If it were advantageous to limit the intercourse between the contractor and the convicts, it was still better to prevent it entirely. However, such a system of administration was found both difficult and expensive.

The contractors, being deprived of the right of inspecting the labor, imposed disadvantageous conditions upon the prison. On the other hand, their exclusion from the work-shops, made it requisite that the jailors should be capable of instructing the prisoners in the respective arts, and such persons, possessing the necessary skill and technical knowl-edge, were not easily found. Finally, the sale of the articles was less easy and productive for the superintendent, than for the contractors, exclusively occupied with commercial operations. The result therefore, has been the adoption of a system of contract such as we have described. This system, surrounded by the guaranties which accompany it, possesses advantages which seem much to outweigh its inconveniences. However, Mr. Elam Lynds seems constantly to fear that the presence of the contractors in the prison, will lead sooner or later to the total ruin of the discipline.

We shall soon see, when we have occasion to treat of the expenses and income, that the labor of the prisoners is in general very productive. Visiting these various establish-ments, we have been surprised by the order, and sometimes the talent, with which the convicts work, and what makes their zeal quite surprising, is, that they work without any interest in its produce. In our prisons, as well as in those of the greater part of Europe, a part of the produce of their labor belongs to the prisoners. This portion, called the *pécule*, is more or less in various countries; in the United States it does not exist. There the principle is adopted, that the criminal owes all his labor to society, in order to indem-nify it for the expenses of his detention. Thus, during the whole time of their punishment, the convicts work without receiving the slightest remuneration, and if they leave the prison, no account is given to them of what they have done. They merely receive a certain portion of money, in order to carry them to the place which they propose to make their new residence.[25]

This system appears to us excessively severe. We do not dispute the right of society to indemnify itself by the labor of the convict for the expenses he causes. It is an incontesta-ble right; moreover we do not know in what degree a consid-erable *pécule* or earning is useful to the convict, who, when he leaves the prison, generally sees in the money earned by him, but a means to satisfy passions, the more excited as they have been the longer repressed. But where would be the inconvenience in giving a slight stimulus to the zeal of the convict, by a small reward to his activity? Why should we not give him in his solitude, and in the midst of his sufferings, an interest in a gain however small, yet to him of immense value? Moreover, is it not necessary that on the day when he re-enters society, he should have, if not a considerable sum at his disposal, at least some means of support while he is in search of labor.[26] Why not adopt the system of the Baltimore prison, where, though the principle of the other American penitentiaries has been acknowledged, yet its rigor has been alleviated? In that prison every prisoner has his fixed task for the day: when that is finished, he does not cease to work, but he begins to work for himself; all that he does after his task, forms his *pécule;* and as he does not receive his earning before he leaves the prison, it is certain that it cannot become injurious to its discipline. There was a time when the prisoners at Baltimore could spend their earnings immediately for eatables. Their labor was then much more productive; but the inconvenience of such indulgence has been acknowledged to be destructive of good discipline; and at present their *pécule* remains untouched until the moment of their leaving the prison.

Such is the order established in the American penitentiaries. We have said that this discipline is applied to all prisoners in the state prison; however, the women have so far not yet been subjected to it, except in Connecticut. Generally they are found together in the American prisons as with us; and in that country, as with us, they are exposed to all the vices growing out of contaminated intercourse.

Some persons believe that it would be extremely difficult to apply to women a system, the basis of which is silence: yet the experiment made at Wethersfield, where the women are, like the rest of the prisoners, subject to isolation in cells during night, and absolute silence during day, proves that the difficulty is not insurmountable. Again, it is not the difficulty of execution in this point which has prevented reform in the prisons of the United States. If, in the application of the new penitentiary system, the women have been omitted, this fact must be ascribed above all, to the small number of crimes

committed by them in that country. It is because they occupy
little space in the prison, that they have been neglected. It is
the same with most evils of society, a remedy for which is
ardently sought if they are important; if they are not alarming they are overlooked.

Disciplinary Means

LET US now examine by what disciplinary means the order of
things which we have explained above, is established and
maintained.

How is silence so rigorously maintained among a number
of assembled criminals? How are they made to work without
any interest of their own?

Here also we have to distinguish between the Auburn and
Philadelphia systems.

In Philadelphia, the discipline is as simple as the system itself. The only critical moment is that when the prisoner enters the prison. The solitary cell of the criminal is for some
days full of terrible phantoms. Agitated and tormented by
a thousand fears, he accuses society of injustice and cruelty,
and in such a disposition of mind, it sometimes will happen
that he disregards the orders, and repels the consolations
offered to him. The only chastisement which the regulations
of the prison permits, is imprisonment in a dark cell with reduction of food. It is rare that more than two days of such
discipline are required, to curb the most refractory prisoner.
When the convict has overcome the first impressions of solitude; when he has triumphed over the terrors which almost
surrendered him to insanity or despair; when, in his solitary
cell, in the midst of the pains of a stinging conscience, and
the agitations of his soul, he has fallen into a dejection of
mind, and has sought in labor a relief from his griefs; from
that moment he is tamed, and forever submissive to the rules
of the prison. What breach of order is it possible to commit
in solitude? The entire discipline consists in the isolation of
the prisoners, and the impossibility of their violating the
established rule. In the other prisons, disciplinary punishments are inflicted on the prisoners who break the law of

silence, or refuse to work. But silence is easy for him who is alone; and labor is not refused by those whose only consolation it forms.[27] We have pointed out the inconvenience of absolute solitude, the deficiency of which is, that it deprives the prisoner's submission of its moral character. But we must at the same time acknowledge its advantages in respect to discipline, and the facility of ruling an establishment of this nature, without the application of severe and repeated punishment, is certainly a very great advantage. There are some persons who consider the order established at Philadelphia complicated, organized with difficulty, and maintained with trouble. They are, in our opinion, greatly mistaken. The Philadelphia system is expensive, but not difficult to be established; and once established, it maintains itself. It is this very system, the discipline of which offers the least embarrassment; each cell is a prison in itself, and the convicts who are detained there cannot render themselves guilty of offenses which can only be possibly committed in company with others. There is no punishment, because there is no infraction.

The discipline at Auburn, Sing Sing, Boston, Wethersfield, and Baltimore, could not have the same character of simplicity: these various establishments themselves, follow, in this respect, different courses.

At Sing Sing, the only punishment for those who infringe the established order, is that of the whip. The application of this disciplinary means is there very frequent; and the least fault is punished with its application. For various reasons this punishment is preferred to all others. It effects the immediate submission of the delinquent; his labor is not interrupted a single instant; the chastisement is painful, but not injurious to health; finally, it is believed that no other punishment would produce the same effects.[28] The same principle is admitted at Auburn, but in its application is extremely rare. The penitentiaries of Boston and Baltimore, a little more severe than that at Auburn, are nevertheless much less so than Sing Sing: Wethersfield differs from all others by its extreme mildness.[29]

In this latter prison stripes are not altogether objected to; but their application is as much as possible avoided: Mr.

Pillsbury, superintendent of the establishment, has assured us, that for three years he has but one single time been obliged to inflict stripes. It is a severity to which recourse is had only if it is well ascertained that every other and milder way has been tried without effect. Before resorting to stripes, absolute solitude day and night without labor is tried: if we believe the officers of the prison, nothing is rarer than to see a prisoner resist this first trial; he has been scarcely subjected to the rigor of absolute isolation, than he solicits the favor of again taking his place in the common workshop, and submits willingly to all that discipline requires. However, if he is not curbed at the first moment, greater severity is added to his solitude, such as entire privation of light, and diminution of food; sometimes also his bed is taken from him, etc. If the prisoner still obstinately resists, then, and then only, the whip is used, as the still more effective means of submission. The directors of this establishment seem to have a decided aversion to corporal chastisement; yet they would regret it much if they were not invested with the right to inflict it. They reject the application of cruel pain, but they find a powerful means of acting upon the criminals in their authority to order it.

The tempered discipline of Wethersfield seems to suffice for the success of the establishment. Yet in the other prisons it is thought that the management of the whole would be impossible without the assistance of the whip. This is the opinion of all practical men whom we have seen in the United States, particularly of Mr. Elam Lynds, whom we have mentioned above.[30] The legislatures of New York, Massachusetts, Connecticut, and Maryland, have had the same conviction, since they have formally authorized the infliction of corporal punishment. These chastisements have also received the sanction of judicial authority; and the country, through the organ of her jury, has given several verdicts in favor of jailors who acknowledged having beaten the prisoners.[31]

We have noticed the remarkable differences which exist in the disciplinary order of the various establishments. All, however, admit the principle of corporal punishment; and it is just to say, that there exist in the particular situation of each of the prisons, certain circumstances, which tend to explain the mildness or severity of its discipline.

If we remember the nature of the labors executed at Sing Sing, and the order established in that prison, we easily understand the insurmountable obstacles with which disciplinary order would meet in this prison, were it not supported by the most energetic measures of repression. Auburn does not require so much severity, because the same dangers do not threaten the order of the establishment. Wethersfield is, in this respect, in a still more favorable position; it contains less than two hundred criminals, while Auburn has six hundred and fifty, and Sing Sing more than nine hundred. It is evident, that the number, more or less considerable, of criminals, and the nature of the labor, render the penitentiary more or less easy of government.

Now, could these various penitentiaries dispense with corporal chastisement? This is a question which we dare not solve. We are merely able to say, that, deprived of this assistance, prison discipline would meet with difficulties very difficult to be overcome. Its embarrassments would be so much the greater, as it is founded on an unique basis, that of absolute silence; and should it ever be deprived of this foundation, the whole fabric must inevitably crumble to pieces; now, how is it possible to maintain absolute silence among criminals, if they are not continually overawed by the fear of a prompt and rigorous chastisement? In the American prisons, this discipline, founded upon stripes, is so much more powerful, as it is practised more arbitrarily.[32] At Sing Sing, and at Auburn, there are no written regulations: the superintendents of these prisons, have only, in their government, to conform themselves to the verbal prescriptions which they receive from the inspectors, and to a few principles expressed in the law. These principles are: solitary imprisonment of the convicts during night, and labor in silence during day. For the rest, they enjoy, as to all acts of execution, a discretionary power.[33] At Sing Sing, the superintendent has even the right to delegate this discretionary power to all his inferior agents; and in fact he has transmitted his power to thirty jailors, who are invested like himself with the power of chastising the convicts. At Auburn, the superintendent alone has the power to punish; yet the same authority belongs to the inferior keepers, in all cases of urgent and absolute necessity. The same is the case in Boston. In Wethersfield, the regulations of the prison are in writing.[34] The subaltern officers can in no case exercise the right of punishing, with which the superintendent alone is invested, and which he uses with so much moderation. Important debates have taken place in the state of New York, on the question whether the presence of an inspector ought to be required when inflicting stripes upon a prisoner. According to the letter of the law, this guaranty was indispensable, but the obligation of the inspectors to be present at such punishments, was so frequently inconvenient, and caused them such painful feelings, that they asked immediately to be absolved from this duty. At present the right of the officers to inflict stripes without these official witnesses is acknowledged. The inspectors have nevertheless a great influence on the application of disciplinary chastisement. Sing Sing is the only prison where their superintendence has appeared to us superficial upon this point. The administration of this vast penitentiary is so difficult, that there seems to be no disposition to dispute the least part of the absolute power of the keepers.

We shall not investigate here whether society has the right to punish, with corporal chastisement, the convict who refuses to submit to the obligation of labor, or to the other exigencies of penitentiary discipline.

Such theoretical questions are rarely discussed, to the interest of truth and human society.

We believe that society has the right to do everything necessary for its conservation, and for the order established within it. And we understand perfectly well, that an assemblage of criminals, all of whom have infringed the laws of the land, and all of whose inclinations are corrupted, and appetites vicious, cannot be governed in prison according to the same principles, and with the same means, as free persons, whose desires are correct, and whose actions are conformable to the laws. We also conceive perfectly well, that a convict who will not labor, ought to be constrained to do so, and that severity ought to be used in order to reduce him to silence, who will not observe it. The right of society seems to us, on this point, beyond all doubt, if it cannot arrive at the same end by milder means, but in our opinion that is not the question.

To what point are corporal chastisements reconcilable with the object of the penitentiary system itself, which is the reformation of the guilty? If this pain be ignominious, does it not go directly against the end which we propose to obtain, viz. to awaken the morality of an individual, fallen in his own opinion?

This question seems to us to be the only one to be examined, but we do not believe that it ought to be solved in an arbitrary manner. It would seem that much depends upon the light in which public opinion, and that of the prisoners, consider bodily punishment.

The discretionary power, by virtue of which, the lowest keeper at Auburn, and even the turnkeys at Sing Sing, lash the prisoners, is little contested in the United States.

"The right of the keepers over the persons of the prisoners, it is said, is that of a father over his children, of the teacher over his pupils, of the master over his apprentice, and of a sea-captain over his crew."

The punishment of stripes is in use in the American navy, with no idea of infamy attached to it. In the beginning, the whip was not admitted as a disciplinary means in the penitentiary system. When it was introduced as an auxiliary to the regulations, some voices were raised against it, but this opposition was much more a dispute of philosophy than one of repugnance to national customs.

Pennsylvania is, perhaps, the only state in the Union which continues to protest against corporal punishment, and which excluded it from the regulations of her prisons. The Quakers cease not to protest against the inhumanity of this punishment, and their philanthropic protestations are joined by the eloquent voice of Edward Livingston, who also rejects this means of discipline from his code. It is chiefly on account of corporal punishment, made use of at Auburn, that he declares himself the adversary of the system which is in practice in that prison.[35]

But their words find few corresponding voices in most parts of the Union, and, at present, all new penitentiaries, that of Philadelphia only excepted, make use of the whip. The laws of the country authorize the discipline which they have adopted, and these laws have the sanction of public opinion.

There is certainly much exaggeration in the reproaches made against the Auburn discipline. First, stripes are not so frequent as is believed. Necessary, as they are, to establish silence in a newly founded prison, they are seldom made use of in order to maintain this regulation if once established.

Now, is the whole system of these prisons, as is asserted, injurious to health, and are the rigors of solitude and the cruelties of the discipline, fatal to the life of the imprisoned? We are able to furnish positive documents upon this point.

All prisoners, whom we have seen in the penitentiaries of the United States, had the appearance of strength and health; and if we compare the number of those who die there with the mortality in the old prisons, we shall see that the new penitentiaries, in spite of their severe regulations and barbarous discipline, are much more favorable to the life of the imprisoned. Mr. Edward Livingston wishes to see solitary confinement during night and day, without labor, and reduction of food substituted for the whip, as a disciplinary measure. It does not seem that at Wethersfield this punishment, which as we have seen, is preferred to stripes, has produced bad effects. However, ten individuals are mentioned as having died in consequence of this kind of punishment in the prison of Lamberton in New Jersey, while there is no case yet on record of a prisoner having become the victim of corporal whipping.

In the old Walnut street prison, there was formerly, during each year, one death out of sixteen prisoners, and in that of New York (Newgate) one out of nineteen. In both these prisons, the criminals were neither in solitary confinement, nor obliged to be wholly silent, nor subjected to corporal punishment.[36]

In the new penitentiaries, founded upon the principles of silence and isolation supported by the discipline of stripes, death takes place in an infinitely smaller proportion.

At Sing Sing, one prisoner died out of thirty-seven; at Wethersfield one of forty-four; at Baltimore one of forty-nine; at Auburn one of fifty-six; and at Boston one of fifty-eight.

Still more: if we compare the mortality of the prisoners to that of persons enjoying liberty and society, we shall yet arrive at a result favorable to the penitentiaries. There dies, in fact, in Pennsylvania, every year, one out of thirty-nine persons, and in Maryland one out of forty-seven. Again, in the old prisons where free communication existed, and where the discipline was mild, one half more died than in society generally. And in the new penitentiaries, subject to the austere system of isolation, silence, and stripes, deaths are less numerous.

These ciphers are better answers than all possible arguments, to the objections which have been raised.

We have said nothing on the sanitary state of the new Philadelphia prison, which has been in existence for too short a time to judge fully of its effects. We have every reason to believe that the system of perpetual and absolute seclusion, established there in full vigor, will prove less favorable to the health of the prisoners than the Auburn system. Yet the physician of that establishment believes himself able already to declare that the mortality will be less there than in the ancient prison of Walnut street.

To sum up the whole on this point, it must be acknowledged that the penitentiary system in America is severe. While society in the United States gives the example of the most extended liberty, the prisons of the same country offer the spectacle of the most complete despotism. The citizens subject to the law are protected by it; they only cease to be free when they become wicked.

CHAPTER THREE

REFORM MEASURES

IN PENITENTIARY SYSTEMS

THERE ARE in America as well as in Europe, estimable men whose minds feed upon philosophical reveries, and whose extreme sensibility feels the want of some illusion. These men, for whom philanthropy has become a matter of necessity, find in the penitentiary system a nourishment for this generous passion. Starting from abstractions which deviate more or less from reality, they consider man, however far advanced in crime, as still susceptible of being brought back to virtue. They think that the most infamous being may yet recover the sentiment of honor; and pursuing consistently this opinion, they hope for an epoch when all criminals may be radically reformed, the prisons be entirely empty, and justice find no crimes to punish.[1]

Others, perhaps without so profound a conviction, pursue nevertheless the same course; they occupy themselves continually with prisons; it is the subject to which all the labors of their life bear reference. Philanthropy has become for them a kind of profession, and they have caught the *monomanie* of the penitentiary system, which to them seems the remedy for all the evils of society.

We believe that both overrate the good to be expected from this institution, of which the real benefit can be acknowledged without attributing to it imaginary effects.

There is, first, an incontestable advantage inherent in a penitentiary system of which isolation forms the principal basis. It is that the criminals do not become worse in the prison than they were when they entered it. On this point this system differs essentially from that pursued in our prisons, which not only render the prisoner no better, but corrupt him still more. With us all great crimes have been planned in some measure in a prison, and been deliberated upon in the midst of assembled malefactors. Such is the fatal influence of the wicked upon each other, that one finished rogue in a prison suffices as a model for all who see and hear him, to fashion their vices and immorality upon his.[2]

Nothing, certainly, is more fatal to society than this course of mutual evil instruction in prisons; and it is well ascertained that we owe to this dangerous contagion a peculiar population of malefactors, which every day becomes more numerous and more alarming. It is an evil which the penitentiary system of the United States cures completely.[3]

It is evident that all moral contagion among the imprisoned is impossible, particularly in Philadelphia, where thick walls separate the prisoners day and night. This first result is important, and we must take good care not to underrate its importance. The theories on the reform of the prisoners are vague and uncertain.[4] It is not yet known to what degree the wicked may be regenerated, and by what means this regeneration may be obtained: but if the efficiency of the prison in correcting the prisoners is yet doubtful, its power of depraving them still more is known, because experience proves it. The new penitentiaries, in which this contagious influence is avoided, have therefore gained a signal advantage; and as long as that prison has not yet been found whose discipline is completely regenerating in its effects, perhaps we may be permitted to say that the best prison is that which does not corrupt.

It is nevertheless clear, that this result, however weighty, does not satisfy the authors of the system; and it is natural that having preserved the prisoner from the corruption with which he was threatened, they aspire at reforming him.

Let us see by what means they endeavor to arrive at this end. We shall then also examine the success of their efforts.

Moral and religious instruction forms, in this respect, the whole basis of the system. In all penitentiary systems, those who have not learned to read are instructed in it. These schools are voluntary. Though no convict is obliged to join them, they consider it as a favor to be admitted, and if it is impossible to receive all who offer themselves, those among the prisoners are selected who are most in need of the benefit of instruction.[5] The free choice left to the prisoners to join or not the school, makes those who enter it thus voluntarily, much more zealous and docile. This school is kept every Sunday. It precedes the morning service. The minister who administers this service, accompanies it almost always with a sermon, in which he abstains from every dogmatical discussion, and treats only of religious morals; so that the instruction of the minister is as fit for the Catholic as for the Protestant, for the Unitarian as for the Presbyterian. The meals of the prisoners are always preceded by a prayer, offered up by the chaplain of the establishment. Each prisoner has a Bible, given by the state, in his cell, in which he may read the whole time that he is not engaged in labor.

This order exists in all the penitentiaries, but we should be much deceived were we to believe that uniformity exists on this point in these various prisons. Some attach to religious instruction much more importance than others. Some neglect the moral reformation of the prisoners, while others make it a particular object. At Sing Sing, for instance, where the nature of things requires so severe a discipline, the directors of the establishment seemed to have in view the support of external order only, and the passive obedience of the convicts. The assistance of moral influence is disregarded. Primary and religious instruction, it is true, is somewhat attended to, but it is manifest that it is considered but a secondary object. In the prisons of Auburn, Wethersfield, Philadelphia, and Boston, the reformation of the criminals occupies a much more prominent place.

In Philadelphia, the moral situation in which the convicts are placed, is eminently calculated to facilitate their regeneration. We have more than once remarked the serious turn which the ideas of the prisoner in this penitentiary take. We have seen convicts there, whose levity had led them to crime, and whose mind had, in that solitude, contracted habits of meditation and of reasoning altogether extraordinary. The system of this prison appeared to us especially powerful over individuals endowed with some elevation of mind, and who had enjoyed a polite education. Intellectual men are naturally those who are the least able to endure a separation from all society.

We can however assert, that this absolute solitude produces the liveliest impression on all prisoners. Generally, their hearts are found ready to open themselves, and the facility of being moved renders them also fitter for reformation. They are particularly accessible to religious sentiments, and the remembrance of their family has an uncommon power over their minds. One who enjoys the intercourse of society, is perhaps incapable of feeling the whole value of a religious idea thrown into the lonesome cell of a convict.

Nothing distracts, in Philadelphia, the mind of the convicts from their meditations. And as they are always isolated, the presence of a person who comes to converse with them is the greatest benefit, and one which they appreciate in its whole extent. When we visited this penitentiary, one of the prisoners said to us: "It is with joy that I perceive the figure of the keepers, who visit my cell. This summer a cricket came into my yard; it looked like a companion. When a butterfly or any other animal happens to enter my cell, I never do it any harm." If the soul is thus disposed, it is easy to conceive what value the prisoners must attach to moral communications, and how great must be the influence of wise advice and pious exhortations on their minds.

The superintendent visits each of them at least once a day. The inspectors visit them at least twice a week, and a chaplain has the special charge of their moral reformation. Before and after these visits, they are not entirely alone. The books which are at their disposal, are in some measure companions who never leave them. The Bible, and sometimes tracts containing edifying anecdotes, form their library. If they do not work, they read, and several of them seem to find in it a great consolation. There were some, who only knew the letters of the alphabet, and have in prison learned, by themselves, to read. Others less ingenious or persevering, have succeeded in it only with the assistance of the superintendent or the inspectors.[6]

These are the means employed in Philadelphia to enlighten and reform the convicts.

Can there be a combination more powerful for reformation than that of a prison which hands over the prisoner to all the trials of solitude, leads him through reflection to remorse, through religion to hope; makes him industrious by the burden of idleness, and which, while it inflicts the torment of solitude, makes him find a charm in the converse of pious men, whom otherwise he would have seen with indifference, and heard without pleasure?

The impression made by such a system on the criminal, certainly is deep; experience alone can show whether the impression is durable.

We have said that his entry into the penitentiary is a critical moment; that of his departure from it is still more so. He suddenly passes from absolute solitude to the ordinary state of society. Is it not to be feared that he will greedily search for those social enjoyments of which he has been deprived so completely? He was dead to the world, and after a loss of several years he reappears in society, to which, it is true, he brings good resolutions, but perhaps also burning passions, the more impetuous, from their being the longer repressed.

This is, perhaps, on the score of reformation, the chief inconvenience of absolute isolation. This system possesses, however, an advantage, which ought not to be passed over in silence; it is, that the prisoners subject to this discipline, do not know each other.[7] This fact avoids serious inconveniences, and leads to happy consequences. There exists always, a tie more or less strong between criminals, who have formed their acquaintance in a common prison, and if they meet again after having gone through their imprisonment, they stand in a reciprocal dependence. Known, mutually, the one is almost forced to assist the other, if the latter will again commit an offense. It would be necessary to have become virtuous in a very elevated degree, in order not to become again criminal. This rock, generally so fatal to delivered convicts, is, indeed, in part avoided in the Auburn system, where the prisoners, seeing without knowing each other, contract no intimate connection. Yet we are still much more certain of avoiding this danger in the Philadelphia prison, where the convicts never behold each other's faces.

He who at the expiration of his punishment leaves this prison in order to re-enter society, cannot find in his former fellowprisoners, whom he does not know, any assistance in doing evil. And if he is willing to pursue an honest course, he meets nobody to prevent him from doing so. If he wish to commit new offenses, he stands alone, and as to this point, he is still as isolated in the world as he was in the prison. If, on the contrary, he is desirous of commencing a new life, he possesses full liberty to do so.

This system of reform is undoubtedly a conception which belongs to the highest philosophy; in general it is simple and easy to be put in practice; yet it presents in its execution, a difficulty sufficiently serious. The first rule of the system being, that the prisoners shall be entirely prevented from holding intercourse with, or even seeing each other, it results that no religious instruction or school can take place in common, so that the teacher or chaplain can instruct or exhort but one person at a time. This occasions an immense loss of time.[8] If the prisoners could be united to participate in the benefit of the same lesson, it would be much easier to diffuse moral and religious instruction, but the principles of the system are opposed to it.

In the prisons of Auburn, Wethersfield, Sing Sing, and Boston, the system of reformation does not rest upon so philosophical a theory as at Philadelphia.[9] In the latter prison, the system seems to operate by itself, by the sole force of its principles. At Auburn, on the contrary, and in the prisons of the same nature, its efficiency depends much more upon the persons charged with its execution. We see, therefore, assistance borrowed from external means, which are not so much employed in the other prison.

The Auburn plan, which permits the prisoners to assemble during the day, seems, indeed, less calculated than that of Philadelphia to produce reflection and repentance, but it is more favorable to the instruction of the prisoners. In all prisons subject to the same discipline, the instructor and the chaplain can address all the prisoners at once. At Auburn there is a chaplain (Mr. Smith) exclusively for the establishment. The same is the case in Wethersfield, where Mr. Barrett, a Presbyterian minister, devotes himself entirely to the penitentiary.[10] After the school, and the service of Sunday, the prisoners return to their solitary cells, where the chaplain visits them; he visits them in a similar way on the other days of the week,[11] and strives to touch their hearts by enlightening their conscience. The prisoners feel pleasure when they see him enter their cell. He is the only friend who is left to them; they confide in him all their sentiments; if they have any complaint against the officers of the prison, or if they have a favor to sue for, it is he who is intrusted with their wishes. By showing the interest which he takes in them, he gains more and more their confidence. He soon becomes initiated into all the secrets of their previous life, and, knowing the moral state of all, he endeavors to apply to each the proper remedy for his evil. For the rest, the minister interferes in no respect with the discipline of the prison. If the convicts are in their workshops, he never draws their attention from their work, and if a complaint is made to him, he does not act, but merely solicits in favor of the unfortunate whose interpreter he is. It would be difficult, indeed, to describe the zeal which animates Messrs. Barrett and Smith in the exercise of their pious functions; yet they sometimes, perhaps, deceive themselves respecting the results of their efforts, though they are at all events sure to earn the veneration of all who know them.

They are admirably seconded in their charitable office by several individuals not belonging to the establishment. The Sunday school is almost entirely managed by citizens residing near the prison. These, guided by a sentiment of humanity with which a profound feeling of religious duty mixes itself, pass on every Sunday two or three hours in the prison, where they act as primary instructors. They however do not only instruct the prisoners in reading, but explain to them also, the most important passages of the gospel. At Auburn, this gratuitous and religious office is performed by the members of the Presbyterian seminary. School is also held at

Sing Sing, Baltimore, and Boston.[12] In the last named city, we have seen men of the highest distinction taking upon themselves this obscure office. They made several criminals, standing around them, repeat their lesson; sometimes they would intersperse their remarks and councils in so affecting a way, that the convicts shed tears of emotion. Certainly, if the reformation of a criminal be possible, it must be obtainable by such means and such persons.

Now, to what point is this reformation actually effected by the different systems which we have examined?

Before we answer this question, it will be necessary to settle the meaning attached to the word *"reformation."*

Do we mean by this expression the radical change of a wicked person into an honest man — a change which produces virtues in the place of vices?

A similar regeneration, if it ever take place, must be very rare. What would it be in fact? To give back its primitive purity to a soul which crime has polluted. But here the difficulty is immense. It would have been much easier for the guilty individual to remain honest, than it is to rise again after his fall. It is in vain that society pardons him; his conscience does not. Whatever may be his efforts, he never will regain that delicacy of honor, which alone supports a spotless life. Even when he resolves to live honestly, he cannot forget that he has been a criminal, and this remembrance, which deprives him of self-esteem, deprives also his virtue of its reward and its guaranty.

Yet if we consider all the means employed in the prisons of the United States, in order to obtain this complete regeneration of the wicked, it is difficult to believe that it should not be sometimes the reward of so many efforts. It may be the work of pious men who devote their time, their cares, and their whole life to this important object. If society be incapable of calming the conscience, religion has the power. If society pardon, it restores liberty to the prisoner's person — this is all. When God pardons, he pardons the soul. With this moral pardon, the criminal regains his self-esteem, without which honesty is impossible. This is a result which society never can attain, because human institutions, however powerful over the actions and the will of men, have none over their consciences.

We have seen some persons in the United States, who have a strong belief in this reformation from the means used to effect it. Mr. Smith said to us at Auburn, that out of the six hundred and fifty prisoners in that prison, already fifty, at least, were radically reformed, and that he considered them good Christians. Mr. Barrett, at Wethersfield, thought that of the hundred and eighty prisoners in that penitentiary, already fifteen or twenty were in a state of complete regeneration.

It would be useless to investigate here, whether Messrs. Smith and Barrett deceived themselves in their estimate; it seems to us that we can admit with them the existence of radical reformation. But, we must be allowed to believe that the cases are still rarer than they themselves believe. This is at least the opinion of almost all enlightened men with whom we have come into contact in the United States. Mr. Elam Lynds, who has great experience in prison matters, goes much further, and considers the thorough reformation of a criminal a chimera.[13] Perhaps he runs into the other extreme, and so discouraging an opinion as his, ought to be founded on incontrovertible truth, in order to be adopted. There exists no human means of proving this complete reformation. How can we prove with ciphers the purity of the soul, the delicacy of sentiments, the innocency of intentions? Society, without power to effect this radical regeneration, is no more capable of proving it if it exist. In the one and the other case, it is an affair of the interior *forum;* in the first case God alone can act; in the second, God alone can judge. However, he who on earth is the minister of God, has sometimes the privilege of reading the consciences of others, and it is thus that the two ministers whom we have mentioned, affect to know the moral state of the prisoners, and what goes on in the depth of their souls. Undoubtedly they are more favorably placed than anybody else, to gain the confidence of these unhappy beings, and we are persuaded that they often receive disinterested avowals, and the expressions of sincere repentance. But how much risk do they run of being deceived by hypocritical protestations! The convict, whatever may be his crime, always looks for pardon. His hope exists, particularly in the prisons of the United States, where, during a long time, the custom of pardoning has been much abused.

The criminal, therefore, has an interest in showing to the chaplain, with whom alone he has moral communications, profound repentance for his crime, and a lively desire to return to virtue. If these sentiments are not sincere, he nevertheless will profess them. On the other hand, the man who sacrifices his whole existence to the pursuit of an honorable end, is himself under the influence of an ardent desire which must sometimes lead to errors. As he desires with ardor the reformation of the criminals, he easily gives credence to it. Shall we find fault with his credulity? No, because success, in which he is confident, encourages him to renewed efforts. Illusions of this nature only become fatal, if on the belief of similar regenerations pardons should be multiplied; as this would encourage hypocrisy, and we should soon see the prisoners reform themselves by calculation.[14] We must say, that in general, this danger seems to be felt very much, and that pardons become rarer and rarer. If the wish of public opinion should be completely satisfied, the governors would make use of their privilege of pardon only in favor of convicts whose guilt has become doubtful, in consequence of circumstances having appeared after their judgment. However, we must also add, that the inconvenience of too great a number of pardons is not yet entirely avoided. At Auburn, one-third of the whole number of pardons is granted on the presumption of reformation.

To resume, we would say positively, if the penitentiary system cannot propose to itself an end other than the radical reformation of which we have just spoken, the legislature perhaps should abandon this system; not because the aim is not an admirable one, but because it is too rarely obtained. The moral reformation of an individual, which is an important affair for a religious man, is little for a politician. Or to express it better, an institution is only political if it be founded on the interest of the mass; it loses its character if it only profit a small number.

But if it be true that the radical reformation of a depraved person is only an accidental instead of being a natural consequence of the penitentiary system, it is nevertheless true that there is another kind of reformation, less thorough than the former, but yet useful for society, and which the system we treat of seems to produce in a natural way.

We have no doubt, but that the habits of order to which the prisoner is subjected for several years, influence very considerably his moral conduct after his return to society.

The necessity of labor which overcomes his disposition to idleness; the obligation of silence which makes him reflect; the isolation which places him alone in presence of his crime and his suffering; the religious instruction which enlightens and comforts him; the obedience of every moment to inflexible rules; the regularity of a uniform life; in a word, all the circumstances belonging to this severe system, are calculated to produce a deep impression upon his mind.

Perhaps, leaving the prison he is not an honest man, but he has contracted honest habits. He was an idler; now he knows how to work. His ignorance prevented him from pursuing a useful occupation; now he knows how to read and to write; and the trade which he has learnt in the prison, furnishes him the means of existence which formerly he had not. Without loving virtue, he may detest the crime of which he has suffered the cruel consequences, and if he is not more virtuous he has become at least more judicious; his morality is not honor, but interest. His religious faith is perhaps neither lively nor deep; but even supposing that religion has not touched his heart, his mind has contracted habits of order, and he possesses rules for his conduct in life; without having a powerful religious conviction, he has acquired a taste for moral principles which religion affords; finally, if he has not become in truth better, he is at least more obedient to the laws, and that is all which society has the right to demand.

If we consider the reformation of convicts under this point of view, it seems to us to be obtained, in many cases, through the system which we are considering; and those Americans who have the least confidence in the radical regeneration of criminals, believe, nevertheless, in the existence of a reformation reduced to these more simple terms.

We must remark here, that the zeal of religious instructors, which is often insufficient to effect a radical reform, has yet a great influence on that of the second grade, which we have just described. It is because their aim is great, that they pursue it with ardor, and the nobleness of their undertaking elevates at once their office, and the functions of those who,

in concert with them, work for the reformation of the criminals; it gives altogether to the penitentiary establishment a
greater interest, and a much higher morality. Thus, though
the preacher does not often arrive at his proposed end, it is
yet important that he should pursue it without interruption,
and, perhaps, that point which we have indicated, is obtained
only because the aim is taken much higher.

The advantages of the penitentiary system of the United
States may then be classed in the following manner: (1)
impossibility of the mutual corruption of the prisoners, (2)
great probability of their contracting habits of obedience
and industry, which render them useful citizens, (3) possibility of a radical reformation.

Though each of the establishments which we have examined
aims at these three results, there are nevertheless, in this respect, some shades of difference, which distinguish the Auburn system from that of Philadelphia.

Philadelphia has, as we have already observed, the advantage over Auburn in respect to the first point. Indeed, the
prisoners, separated by thick walls, can communicate with
each other still less than those who are separated by silence
only. The Auburn discipline guaranties the certainty that
silence shall not be violated, but it is a mere moral certainty,
subject to contradiction; while at Philadelphia, communications among the convicts is physically impossible.

The Philadelphia system being also that which produces
the deepest impressions on the soul of the convict, must effect
more reformation than that of Auburn. The latter, however,
is perhaps more conformable to the habits of men in society,
and on this account effects a greater number of reformations, which might be called "legal," inasmuch as they produce the external fulfilment of social obligations.

If it be so, the Philadelphia system produces more honest
men, and that of New York more obedient citizens.

Some Statistical Evidence of Reform Measures

AFTER HAVING SHOWN the consequences of the penitentiary
system, such as we understand them, shall we find in statistics

the proof of those facts, which we believe we can attribute
to it?

It is customary, in order to know what influence the penitentiary system has upon society, to meet the question thus:

Has the number of crimes augmented or diminished since
the penitentiary system has been established?[15]

The solution of all questions of this kind in the United
States, is extremely difficult, because it requires statistical
documents, which it is almost impossible to procure. There
is neither in the Union nor in the different states, any central
authority which possesses them. With difficulty the statistics
of a town or county can be obtained, but never those of a
whole state.[16]

Pennsylvania is the only state in which we have been able
to learn the total number of crimes. During the year 1830,
there were 2084 individuals condemned in this state to imprisonment; which, if compared to a population of 1,347,672
inhabitants, gives one conviction for 653 inhabitants.

In other states we have obtained very exact materials respecting the number of certain crimes, but never the totality
of offenses. Thus we know merely the number of burglaries
committed in the states of New York, Massachusetts, Connecticut, and Maryland, which caused the criminals to be
sent to the state prison.

If we take these special convictions for the basis of our
observations, we shall see that in the states of New York,
Massachusetts, and Maryland, the number of criminals, compared to the population, decreases; that in the state of Connecticut it increases; while it is stationary in Pennsylvania.

Shall we conclude from this statement that the prison of
Connecticut is very bad; that those of New York, Massachusetts, and Maryland, are the only good penitentiaries;
and that those of Pennsylvania are better than the first, but
worse than the others?

This conclusion would be strange, because it is an incontestable fact, that the penitentiary of Connecticut is better
than the prisons of Maryland and Pennsylvania.[17]

If we examine with attention the situation of these different
states, and the political circumstances which surround them,
we shall see that the number, more or less considerable, of

crimes, and even their decrease or increase, may be owing to causes entirely foreign to the penitentiary system.

First, a difference must be made between the number of crimes and their increase: in the state of New York there are more crimes committed than in Pennsylvania; yet the number of crimes is stationary in the latter state, while it diminishes in the former. In Connecticut, where crimes increase, there are, in the whole, but half the crimes committed, in proportion, to those in all other states.

We would add, that, in order to establish well-founded points of comparison between the various states, it would be necessary to deduct from the population of each the foreigners, and to compare only the crimes committed by the settled population; proceeding thus, it would be found that Maryland is that state the settled population of which commits most crimes. This fact is explained by a cause peculiar to the southern states — the colored race. In general, it has been observed, that in those states in which there exists one Negro to thirty whites, the prisons contain one Negro to four white persons.

The states which have many Negroes must therefore produce more crimes. This reason alone would be sufficient to explain the large number of crimes in Maryland: it is, however, not applicable to all the states of the south; but only to those in which manumission is permitted: because we should deceive ourselves greatly were we to believe that the crimes of the Negroes are avoided by giving them liberty; experience proves, on the contrary, that in the south the number of criminals increases with that of manumitted persons; thus, for the very reason that slavery seems to draw nearer to its ruin, the number of freed persons will increase for a long time in the south, and with it the number of criminals.[18]

While the southern part of the United States contains in its bosom this fertile cause of crimes, there are in the states of the North, on the other hand, such as New York and Massachusetts, several political causes which tend to diminish the number of crimes.

The colored population decreases here every day, compared to the white population which goes on continually increasing.

Moreover, the foreigners who arrive every year from Europe without means of existence, in these states are a cause of crime which is continually becoming less.

In the same measure as the population increases, the number of emigrants, though not decreasing in itself, becomes less in relation to the sum total of the inhabitants.

The population doubles in thirty years; while the number of emigrants remains about the same. So that this cause of increase of crime in the North, though apparently stationary, loses every year its force in a statistical point of view; the cipher which represents it remains always the same considered by itself; but it becomes less compared with another cipher which daily increases.

Some Americans believe also that knowledge and education, so much diffused in the states of the North, have a tendency to diminish the number of crimes.

There are in the state of New York, with a population of 2,000,000 of inhabitants, 550,000 children instructed in the schools, and the state alone spends for this object nearly Fr. 6,000,000 every year. It seems that an enlightened population, to whom no opportunity is wanting which agriculture, commerce, and manufactural industry can offer, should commit less crimes than that which possesses these latter advantages without having the same intellectual means to make use of them. Nevertheless, we do not believe that to the diffusion of knowledge this decrease of crimes in the North is to be attributed, because in Connecticut, where knowledge is still more diffused than in the state of New York, crimes increase with extreme rapidity. And if we cannot reproach knowledge with this prodigious increase, we are at least constrained to acknowledge that it has not the power of preventing it. For the rest, we do not pretend to explain these strange anomalies exhibited by states whose political institutions are almost the same, and in which, nevertheless, the proportion of crimes to the population is so different. These difficulties belong to that class which never fails to lead to every kind of statistical labors.[19] But the considerations which we have just offered, serve at least to prove how many important causes, unconnected with the penitentiary system, influence the increase or decrease of crime.

Sometimes a crisis in the industry of a country, the disbanding of an army, etc., are sufficient to increase the number of offenses during a year.

Thus in the year 1816, the number of criminals increased in an extraordinary degree in all American prisons. Had the penitentiary system anything to do with it? No, it was simply in consequence of the war between America and England; peace having been concluded, a number of regiments were disbanded, and the soldiers thus deprived for the moment of employment.

There is another difficulty; even if we agree respecting the cause of crimes, we do not know exactly that of their increase.

How shall the number of crimes be proved? By that of the convictions? Several causes, however, may produce more frequent convictions, though the number of crimes be the same.[20]

This may happen, if the police pursue crimes with more activity — a circumstance which generally occurs, if public attention is more actively directed to the subject. In such case the number of crimes is not increased, but more crimes are proved. The same is the case when courts of justice are more exact; which happens always when the penal law is mitigated. Then the number of acquittals diminishes. There are more convictions, though the number of crimes has not varied. The penitentiary system itself, which is intended to diminish the number of crimes, has for its first result, the increase of convictions. In the same degree as magistrates feel repugnant to condemn the guilty, since they know the corrupting influence of the prison which receives them; in the same degree, they show themselves more ready to pronounce a condemnation as soon as they know that the prison, far from being a school of crime, is a place of repentance and reformation.[21]

However this may be, it is clear from the above, that the increase of crimes or their decrease, is produced sometimes by general causes, and sometimes by accidental ones, which have no direct connection with the penitentiary system.

If we consider the object of the penitentiary system and its natural extent, we shall see that it cannot have that general influence which is often attributed to it, and that the question is not put as it ought to be, if we intend to judge of it by the absolute number of crimes. A prison discipline, good or bad, cannot have any influence except on those who have been imprisoned. Prisons may be very good in a country where there are many crimes, and very bad in another in which few are committed. Thus in Massachusetts, where there are less convicts, the prisons are bad, while they are good in the State of New York in which crimes are much more numerous.[22] A bad prison cannot corrupt those who have not been exposed to its influence, any more than a good penitentiary can correct those who have remained out of the reach of its beneficial discipline.

The institutions, the habits,[23] and political circumstances — these influence most the moral state of men in society. Prisons act but on the morality of prisoners.[24]

The penitentiary system then has not that extended circle of action which sometimes is attributed to it. If we reduce it as we ought to do, to the inmates of the prison, its influence is sufficiently important not to attribute to it another that is foreign to it. And, in fact, if this part of the social body on which the penitentiary system operates is but small, it is at all events the most diseased, and its disorder is both the most contagious and the most important to be remedied.

Hence, if we wish to appreciate the merit of a prison and the system which has been put in practice, we ought to observe not the morality of society in general, but only of those individuals who, having been imprisoned in such establishments, have returned to society. If they commit no new offense, we have a right to believe that the influence of the prison has been salutary, and if they relapse into new crimes, it is a proof that the prison has not made them better.

While it is true that a large or small number of recommittals alone can prove the deficiency or excellence of a prison, we must add, that it is impossible to obtain, on this point, a perfectly exact statement.

On the one hand, it is difficult to obtain proof that liberated convicts have led an honest life; on the other, we have not always a knowledge of the new crimes which they commit.

To these considerations, which appear to us necessary to reduce the question to its true limits, we shall add another, which seems to us equally important; that is, in order to ap-

preciate the effects of the penitentiary system, we ought not
to consider the epoch of its creation, but the period which
follows it. This truth, which it seems idle to mention, has
nevertheless been forgotten by writers of great merit. We
will quote an example.

We have said already that in the year 1790, a new system
of imprisonment was established in Philadelphia, and the
Walnut street prison organized on a plan which we have
pointed out as entirely deficient; yet by some accidental circumstance, or from some unknown reason, the number of
crimes in Pennsylvania during the years 1790, 1791, 1792,
and 1793, was considerably less than during the preceding
years. Mr. Livingston and Mr. Roberts Vaux, in the United
States, and in France, the Duke de Larochefoucauld-
Liancourt and Mr. Charles Lucas, have drawn from this decrease of crimes, the proof of the efficiency of the system,[25]
but their arguments seem to be founded on a fact erroneously
appreciated. To ascribe this result to the new system, it
would have been necessary to prove that the individuals, once
imprisoned in Walnut street, had not committed new crimes.
This proof could not be made. In fact, the system commences
in 1790, and already in the years 1791, 1792, and 1793, the
effects are sought for, i. e. before most of the prisoners, on
whom the new system could have any effect, were released.[26]

It is easy to conceive that the effect of the penitentiary
system cannot be appreciated except after a certain series of
years, and only after the convicts, whose terms have expired,
have had time to commit new crimes, or to give assurance of
an honest life.

On this account we shall pass over the results obtained in
the new penitentiaries of Philadelphia, Sing Sing, Boston,
and Baltimore. By giving up the arguments which we might
draw from these different prisons, we shall very much narrow
the circle of disagreement, but we shall have at least the advantage of giving to our arguments none but solid founda-
tions.

Let us then compare the effects produced by the ancient
prisons of the United States, with those resulting from the
new system practised in the penitentiaries of Auburn and
Wethersfield, the only ones which have been established for a

time sufficient to draw just conclusions as to their influence.

In the ancient prison of New York (Newgate), recommittals took place (in proportion to the whole number of convictions) as one to nine; in the prison of Maryland as one to seven; in that of Walnut street as one to six; in the ancient Connecticut prison as one to four; and in the Boston jail also, as one to six.

The number of recommittals is considerably less in the new prisons at Auburn and Wethersfield. In the former, recommittals form the nineteenth part of the whole number, and of one hundred individuals released from the latter, since its creation, five only have been recommitted for new offenses; which gives the proportion of one to twenty.

At Auburn not only those criminals are noted down who are recommitted, but an attempt has also been made to watch the conduct of delivered prisoners who have remained in society. Of one hundred and sixty individuals, in respect to whom it was possible to obtain information, one hundred and twelve have conducted themselves well; the others have returned to bad or at least doubtful habits.[27]

These statistics, however conclusive they may appear, are the result of too short a period to justify an invincible proof of the efficiency of the system to be deduced from them. But we must nevertheless acknowledge, that they are extremely favorable to the new penitentiaries, and the presumption in their favor, caused by this result, is so much the stronger as the effect obtained perfectly accords with that promised by the theory. It must be added, that in spite of the impossibility of drawing any conclusive argument from the penitentiaries of Sing Sing, Boston, and others of the same kind, on account of their having been so recently established, it cannot be doubted, that the success of Auburn and Wethersfield, renders that of establishments on the same model, extremely probable.

In offering these statistical documents, we have not compared the number of crimes and recommittals in the United States and in France; persuaded as we are, that the foundation for such a comparison would be imperfect. The modes of existence in the two countries do not resemble each other, and the elements composing them are essentially different.

A young society, exempt from political embarrassments, rich both by its soil and its industry, should be supposed to furnish less criminals than a country where the ground is disputed foot by foot, and where the cries produced by political divisions tend to increase the number of offenses, because they increase misery by disturbing industry.

Yet if the statistical documents which we possess of Pennsylvania, should be applied to the rest of the Union, there are in this country more crimes committed than in France, in proportion to the population.[28] Various causes of another nature explain this result: on the one hand, the colored population, which forms the sixth part of the inhabitants of the United States, and which composes half of the inmates of the prisons; and on the other hand, the foreigners pouring in every year from Europe, and who form the fifth and sometimes even the fourth part of the number of convicts.

These two facts, explaining the great number of crimes in the United States, make it not a subject of comparison with the number of offenses in a country where we are met with no similar facts.

If we should deduct from the total number of crimes, those committed by Negroes and foreigners, we should undoubtedly find that the white American population commits less crimes than ours. But proceeding thus, we should fall into another error; in fact, to separate the Negroes from the whole population of the United States, would be equal to deducting the poorer classes of the community with us. That is to say, those who commit the crimes. One obstacle is here avoided only to meet with another; in this respect, the only certain, incontestable fact, which we have remarked in the United States, and which may offer an opportunity for comparison, is the peculiar and extraordinary morality of the women belonging to the white race. Out of one hundred prisoners in the United States, we find but four women; while with us there are twenty in a hundred. Now this morality of the female sex must influence the whole society, because it is upon them that the morality of a family chiefly depends.

At all events, as the elements of comparison are otherwise different, we can on the whole but hazard probabilities.

Difficulties abound if we wish to make approximations of

this kind between the two nations. The difference which exists between the penal laws of the United States and ours, adds greatly to them.

In the United States, things are punished as crimes which with us are beyond the reach of the laws. And again, our code punishes offenses which in the United States are not considered as such. Thus, many offenses against religion and morals, such as blasphemy, incest, fornication, drunkenness, etc., are in the United States repressed by severe punishments; with us they are unpunished. Again, our code punishes bankruptcy, against which the laws of the United States have no provisions.

How then can we compare the number of crimes committed in countries the legislation of which is so different? And yet, we must add, that this comparison, were it made exactly, would hardly afford conclusive results: thus, it may well be said, in general, that the number, more or less considerable, of convictions in a country, proves its corruption or its morality. Yet there exist exceptions to this rule, which throw a great uncertainty upon these calculations: thus, in one of the most religious and most moral states of the Union (Connecticut), there are more convictions for offenses against morals than in any other state. To understand this result, it is necessary to remember that crimes of this nature are punished only where they are rare: in societies in which adultery is frequent, it is not punished. No bankrupts are found in the prisons of the United States. Shall we conclude from this that the crime of bankruptcy is never committed there? This would be a strange mistake, because in no country perhaps more bankruptcies take place than there: it is necessary, therefore, in order not to admire on this point the commercial morality of the United States, to know whether a matter is in question which the law regards as a crime. Again, if we know that there are in the United States ten criminals committed for forgery out of one hundred prisoners we are not authorized to take this as a proof of greater corruption in that country than in ours, in which those sentenced for forgery are but two out of the hundred. In the United States the whole population is in some degree commercial, and in addition, there are three hundred and fifty banks, all emitting paper money. The ingenuity of the forger therefore has in that country a much wider field, and much stronger temptation, which is not the case with us, where commerce is but the business of a single class, and where the number of banks is so small.

There is again a difficulty in comparing the crimes committed in the two countries. It is, that in those cases even, in which the legislation of both punishes the same act, it inflicts different punishments; but as the comparison of crimes is made by that of the punishments, it follows that two analogous results, obtained from different bases, are compared together; which is a new source of mistake.

If it is difficult to compare, for any useful purpose, the number and nature of crimes committed in the United States and in France, it is perhaps still more so to compare the number of recommittals, and to arrive by this comparison at a conclusive result, in respect to the prisons of the two countries.

In general, those recommittals only, which bring back the prisoner to the prison where he has been detained the first time, are calculated in the United States.[29] His return to the same prison, is in fact the only means of proving his relapse. In that country, where passports do not exist, nothing is easier than to change one's name. If therefore a delivered convict commits a new crime under a fictitious name, he can very easily conceal his relapse, providing he is not brought back to the prison where he underwent his first punishment. There are, besides, a thousand means of avoiding the chances of being recognized. Nothing is easier than to pass from one state to another, and it is the criminal's interest to do so, whether he intends to commit new crimes, or has resolved to lead an honest life. We find therefore among a hundred criminals convicted in one state, thirty, upon an average, who belong to some neighboring state. This emigration is sufficient to make the proof of recommittals impossible. The tie between the various states being strictly political, there is no central power to which the police officers might refer to obtain information respecting the previous life of an indicted person: so that the courts condemn, almost always, without knowing the true name of the criminal, and still less his previous life. It is clear, therefore, that in such a state of things the number of known recommittals is never that of all the existing ones.[30] The same is not the case with us. There are a thousand ways in France to prove the identity of the indicted and the convicted prisoner, by means of the mutual information which all the agents of the judicial police keep up among themselves. The convictions pronounced by a *cour royal* in the south are known by a court in the north, and the judiciary possesses on this point all the means of investigation which are wanting in the United States. If, therefore, in France, no more recommittals should take place than in the United States, a greater number, nevertheless, would be publicly known. And as the means of proving them in the two countries are so different, it would be useless to compare the number.

All comparisons of this kind then, between America and Europe, lead to no satisfactory result. America can be compared only with herself; yet this comparison is sufficient to shed abundant light upon the question we are considering. We acknowledged the superiority of the new penitentiary system over the old prisons, when we found that the number of recommittals in the ancient prisons, compared to all convictions, was in the proportion of one to six, and in the new penitentiaries in the proportion of only one to twenty.

SOME

FINANCIAL CONSIDERATIONS

OF PENITENTIARY SYSTEMS

At present, after having stated the principles and effects of the penitentiary system in the United States, with regard to the reformation of the prisoners, it only remains to treat of its result in a financial view.

The latter comprises the manner of constructing prisons, and the expenses of the support of the prisoners, compared to the produce of their labor.

Construction of the Prisons

we must in this respect distinguish between the systems of Philadelphia and Auburn.

The penitentiary of Philadelphia (Cherry Hill) will, at the time of its completion, have cost $432,000 which makes the price of each cell $1624.[1]

It is true that enormous unnecessary expenses have been incurred in its construction. The greater part had no other object than the ornament of the edifice. Gigantic walls, gothic towers, a wide iron gate, give to this prison the appearance of a fortified castle of the middle ages, without affording any real advantage to the establishment.[2]

Yet even if these unnecessary expenses had been wisely avoided, there would yet remain a considerable amount inherent in the Philadelphia system, which it would have been impossible to avoid. The convict being condemned, according to this system, to constant confinement, his cell must necessarily be spacious and well ventilated, provided with all proper wants, and large enough to permit him to work without much constraint. It is besides necessary that a small yard should be joined to the cell, surrounded by walls, in which he may, each day, during the hours prescribed by the rules, breathe the fresh air. Now, whatever pains may be taken to construct this cell with its appendage in the most economical manner, it must necessarily be much more costly than one that is narrower, without a particular yard, and destined only to receive the convict during night.

The prisons, constructed on the Auburn plan, are infinitely cheaper. Yet there are very considerable differences in the respective costs of their construction.

This disparity seems at first difficult to be accounted for, but upon investigating the causes, we find, that the construction of new penitentiaries is either expensive or cheap, according to the means employed in erecting them.

The penitentiary at Washington for the District of Columbia will have cost, when finished, $180,000. It contains only 160 cells, each of which, therefore, will cost $1125; while the penitentiary at Wethersfield, established on the same plan, has cost $35,000 for 232 prisoners, so that each cell has cost but $150.86.

As all public expenses are incurred with great economy in the small state of Connecticut, we might believe that the small expense of the building of the prison is the effect of extraordinary efforts, of which a larger society, occupied with other interests, would not be capable.

But the penitentiaries of Sing Sing and Blackwell Island, (erected for the same price as that of Wethersfield) in the State of New York, the largest of all the members of the Union, prove that Connecticut has done nothing extraordinary, and the construction of the Baltimore penitentiary has caused no greater expense.

The care which some states take to avoid in this matter every kind of useless ornament, while others do not pay the same attention to economy, produces this difference in the expense of construction.

The Washington penitentiary has been built on a sumptuous plan, more fit for a palace than a prison.

The greatest difficulty to be avoided in similar constructions, is the ambition of the architect, who will always strive to erect an edifice of great size, and will reluctantly submit to the adoption of a simple and strictly useful plan. Several states have triumphed over this difficulty, though at Philadelphia, Pittsburgh, and Washington, it has not been avoided.

Of all the establishments founded on the Auburn plan, the construction of the Washington penitentiary has been the most expensive.

The reason of this circumstance perhaps is to be found, in the nature of the authority itself, which directed this building to be constructed.

Particular states of the United States adopt generally the simplest plants for their prisons: they superintend the execution, and aim at strict economy in the most minute details. On the contrary, the administration at Washington, more elevated in its views, admits more easily of great designs, and as it is absorbed by a number of general interests, it is obliged to leave everything which belongs to the execution of the plan, to agents whom it has neither the time nor the power to superintend.

All practical men in the United States, believe that the Auburn system satisfies all claims of economy as far as regards construction.

In those prisons in which the whole discipline consists in the strength of the walls and the solidity of bolts, heavy walls and strong locks are requisite to master the prisoners.

In the new penitentiaries, so much material strength is not necessary, because it is not the point against which the prisoners direct their continual efforts. The moral superintendence forms the chief object with which they have continually to struggle. Isolated by the cell or by silence, they are more-over reduced to their individual strength. To curb them, therefore, does not require so much material force as if they were able to unite their efforts.

The necessity of having a cell for each prisoner, multiplies indeed the walls, and requires a greater extent of building. But this increase is compensated by a circumstance favorable to economy.

As the prisoners have no communication whatever with each other, every classification becomes useless, and it is not any longer necessary to have a separate division for young convicts, another for criminals more advanced in age, and another for recommitted convicts, etc. In short, the principles of the penitentiary system being directly opposed to every communication of the prisoners with each other, there is no yard for recreation required in the modern penitentiaries. Much, therefore, is saved in building and enclosing walls, which exist, or at least ought to exist, in the system of our prisons.

In short, it may be said, that the construction of a modern penitentiary may be effected at a cheap rate, if proper views of economy are adopted.

Mr. Welles, one of the inspectors of the Wethersfield prison, whose correct views and experience we have always appreciated, has told us repeatedly, that in this affair every-thing depended upon economy in the most minute details. He thinks that a penitentiary of five hundred cells might be constructed for about $40,000; which would make $80.00 for each cell.[3]

It would be impossible to estimate exactly the cost of a prison in France, by that of one in the United States.

However, we believe that this expense would be about the same in France as in America. Because if it is true that the raw materials are much costlier with us than in the United States, it is also incontestable, that wages for daily labor are much higher in America than in France.

We have seen that in the United States the prisoners are sometimes employed to build the prisons. The penitentiaries of Sing Sing, Blackwell Island, and Baltimore, have been thus erected. Yet there are many persons in America, who believe that this is not the most economical way, and that it is more profitable to have them built by free laborers. This opinion seems at first glance to be opposed to the nature of things, particularly in a country where labor is so dear as in the United States. But it is answered, that for this very reason, viz. the high price of labor, manufactured articles are sold at a high price. Thus the labor of the prisoners applied to productive industry, yields more for the state than it has to spend for the work of free laborers.

This question, therefore, must be decided according to place and circumstances. Its solution, says Judge Welles of Wethersfield, depends likewise upon the situation of the prisoners: it is better to leave those in their workshops whose labor is applied to branches which are very productive, but such as are not particularly skilful may be used for the rougher kind of labor in the construction of a penitentiary.[4]

In France, the construction of prisons by the prisoners, might be still more advantageous than in America, if we look at the question simply on account of its economy, and disregard the difficulties which, with us, the superintendence of prisoners occupied in building their own prison, would present.

The rate of manufactured articles does not present in France the same chances of profit as in the United States, and the prisoners, therefore, may be employed in the construction of the prison, without risk of loss in the productiveness of their labor.

We are sure that the walls to be erected would be profitable, since they have their destination fixed before being built: while nothing is more accidental and uncertain that the future profit yielded by the sale of merchandise.

If we employ free workmen, we pay their wages without diminution; while prisoners, occupied with any branch of industry, work with all the chances of loss and depreciation, incident to manufactured articles. If, on the contrary, the prison is built by the prisoners themselves, the fruit of their labor is immediately collected. This labor does not produce a gain, properly so called, but it dispenses with an unavoidable charge.

We are well aware that in America the case is not the same.

There, manufacturers stand a favorable chance on account of the various fields opened to industry: the object there is to gain, while we only aim at avoiding losses. Finally, it is a great advantage in France to be able to employ the prisoners in a labor useful, and sometimes necessary, without injuring by way of competition the manufactories of free labor.[5]

Annual Expense of the Prisons

THE NEW SYSTEM in practice in the United States, promises also great advantages on the score of *annual* expense; its effects have already, in this respect, surpassed the expectations of its promoters.

As long as the ancient prison discipline was in practice, the support of the prisoners was in all the states a source of considerable expense. We will cite but two instances: From the year 1790 to 1826, the state of Connecticut has expended for its prison (Newgate), $204,711, and the state of New York has paid for the support of the ancient prison of Newgate, during twenty-three years, (from the year 1797 to 1819) $646,912. The new system was established in 1819 in the state of New York, and in 1827 in Connecticut. In the former, the expenses immediately diminished; in the latter they changed directly into an annual revenue.

At Auburn, the income resulting from the labor of the prisoners, has, during the last two years, exceeded the expenses of support, and the period is already foreseen, when, after the construction of Sing Sing shall be finished, the labor of its prisoners, applied solely to productive industry, will cover the expenses of the prison.

From the first year of its institution, the new Connecticut prison (Wethersfield,) has produced $1,017.16, expenses deducted. Every year the revenue has increased, and the gain of the year 1831, was $7,824.02. In short, the new penitentiary, which cost so much, produced during three years and a half, expenses of all kinds deducted, a net income of $17,139.53.

The Baltimore penitentiary has, during three years, beginning with the day of its institution, yielded to the state of Maryland $44,344.45, all expenses deducted.

These results, assuredly, are not owing altogether to the penitentiary system: and that which proves it is the circumstance that the Baltimore prison was productive even previously to the introduction of the penitentiary system. We allow even, that the best penitentiary is not that which yields the most; because the zeal and talent of the prisoners in the workshops, may be stimulated to the detriment of the discipline. Yet we are obliged to acknowledge, that this system, once established, is powerful in maintaining order and regularity in the prison; it rests on an uninterrupted watchfulness. The labor of the prisoners, therefore, is with such a system more constant and more productive.

At all events, after having seen the above statements, it would be unreasonable to reject the penitentiary system as expensive, since the discipline which has been established in the United States with so little expense, supports itself in some states, and has become in others a source of revenue.[6]

Every prisoner in the new penitentiaries costs, on an average, for his support, food, clothing, and surveillance, fifteen cents. In Wethersfield and Baltimore, the support of the prisoner is the cheapest; at Auburn the most expensive: the food costs in the various penitentiaries, on an average, five cents a day per head. At Wethersfield it costs but four cents, and at Sing Sing, five cents.

The expenses for clothing and bedding, amount in general to nothing, owing to the care which is taken to have them made in the prison by the prisoners themselves. The expenses of surveillance amount on an average to six cents a day per head. At Auburn they are the least, and at Sing Sing the most.

In all the new prisons, the expenses of surveillance are greater than those incurred for food and clothing. All economy on this point would be destructive to a system which rests entirely upon discipline, and consequently upon the good choice of officers.

We see that in all the new prisons, the sum total of the expense, though varying in some points, is nevertheless always, nearly the same, and it is clear, that as long as the administration of these establishments is directed by men of probity, and with similar economy, the expenses of each year will not vary much. There is a minimum below which it cannot fall without becoming detrimental to the well being of the prisoners, and a maximum beyond which it ought not to rise, without extravagance in the administration, or misconduct on the part of the officers.

The same is not the case with a production which by nature is variable. We may certainly presume that the prison which produces most is that in which the prisoners work most. Yet the difficulty attending the sale of the articles, produced by their labor, often defeats this presumption. Even in the United States, where labor is so costly, the demand for articles undergoes numerous variations, which raise or lower their price.[7]

In short, the financial administration of Auburn, Wethersfield, Sing Sing, and Baltimore, has appeared to us to be directed with extreme skill, and the discretionary power with which the superintendents are invested, is perhaps one of the principal causes of economy. They govern the prison, as it seems best to them, under the superintendence of the inspectors. They are responsible, but they act freely.

The administration of these prisons, which combines the system by contract with the *régie* (management of sale, etc., by its own officers) appears to us very conducive to economy.

There are in our prisons many things for which a very high price is paid to the contractor, and which are obtained for very little expense in a prison which manages its own affairs.

At Auburn (in 1830) 160 prisoners out of 620, are occupied in the service of the prison. They make everything which serves for the clothing, linen, and shoes, and conduces to the neatness and order of the prison; only 462 work for the contractor.

At Wethersfield, the number of prisoners who work for the contractor is proportionately still smaller. It is believed in America that it is more profitable to employ a large number of contractors, because more favorable agreements can be made for each branch of industry.

Particular care is taken never to make contracts for any great length of time: the contractors, therefore, cannot exact contracts disadvantageous to the prison, under the pretense of injurious contingencies to which the possible depreciation of the manufactured articles may expose them.

The duration of a contract often does not exceed a year; it is sometimes of less duration for the labor, and generally of six months only for the food.

The contractor pays for a day's labor of a prisoner, about half of what he would pay to a free workman.[8]

The constant renewal of the contracts makes it possible for the administration to seize upon all the chances of economy. It profits by the cheapness of provisions, and if the price of manufactured articles is high, it obtains better conditions from the contractors to whom it hires the labor of the prisoners: it makes these calculations for each contract, and must on this account be acquainted with the rise and fall of the various branches of industry. One often prospers to the disadvantage of another, and in such a case the prison will regain from one contractor the loss which it has suffered with another.

It is evident that such an order of things requires in the superintendent a constant attention, an accurate knowledge of affairs, and a perfect probity, which procures him the confidence of the state, and of all those who have business with him. The superintendent is not only the director of a prison, but he is also the agent who, attentive to the movements of commerce, must watch without interruption how he can apply the labor of the prisoners in the most advantageous way, and find the most profitable sales for his products. This system, which unites the contract and the *régie*, necessarily produces a responsibility of a very complicated character, and on this account will not meet with the approbation of those who, in all matters of administration, wish to see but one individual; in the accounts but one column, and in this column but one number; this simplicity is not to be found in the American prisons. It requires in the superintendent constant activity, in the inspectors a minute surveillance, and in the comptrollers of the state a thorough examination.

We may yet remark, that this variety of duties, this power of governing the prison, or of making contracts for its labor, this vast administration at once moral and physical, serve to explain also, why the office of superintendent is sought for by persons at once intelligent and respectable.

CHAPTER FIVE

THE

PRISON SYSTEMS OF FRANCE

D URING THE YEARS 1827, 1828, 1829, and 1830, government paid Fr. 3,300,000 every year for the support of eighteen thousand prisoners in the *maisons centrales* (state prisons). Thus the prisons, which, in the United States, yield an income, form with us a heavy charge upon the public treasury. This difference is owing to various causes.

The discipline of our prisons is less severe, and the labor of the prisoners necessarily suffers from every relaxation of discipline.

The saving (*pécule*) of the prisoners absorbs, with us, two-thirds of the produce of their labor, while in America it does not exist at all.

Finally, the manufactured articles are sold in France with much more difficulty, and with less profit, than in the United States.

The object of punishment is to punish the guilty and to render them better, but as it is at present, it punishes little, and instead of reforming, it corrupts still more. We would develop this melancholy truth, if we believed that there is a single individual who contests it. Of sixteen thousand prisoners, at present in the *maisons centrales,* there are four thousand held upon recommittals.[1] And it is now acknowledged by government itself, that the number of recommittals goes on continually increasing. The same was formerly the case in America, but since the new penitentiary system has been established, the number of recommittals diminishes.

The corruption of our prisons is owing chiefly to two causes. The first and the most important, is the free communication of the prisoners both night and day. How can a moral reformation of the prisoners take place in the midst of this assemblage of all crimes and all vices? The convict who arrives at the prison half depraved, leaves it in a state of complete corruption, and we may well say that in the bosom of so much infamy, it would be impossible for him not to become wicked.

The second cause of the depravity of the prisoners is found in the bad use which they make of their saving. They spend that part of it which is allowed to them in the prison, in excess of food or other superfluities, and thus contract fatal habits. Every expense in the prison is destructive of order, and incompatible with the uniform discipline, without which there is no equality of punishments. The saving is of no real use whatever to the convict before he leaves the prison. And we must add, that, in the actual state of things, that part even of the saving which is given to the convict on his leaving the prison, is neither more useful than that which he has spent in the prison. Had he contracted, during his imprisonment, habits of order, and some principles of morality, the sum, sometimes very considerable, then placed at his disposal, might be employed in a judicious way and for his future benefit. But, corrupted as he is by his imprisonment itself, he hardly feels himself free, than he hastens to spend the fruit of his labor in debaucheries of all kinds, and continues this kind of life until the necessity of recurring to crime brings him back to the arm of justice and thence to the prison.

The prison, the system of which is corrupting, is at the same time fatal to the life of the prisoners. With us one prisoner dies out of fourteen in the *maisons centrales.* In the penitentiaries of America, there dies on an average one out of forty-nine.

In these prisons, in which death is so rare, the discipline is austere, the law of silence is imposed upon the prisoners. All are subject to a uniform discipline, and the produce of their labor is not lost either in debaucheries or superfluous expenses; the most rigorous punishment reaches, without pity, every one who breaks orders; not one hour of rest is granted them during the day; and the whole night they are in solitude.

In our prisons, where death makes so many ravages, the prisoners talk freely together; nothing separates them during day or night; no severe punishment is inflicted upon them. Every one may, by the earning of his labor, alleviate the severity of his imprisonment; and finally, he can enjoy hours of recreation.

This severe discipline of the American penitentiaries, this absolute silence imposed upon the prisoners, this perpetual isolation, and the inflexible uniformity of a system, which cannot be alleviated for one without injustice to others, do they not altogether constitute a rigor which is yet full of humanity?

The contagion of mutual communications, which in our prisons corrupts the inmates, is not more fatal to their souls than their bodies.[2]

We notice here the principal vices which have most attracted our attention in our central prisons. It is easy to see that we do not present them as a complete picture; moreover, we add nothing on the "houses of arrest" and "of justice," the other departmental prisons and the bagnes. We only speak of the central prisons destined for great criminals, because they alone contain a population analogous to that within the penitentiaries of America.

CHAPTER SIX

APPLICATION OF AMERICAN

PENITENTIARY SYSTEM

IN FRANCE

WOULD IT BE POSSIBLE to establish the American penitentiary system among us?

It seems to us that this system, considered theoretically
(if we abstract the particular difficulties which its execution
would meet with in France) is both sound and practicable.
Various objections are made against it which we shall examine.

Many persons see in the penitentiary system a philanthropic conception which has for its sole object the amelioration of the physical situation of the prisoners, and as they
believe that the criminals are not too severely punished in
their present prisons, they reject the system which would
make them more comfortable. This opinion rests upon a fact;
for a long time those who have raised their voices in France
in favor of reforms in the prison discipline, have called public attention simply to clothing, food, and all those matters
which contribute to make the convicts more easy.[1] So that in
the eyes of a great number, the adoption of a penitentiary

system, which makes innovations necessary, tends only to the physical amelioration of the prison.

Others engaged in a way entirely opposite, believe that the condition of the prisoners is so unfortunate that it would be wrong to aggravate it. If they hear of a system which is founded on isolation and silence, they say that society has not a right to punish men with such severity.

Finally, there is a third class of persons who, without expressing themselves on the advantages or inconveniences of the penitentiary system, consider it as a utopian scheme, destined only to enlarge the number of human errors. It must be acknowledged that the opinion of the latter has been in some cases supported by the writings of the most distinguished publicists, whose mistakes in this matter have been received together with their soundest opinions.

Thus, Bentham wishes in his *panoptic* prison the continual sound of music, in order to soften the passions of the prisoners. Mr. Livingston asks for the young prisoner, and for the convicts themselves, a system of instruction almost as complete as that established in any of the free academies. And Mr. Charles Lucas indicates, as a mode of executing the punishment of imprisonment, a penitentiary system which it would be difficult to reconcile with the principles essential in criminal matters.

Is it just to blame the severity or mildness of the penitentiary system? Must we condemn this system on the exaggeration of writers who, preoccupied with philosophical doctrines, have not guarded themselves against the danger attending any theory if carried to its full consequences?

The new system, on the contrary, seems to us to have been conceived for the very object of avoiding those excesses with which it is reproached: freed from severities which are not necessary for its success; unencumbered by indulgences which are asked for only by mistaken philanthropy.

Finally, its execution presents itself with all the advantages of extreme practical simplicity.

It is believed that two depraved individuals, kept in the same place, must corrupt each other. They are therefore separated. Their passions, or the bustle of the world, had deafened or misled them: they are isolated and thus brought to reflect. Their intercourse with the wicked had perverted them: they are condemned to silence. Idleness had depraved them: they are made to work. Misery had conducted them to crime: they are taught a useful art. They have violated the laws of their country: a punishment is inflicted upon them. Their life is protected, their body is safe and healthy: but nothing equals their moral suffering. They are unhappy, they deserve to be so: having become better, they will be happy in that society whose laws they will have been taught to respect. This is the whole system of American penitentiaries.

But, it is objected, that this system, tried in Europe, has not succeeded, and to prove it, the instances of Geneva and Lausanne are mentioned. There penitentiary systems have been established at great expense without producing the results which were expected from them for the reformation of the convicts.

We believe that the example of that which has been done in Switzerland ought in no respect to influence what France might do. In fact, the same mistake in respect to the construction of prisons, has been fallen into in Switzerland, which has not been always avoided in the United States, viz. the desire of elevating architectural monuments instead of simply constructing useful establishments. The expense incurred for the Swiss penitentiaries, therefore, ought in no way to be taken as a basis for calculating the probable expenses of prisons of the same nature in France. On the other hand, if the system of these penitentiaries has not been efficient for the reformation of prisoners, we must not seek for the cause in the system of the United States: it is a mistake to believe that the discipline of the prisons in Geneva and Lausanne is the same with that of the American penitentiaries. The only point common to both is, that the prisoners pass the night in solitary cells: but that which makes a difference of primary inportance in the penitentiary systems of the two countries, is, that in the United States the discipline rests essentially on isolation and silence, while in Switzerland the prisoners have free intercourse with each other during the day.

It cannot be denied that the liberty of communication granted to the prisoners, changes the very nature of the

American system, or to speak more correcely, it produces a new system without any resemblance to the latter.

As for us, as much as we believe that the system founded on isolation and silence is favorable to the reformation of criminals, we are equally inclined to believe that the reformation of convicts who communicate with each other is impossible.

It seems to us, therefore, that, speaking in the abstract, the penitentiary system of the United States (the superiority of which over every other prison discipline appears incontestable) presents itself to France with all the chances of success which a theory can offer, the first experiment of which has already succeeded. In stating this opinion, we are not blind to the difficulties which this system would have to overcome in being established with us. These difficulties are in the nature of things ; in our customs, and in our laws.

The first of all is the existence of another order of things, founded upon a different basis, and upon principles diametrically opposed. The American system has for its foundation the separation of the prisoners, and for this reason we find in each penitentiary as many cells as convicts. In France, on the contrary, the system of cells established in a general way is unknown, and in all our prisons, the greater part of the convicts are huddled together during night in common dormitories. This circumstance alone is sufficient to render, for the present, a system which rests entirely upon the isolation of the prisoners, impracticable with us. Should, therefore, this system be adopted, new prisons, constructed upon the model of the modern penitentiaries, must be raised. Here a grave difficulty presents itself in the first expenses of their construction.

We are far from believing that the expense of this would be as considerable as is generally presumed. Those who see in Paris a model prison, destined for four hundred prisoners, and costing Fr. 4,000,000,[2] conclude with apparent reason, that it would require Fr. 320,000,000 to lodge, upon the same plan, thirty-two thousand criminals ; i. e. Fr. 10,000 for each. But we must remember, that this enormous expense has been occasioned by the deplorable extravagance with which the construction of that prison was attended.

The elegance, the regularity of its proportions, and all the ornaments with which it is embellished, are of no use whatever for the discipline of the establishment. They exhausted the public treasure, and are of service to the architect alone, who strove to erect a monument, to hand down his name to posterity.

We must remark again that a distinction ought to be made between the expenses of construction upon the Philadelphia and the Auburn system. We have acknowledged, that there are great advantages resulting from the plan of absolute confinement adopted in Pennsylvania, and if the question were only on a theoretical point, perhaps we should prefer it to the Auburn system, but the expense of penitentiaries built upon the Philadelphia plan is so considerable, that it would seem to us imprudent to propose the adoption of this plan for our country. Too heavy a burden would be thrown on society, for which the most happy results of the system could hardly offer an equivalent. Yet the Auburn system, whose merit in theory is not less incontestable, is, as we have shown above, much cheaper in its execution. It is therefore this system which we should wish to see applied to our prisons, if the question were only to choose between the two.

But the Auburn system itself could not at once be established in France without great expense, which certainly would be incomparably less than that incurred for the prison which we just mentioned. We believe even that the construction, if judiciously directed, of a modern penitentiary, would in the whole cost no more here than in the United States.[3] Yet, however great the economy might be, which would preside over such an undertaking, it is certain that more than Fr. 30,000,000 would be necessary for the general establishment of this system. It will easily be believed that France would not burden her budget with a similar item in the midst of political circumstances which require from her still more urgent sacrifices.

Is it not also to be feared that the grave interests which absorb the treasures of France, are injurious in another way to the reform of prisons? Do not political events preoccupy the minds of men to such an extent, that questions, even the most important, or internal reforms, excite public attention but feebly? Talent and capacity are directed towards one single object — politics. Every other interest meets with indifference, and the results of this is, that the most talented men, distinguished writers, experienced members of the administration — in one word, all those who exercise influence on public opinion, spend their energy in discussions useful to the government, but not conducive to the welfare of society. Shall we not fear the consequence of this disposition in respect to the penitentiary system? Will not this institution, which requires for its execution public attention and favor, be received with coolness?

But even if the pecuniary and political objections, just indicated, did not exist, and nothing in the actual state of things were opposed to internal reforms, the introduction of the penitentiary system into France would nevertheless meet with grave difficulties.

The American discipline is, as we have seen, principally supported by corporal punishment. But is it not to be feared that a system, of which these punishments are the most powerful auxiliary, will be ill received by public opinion? If it is true, that with us an idea of infamy is attached to this punishment, how could it be inflicted on persons whose morals it is our intention to improve? This difficulty is a real one, and it appears still more serious, if we consider the nature of the discipline itself, which is to be maintained. Silence is the basis of the system: would this obligation of absolute silence, which has nothing incompatible with American gravity, be so easily reconciled with the French character? If we believe Mr. Elam Lynds, the French are, of all nations, those who submit the easiest to all the exigencies of the penitentiary system. Yet the question seems to us yet undecided, and we do not know to what point Mr. Elam Lynds has had an opportunity of judging of the docility of French convicts in general, by observations made in American prisons, where he has seen but a small number of French dispersed among a multitude of Americans.[4]

As for ourselves, without pretending to solve this problem, we believe that the law of silence would be infinitely more painful to Frenchmen than to Americans, whose character is taciturn and reflective. For this reason, it seems to us that it would be still more difficult with us than in America, to maintain the penitentiary discipline whose foundation is silence, without recurring to corporal punishment. We are the more induced to believe so, as the discipline of American penitentiaries is favored by another circumstance, on which we cannot calculate. There is a spirit of obedience to the law, so generally diffused in the United States, that we meet with this characteristic trait even in the prisons. Without being obliged to indicate here the political reasons of this fact, we only state it as such: but this spirit of submission to the established order does not exist in the same degree with us. On the contrary, there is in France, in the spirit of the mass, an unhappy tendency to violate the law, and this inclination to insubordination seems to us also to be of a nature to embarrass the regular operation of the discipline.

The penitentiary system, to which it would be difficult to give, in France, the physical support of stripes (that would seem in this country more necessary than in others) would perhaps be deprived also of a moral auxiliary, which contributes in the United States much to its success.

In America, the progress of the reform of prisons has been of a character essentially religious. Men, prompted by religious feelings, have conceived and accomplished everything which has been undertaken. They were not left alone, but their zeal gave the impulse to all, and thus excited in all minds the ardor which animated theirs. So also is religion to this day in all the new prisons, one of the fundamental elements of discipline and reformation. It is its influence alone which produces complete regeneration, and even with regard to reformations less thorough, we have seen that it contributes much to obtain them.

It is to be feared that in France the penitentiary system would not find this religious assistance. Would not the clergy receive with lukewarm feelings this new institution, on which philanthropy seems to have seized? And on the other hand, if the French clergy should show themselves zealous for the moral reformation of the criminals, would public opinion be satisfied to see them charged with this duty?

With us there exist, in a great number of persons, prejudices against religion and her ministers, which are unknown in the United States, and our clergy in turn are subject to impressions unfelt by the religious sects of America.

In France, where, during a long period, the altar has struggled in concert with the throne to defend royal power, the people are not yet accustomed to separate religion from authority, and the feelings directed against the latter usually extend to the former.

It thus happens, that in general public opinion shows itself little favorable towards anything protected by religious zeal; and the clergy, on their part, show little sympathy for anything which presents itself under the auspices of public favor.

In America, on the contrary, church and state have always been separated, and political passions erect themselves against the government and never against religion. For this reason, religion there always remains out of the struggle, and there exists an absence of all hostility between the people and the ministers of every sect.

We must add an observation on this point: it is, that in the United States, should the support of the clergy fail, the reform of prisons would not thereby be deprived of the assistance rendered by religion.

In fact, society in the United States is itself eminently religious — a circumstance which has a great influence upon the direction of penitentiaries. A multitude of charitable persons, who are not ministers by profession, sacrifice nevertheless a great part of their time to the moral reformation of criminals. As their religious belief is deeply rooted in their customs, there is not one among all the officers of a prison who is destitute of religious principles. For this reason, they never utter a word which is not in harmony with the sermons of the chaplain. The prisoner in the United States, therefore, breathes in the penitentiary a religious atmosphere, and is more accessible to this influence because his primary education has disposed him for it.

Generally speaking, our convicts have not such favorable dispositions, and without the walls of the prison, religious ardor is met with in the ministers of religion only.

If they are kept from the penitentiary, the influence of religion will disappear: philanthropy alone would remain for the reformation of criminals. It cannot be denied that there

are with us generous individuals, who, endowed with profound sensibility, are zealous to alleviate any misery, and to
heal the wounds of humanity: so far, their attention, exclusively occupied with the physical situation of the prisoners,
has neglected a much more precious interest, that of their
moral reformation. It is clear, however, that called to this
field, their charity would not be tardily dispensed, and their
efforts would undoubtedly be crowned with some success.
But these sincere philanthropists are rare. In most cases
philanthropy is with us but an affair of the imagination. The
life of Howard is read, his philanthropic virtues are admired,
and it is confessed that it is noble to love mankind as he did;
but this passion, which originates in the head, never reaches
the heart, and often evaporates in the productions of the pen.

There are, then, in our customs and morals, and in the
actual disposition of the people, moral difficulties, with which
the penitentiary system would have to struggle, if ever it
could be established such as it exists in the United States.
These obstacles certainly would not always exist. A lasting
public prejudice against religion and her ministers, is not
the natural state of things. And we do not know what point
a society may reach, without the assistance of religious
belief. But here we must not go beyond the actual state of
things, and among the difficulties actually existing, which
would injure the penitentiary system in France, that which
we have just pointed out would without contradiction be
one of the gravest.

Our legislation also presents difficulties. The first results
from the very nature of some of our penal laws.

At the time when the brand was prescribed by our code,
the penitentiary system could not have been established; because it would have been contradictory to pursue the moral
reformation of criminals who had been disgraced already
with indelible infamy. This punishment has disappeared
from our laws, and its abolition, which reason and humanity
imperiously claimed, is one impediment the less to the efficacy of a good prison discipline. But there are yet some
provisions in our penal code, which are not less irreconcilable
to a complete system of reform. We mean the infamy attached to most punishments, and their great diversity.

There are in our laws eight punishments which are expressly called infamous; without courting public exposure, which is considered only as accessory to certain punishments, and that of the ball, which only figures in the law as a mode of enforcing labor.

If you attach infamy to a perpetual punishment, we see little inconvenience in it, provided the principle of perpetuity is once admitted. But is it not an inconsistency, to declare by judgment a person infamous, who may at some future period reappear in society. To be logical, the law should also declare, that at the expiration of the punishment the prisoner should receive back his honor and his liberty. It does not do so, because the infamy so easily imprinted on the forehead of the guilty, cannot be effaced with the same facility. However this may be, the perpetual dishonor attached to a temporary punishment, seems to us little compatible with the object of the penitentiary system, and we do not know how it would be possible to awaken sentiments of honor and virtue in those whom the law itself has taken care to disgrace and to debase. In order to make, in this respect, our penal legislation agree with the essential principles of the penitentiary system, few changes would be required. It would be sufficient not to call any longer the punishments pronounced by the code infamous, and in all cases to spare the convict the transitory shame of the pillory and the lasting humiliation of hard labor in public.

It would be necessary, lastly, to abolish, if not the diversity of punishments, at least the difference which exist in the manner of suffering them.

The variety of punishments and of imprisonment, prescribed by each of them, have rendered necessary a great number of different prisons. As there are criminals of various degrees and as they are thrown together in our prisons, it has been justly believed that it would be immoral to confound all, and to place under the same roof, in the same workshop, and in the same bed, the man who has been sentenced to twenty years of forced labor, and him who has to undergo but one year's imprisonment. There is, therefore, a separate prison for the galley slaves, another for *réclusionnaires*, (simply), and if the law were strictly executed, there would be a third class of prisons, for persons sentenced for police offenses to more than a year's imprisonment, and a fourth class, for those whose confinement would be for less than a year. These classifications, the reason of which we understand, if in principle the assemblage of the prisoners is admitted, become evidently useless, if the system of separation during night and silence during day is introduced. This system once established, the least guilty of all the convicts may be placed by the side of the most consummate criminal without fearing any contamination.

It is even well to unite the criminals of various kinds in establishments of the same nature. All are subject to a uniform system; punishment varies only in its duration. We thus lose the exceptionable system of the bagnes, and see the government of the French prisons freed from this strange anomaly which places the third of all convicts under the direction of the minister of the marine.

It would then be necessary, in order to put our legislation in harmony with the penitentiary system, to abolish those provisions in the penal code which prescribe distinct prisons, subject to a special system for each species of convicts.[5]

The second obstacle in our laws, is the too great extent to which the principle of centralization has been carried, forming the basis of our political society. There are, no doubt, general interests, for the conservation of which the central power ought to retain all its strength and unity of action.

Every time that a question arises concerning the defense of the country, its dignity abroad, and its tranquility within, government ought to give a uniform impulse to all parts of the social body. This is a right which could not be dispensed with, without compromising public safety and national independence.

But however necessary this central direction respecting all subjects of general interest may be to the strength of a country like ours, it is as contrary, it seems to us, to the development of internal prosperity, if this same centralization is applied to objects of local interst.

It has appeared to us, that the success of the new prisons in the United States, is principally owing to the system of local administration under the influence of which they have originated.

In general, the first expenses of construction are made with economy; because those who execute the plan, pay also the expenses. Little mismanagement is to be feared from the inferior agents, because those who make them work are near to them; and even after the system which they have thus introduced is put into practice, they do not cease to watch its operation. They are occupied with it as with their own work, and one, in the success of which, their honor is interested.

As soon as a state has founded a useful establishment, all others, animated by a happy spirit of emulation, show themselves zealous to imitate it.

Would our laws, and our customs, which leave everything to the central power, offer to the penitentiary system the same facilities for its foundation and support among us? We do not believe it.

If the question were, of enacting a law, this centralization would be far from throwing difficulties in the way. In fact, it would be much easier for our government to obtain from the chambers, the adoption of the penitentiary system for all France, than it has been in America, for the governors of the various states, to get this same principle sanctioned by the various legislatures, without whom it could not be acted upon.

But after this principle has been adopted by law, it yet remains to be executed. It is here, where with us the difficulties begin.

It is to be feared that the building which the government would cause to be erected for this purpose, would not be on a very economical plan; and that the expenses of construction, superintended by secondary agents, would much exceed the original estimates. If the first experiments prove too expensive, they will discourage public opinion, and the most zealous partisans of the penitentiary system. Supposing these first difficulties conquered, is not the indifference of the different communities towards the success of an establishment which is not their own work, to be feared? and yet this system cannot prosper without the especial zeal of the officers of the prison. Finally, how could the central power, the action of which is uniform, give all those modifications to the penitentiary system, which are necessary on account of local customs and wants?

It seems to us difficult to expect the penitentiary system to succeed in France, if its foundation and erection are to be the work of government, and if it should be thought sufficient to substitute for the central prisons (*maisons centrales de détention*) others built merely on a better plan.

Would not the chances of success be far greater, if the care of constructing, at their own expense, and of directing (according to certain general principles expressed in a law common to all) the prisons of all kinds, (those destined for great criminals not excepted) were conferred upon the departments themselves?

The laws of 1791 laid down the principle, that the superintendence of the prisons belongs essentially to the municipal authority, and their direction to the administrative authority of the department. These same laws prescribe, as to the administration of the prisons, a great number of important innovations, and contain even the germ of the penitentiary system since adopted in the United States.[6]

But the principles thus proclaimed, were but imperfectly executed. As soon as Bonaparte had been invested with consular dignity, he decreed the establishment of "central houses of detention," without taking the pains to cause the abolishment by the constitutional powers, of the laws contrary to this decree. This institution was destructive to all local direction and superintendence. In fact, most of the central prisons now existing, are nothing but ancient convents dispersed through France, some near towns, others in the midst of fields.

Bonaparte, however, declared in 1810, that each department should have, besides the "houses of justice and arrest," a prison destined to contain prisoners convicted for police offenses.

If, then, the system of one general prison for each department should be adopted, we would return to the principle of the laws of 1791; and we should extend to all criminals the local imprisonment, which Bonaparte himself intended to establish for those convicted of police offenses. This extension would be without inconvenience in regard to prison discipline, since we always reason on the supposition of a change in the penitentiary system, founded on silence and isolation of the prisoners.

Government depriving itself of the privilege of directing the central prisons, would abandon a prerogative which is but onerous to itself, without being beneficial to the departments. It would retain a right of impulse, control, and superintendence, but instead of acting itself, it would make others act.

We here only throw out hints of a system, which, to be adopted, ought to be matured; we have the certainty of that which exists being bad; but the remedy seems to us not so certain as the existence of the evil.

Our prisons created and entirely governed by a central power, are expensive and inefficient for the reformation of the prisoners: we have seen in America, cheap prisons, in which all contamination is avoided, springing up in small states under the influence of local authorities: it is under the impression of this contrast that we write.

We are well aware that the situation of the various American states and that of our departments, is not the same. Our departments possess no political individuality; their circumscription has been to this day of a purely administrative character. Accustomed to the yoke of centralization, they have no local life. And we must agree, that it is not the duty of governing a prison which would give them the taste and habits of individual administration; but it is to be hoped that "political life" will enter more into the habits of the departments, and that the cares of government will have, more and more, a tendency to become local.

If our hopes in this respect should be realized, the system which we indicate would become practicable, and the penitentiary system in France would find itself surrounded by a great many favorable circumstances, which, in the United States, have effected its success.

Each department having its central prison, would only contribute to the support of its own convicts; while at present the rich and well populated department, whose inhabitants commit few crimes, pays more for the support of central prisons, than the poor department, whose population, less numerous, furnishes more criminals.

If each department should construct its own prison, it
would vote with less repugnance the funds which it would
itself dispose of. The construction, which would be its own
work, would, undoubtedly, be less elegant and less regular
than if it had been directed by the central power, assisted by
its architects. But the beauty of the fabric adds little to the
merit of the establishment. The great advantage of a local
construction would be to excite the lively interest of its
founders. The French government, acknowledging how necessary local direction and superintendence are for the prosperity of the prisons, has tried at various times to interest
the departments in the administration of their prisons, but
its attempts have always been without success.[7] Whatever
government may do, the various bodies will never take an
interest in that which they have not made themselves.

Would not this constant watchfulness, this continual and
mute care, this constant solicitude and zeal, indispensably
necessary to the success of a penitentiary prison, be extended
to an establishment created by the department, the witness of
its birth, its development, and its progress?

Among the difficulties which would be opposed to the execution of this system, there are some which are perhaps not
so serious as some think, and which we believe it our duty to
indicate. It is feared, with reason, that by increasing the
number of central prisons, the expense of their construction
would proportionally increase. In fact, eighty prisons destined to contain thirty-two thousand prisoners, would cost
more than the erection of twenty prisons fitted to contain
the same number of individuals. But if the advantage of
economy is inherent in vast constructions, on the other hand,
that of a better discipline is inherent in establishments less
considerable.

It is certain that a prison, in order to be well governed,
ought not to contain too great a number of criminals. The
personal safety of the officers and the order of the establishment are in continual danger in prisons, where two or three
thousand malefactors are assembled (as is the case in the
bagnes). It is the small number of the prisoners in Wethersfield which forms one of the greatest advantages of that
penitentiary; there the superintendent and the chaplain are
thoroughly acquainted with the moral state of each indi-

vidual, and after having studied his evil, they endeavor to cure it. At Sing Sing, where there are one thousand prisoners, a similar care is out of the question, and it is not even attempted. Supposing that the 32,000 prisoners of France were distributed in eighty-six departmental prisons, there would be on an average 400 in each of them. There are some departments, indeed, whose large and corrupted population furnishes many criminals, while others, whose inhabitants are less numerous and more honest, send few criminals to the prisons. But what would result from this fact? That those departments in which most crimes would be committed would be forced to build larger prisons, while the others would erect smaller penitentiaries. Our departments would be in this respect precisely in the same position with the different states of the American Union.

The state of New York, which contains 2,000,000 of inhabitants, has two central prisons; of which one alone contains 1,000 prisoners. Connecticut, with but 260,000 inhabitants, possesses a single prison containing but 200 criminals. Few departments would have a prison so numerously filled as that of Sing Sing, the principal defect of which consists in the great number of its inmates. Many departments, whose population is similar to that of Connecticut, would not have more criminals in their prisons than we find at Wethersfield, and we have a right to believe that this limitation of number would be an advantage, since Wethersfield, the smallest penitentiary in America, is also the best. And would not the example of this penitentiary, which, though less extensive, cost less in its construction than all the others, prove that we are enabled to compensate, by a spirit of economy and by local superintendence, for the greater expense occasioned by the construction on a small scale?

It is perceived with what reserve we have communicated these ideas. In order to proceed safely and steadily on a similar path, it would be necessary to possess information which we have not, and to be supported by documents which are not at our disposal. Deprived as we are of this guidance, we do not present a system. We have only started a question, the solution of which is of vital interest to society, and to which we call the attention of all enlightened men.

Supposing the penitentiary system established and prospering in France, we cannot perhaps expect from it all the happy effects which it has produced in the United States.

Thus we doubt whether the labor of the prisoners would be as productive as it is in America, even allowing that the saving (*pécule*) of the convicts should be entirely suppressed. Indeed it is incontestable, that manufactured articles do not find with us the same market which is offered in the United States, and in order to estimate the revenue of a prison, it would be necessary to take into account articles which would remain unsold.

The penitentiary, which on this account would be less productive with us, would for a similar reason also be less efficient in respect to the reformation of the convicts. In America, where wages are extremely high, the convicts easily find labor when they leave the prison, and this circumstance favors their good conduct, when they have re-entered society.[8] In France, the situation of delivered convicts is infinitely less favorable, and even if they are resolved to lead an honest life, they are not infrequently brought back to crime by a fatal necessity. In the United States, the delivered convict generally leaves the state where his conviction is known; he changes his name and takes up his residence in another state, where he may begin a new life: with us, the convict, whose punishment has expired, meets everywhere with obstacles and embarrassments. The surveillance of the police, to which he is subject, obliges him to a fixed residence, which he cannot change, without committing a new offense against the laws. He is condemned to live in the place where his first crime is officially known, and everything conspires to deprive him of the means necessary to his existence. The defect of a similar state of things is felt by all the world, and we doubt whether it will be long continued.

The surveillance of the "high police," such as it is practised at present, is less useful to society than fatal to the delivered criminal. It would be of some advantage, if, by its influence, society, informed of the real situation of each released criminal, had some means of procuring labor for those who have none, and assistance for those who stand in need of it. Might not government find this means in the foundation of agricultural colonies, similar to those which at present are so flourishing in Belgium and Holland? If such colonies were established in France on the yet uncultivated districts of our soil, no idler could complain of not finding labor; the beggars, vagrants, paupers, and all the delivered convicts, whose number, continually increasing, threatens incessantly the safety of individuals and even the tranquility of the state, would find a place in the colony, where they would contribute by their labor to increase the wealth of the country.

Perhaps persons convicted for a short time, might also be sent there. There would be an incontestable advantage in introducing the greatest possible number of prisoners. One of the principal advantages of agricultural colonies, indeed, consists in not injuring the industry of citizens: they thus obviate one of the greatest dangers presented by the establishment of manufactories in prisons. The system of agricultural colonies deserves, therefore, a serious attention on the part of politicians. It seems that after having admitted its principle, it ought to be extended as much as possible, and that it would be easy to reconcile its application with the principles of the penitentiary system. Lastly, the establishment of agricultural colonies would have, among other advantages, that of deriving happy effects from that administrative superintendence, of which almost all the consequences are otherwise fatal, and it would thus cause one of the difficulties, obstructing the introduction of the penitentiary system, to disappear.

We have pointed out the difficulties which the penitentiary system would meet with in France, and have not disguised their importance. We do not deny that we see very great obstacles to the introduction of this system, such as it is in the United States, and surrounded by all the circumstances which accompany it in that country. We are, nevertheless, far from believing that nothing can be done towards the amelioration of our prisons.

We never have entertained the idea that France could attempt a sudden and general revolution in its prison system; to raze the old establishments, to erect new ones, and to sacrifice, for this single object, in one moment, enormous sums, which are urgently claimed by interests of another nature. But we can reasonably demand progressive reforms in the system of our prisons; and, if it is true, that it would be impossible to found in France a discipline supported by the assistance of the whip; if it is true, that with us the assistance of local influence is wanting to the success of the establishment, and the support of religion to the progress of moral reformation; it is also certain, that, though not adopting the American prison discipline without modification, we might borrow from it a number of its principles and its advantages. Thus every new prison which would be built according to the system of cells, would have an incontestable superiority over the present prisons. The separation of the prisoners during night, would put a stop to the most dangerous communications, and destroy one of the most active agents of corruption. We cannot imagine what objection, possibly, could be made against the system of cells, if, as we believe it to be the case, the prisons built according to this system, would not cost more than the others. We have said that it seems to us difficult to maintain absolute silence among the convicts without the assistance of corporal punishment. However, this is only an opinion, and the example of Wethersfield, where the prisoners have been governed without beating for several years, tends to prove that this severe means of discipline is not absolutely necessary. It seems to us, that the chance of success would make the trial on the part of government well worth the attempt—a trial which seems to us the more reasonable, as we would be sure at least of approaching our end, in case we should not succeed entirely: thus even if public opinion should show itself decidedly hostile to corporal punishments, we would be obliged, in order to establish the law of silence, to resort to disciplinary chastisements of another nature, such as absolute solitude without labor, and a reduction of food. There is good ground to believe, that with the assistance of these latter punishments, less rigorous than the first, but nevertheless efficient, silence would be sufficiently maintained to avoid the evil of moral intercourse between the prisoners. The most important point would be, first to declare the principle of isolation and silence as a rule of discipline of the new prisons. The application of the principle would meet, perhaps with us, with

more obstacles, because it would not be aided by such energetic auxiliaries, but we have no doubt, that regarding the
great general end, much good would already thus be effected.
Radical reformations, perhaps, would not be obtained by this
imperfect system, but great corruptions would be prevented,
and we would thus derive from the American system, those
advantages which are the most incontestable.

We believe that government would do something useful in
establishing a model penitentiary, constructed upon the
American plan, and governed as much as possible according
to the disciplinary rules which are in force in the penitentiaries of the United States. It would be necessary that this
construction, planned according to all the simplicity of the
models we have brought with us, should be executed without any architectural elegance. Care should be taken to place
in the penitentiary new convicts only; because if the nucleus
of an old prison should suddenly be introduced into the new
penitentiary, it would be difficult to submit to the severities
of the new discipline, individuals accustomed to the indulgent
system of our "central houses."

To recapitulate, we have signalized in the two first parts
of this report, the advantages of the penitentiary system in
the United States. The inflexible severity of a uniform system, the equality of punishments, the religious instruction
and the labor substituted for the system of violence and
idleness; the liberty of communication supplanted by isolation or silence; the reformation of the criminals instead of
their corruption; in the place of jailors, honorable men who
direct the penitentiaries; in the expenditure, economy, instead of disorder and bad management: these are the characteristics which we have acknowledged in the new American
system.

The necessity of a reform in the prison discipline in France
is urgent, and acknowledged by everyone: the number of
recommitted criminals regularly increasing, is a fact which
strikes every thinking mind. The delivered convicts, who are
but criminals still more corrupted for their having been confined in the prison, become, wherever they show themselves,
just objects of fear. Incapable, as society thus is, to correct
the guilty, will it resort to transportation? Let France look

at England; let her judge whether it would be wise to imitate her in this respect.

The defect is in our prisons, infected with a frightful corruption; but cannot this cancer, which every year increases, be healed? And do we not see prisons efficient for the reformation of the wicked, in a country whose prisons, but fifteen years ago, were worse than ours are now?

Let us not declare an evil incurable, which others have found means to eradicate; let us not condemn the system of prisons; let us labor to reform them.

To arrive at this end, the united efforts of many are necessary. And first, it is requisite that all writers, whose talent influences public opinion, should strive to give it a new direction, and to succeed so far, that the moral part of the discipline should be no more neglected than the amelioration of the administration of the physical part. It is necessary that the interests of reform should seize every mind, and become the conviction of all. A controversy even, would be desirable between the organs of public opinion, in order to find out which are the disciplinary punishments that might be admitted without wounding public feeling, and which are incompatible with our civilization and our customs.

Lastly, it would be necessary that the government should put our legislation in harmony with the principles of the penitentiary system, and above all, that it invite the deliberation of the most enlightened men on these grave matters.

The future success of the penitentiary system, depends much upon the first step we take. It is important, therefore, that all possible precaution be taken to secure success to the first establishment which may be erected in France. It is particularly necessary for the success of this establishment, that public attention should be turned towards it, should receive it favorably, and instead of throwing obstacles in its way, surround it with that moral assistance, without which no institution can prosper in a free country.

CHAPTER SEVEN

HOUSES OF REFUGE

IN AMERICA

GOVERNOR CLINTON, whose name is forever celebrated in the state of New York, said: "The houses of refuge are the best penitentiary establishments which have been conceived of by the genius of man, and instituted by his benevolence." With an examination of them we will finish our work, as we announced in the beginning.

The first house of refuge was established in the city of New York, in the year 1825; Boston followed in 1826, and Philadelphia in 1828; and there is good reason to believe that Baltimore will soon have a similar one. This offers an opportunity of judging of the power of association in the United States.

Touched by the shocking fate of young delinquents, who were indiscriminately confounded in the prisons with inveterate criminals, some individuals of New York sought a remedy for the evil. They united their efforts; labored, first to enlighten public opinion, and then, setting themselves the example of generosity, soon found sufficient funds, by voluntary subscriptions, for the establishment of a house of refuge.

The houses of refuge, thus called into existence by the combination of individual charity, are, as is seen in their origin, private institutions; yet they have received the sanction of public authority. All the individuals whom they contain are legally in custody. But in approving of the houses of refuge, government does not interfere in their management and superintendence. It leaves all the care to the private individuals who founded them. Every year the state grants some pecuniary assistance to these establishments, and yet it never takes the least part in their administration.

The supreme authority over the houses of refuge, resides in the entire body of the subscribers, who have contributed to their erection, or who continue their contributions for their support. The subscribers elect the directors (managers) on whom they confer the power of ruling the establishment in the manner which they judge the most advantageous. These managers appoint the officers, and make all the necessary regulations for the administration of the house. Some of them compose a permanent acting committee, charged with superintending the execution of the several resolutions. This composes the executive power of the institution. The officers of the house of refuge are the immediate agents of the acting committee, to whom they submit all their acts. They give no accounts to government, which does not demand any. Among the officers, the choice of the superintendent requires the chief care of the directors, because he is the soul of the whole administration.

Thus left to themselves, and subject to the control of public opinion alone, the houses of refuge prosper. The efforts, through the assistance of which they maintain themselves, are the more powerful as they are spontaneous and free. The expenses which they cause are incurred without trouble or regret, because they are voluntary, and because the lowest subscriber has his share in the administration, and consequently, his interest in the success of the establishment. Though the expenses of construction and support are not paid by the state, they are not the less a charge upon society; but they weigh upon those who can best sustain them on account of their fortunes, and who find a moral indemnity in the sacrifice which they have had the merit of imposing upon themselves.

The houses of refuge are composed of two distinct elements: there are received into them young people of both sexes under the age of twenty, condemned for crime, and also those who are sent there by way of precaution, not having incurred any condemnation or judgment.

Nobody contests the necessity of houses of refuge for young convicts. In all ages and in all countries, the disadvantage has been acknowledged which results from placing in the same room, and submitting to the same discipline, the young delinquents and the guilty offenders whom age has hardened in crime: the prisoner, yet of tender age, has often committed but a slight offense. How can we justly make him the associate in prison of another, who is doomed to expiate heavy crimes? This defect is so serious, that magistrates hesitate to pursue young delinquents, and the jury to condemn them. But there another danger presents itself. Encouraged by impunity, they give themselves up to new disorders, which a punishment proportionate to their offense would perhaps have prevented them from committing.

The house of refuge, the discipline of which is neither too severe for youth, nor too mild for the guilty, has therefore for its object both the withdrawal of the young delinquent from a too rigorous punishment and from the dangers of impunity.

The individuals, who are sent to the houses of refuge without having been convicted of some offense, are boys and girls who are in a position dangerous to society and to themselves: orphans, who have been led by misery to vagrancy; children, abandoned by their parents and who lead a disordered life; all those, in one word, who, by their own fault or that of their parents, have fallen into a state so bordering on crime, that they would become infallibly guilty were they to retain their liberty.[1]

It has, therefore, been thought that the houses of refuge should contain at once juvenile criminals and those on the point of becoming such. The latter are spared the disgrace of judgment, and all protected against the pollution of the prison. And that no disgrace should be attached to confinement in the house of refuge, a name has been given to this establishment, which reminds us of misfortune only. The house of refuge, though containing a certain number of convicted youths, is nevertheless no prison. He who is detained in it undergoes no punishment, and in general the decision by which the children are sent to the refuge, has neither the solemnity nor the forms of a judgment. And it is here that we will mention a fact which seems to us characteristic of this institution. The magistrates who send the children to the refuge, never determine what length of time the delinquent must remain there. They merely send them to the house, which from that moment acquires all the rights of a guardian. This right of guardianship expires when the lad arrives at his twentieth year, but even before he has attained this age, the managers of this establishment have the right to restore him to liberty if his interest require it.

The house of refuge is a medium between a school and a prison. The young delinquents are received much less for punishment than to receive that education which their parents or their ill fate refused them; the magistrates, therefore, cannot fix the duration of their residence in the house of refuge, because they cannot foresee how much time will be necessary to correct the children, and to reform their vicious dispositions.[2]

The office of judging whether a child is fit to leave the refuge, is left to the managers of the establishment, who see every day the children confided to their superintendence, judge of their progress, and designate those to whom liberty may be restored without danger. But then even when a child leaves the house of refuge in consequence of good conduct, he does not cease to be under the supervision of the managers during minority; and if he does not realize the hopes which had been entertained, the latter have the right to call him back to the house of refuge, and may employ the most rigorous means in order to effect it.

Some objections have been made in Pennsylvania against the right granted to the houses of refuge to receive individuals who had neither committed a crime nor incurred a conviction. Such a power, it was said, is contrary to the Constitution of the United States: it was added, that the power of the managers to shorten or prolong, at their pleasure, the duration of detention, is arbitrary, and cannot be tolerated in a free society. It would have been difficult to refute theoretically these objections, but the public saw that the houses of refuge alleviated the fate of juvenile criminals, instead of aggravating it, and that the children brought into it without being convicted, were not the victims of persecution, but merely deprived of a fatal liberty.

Nobody raises at present his voice against the houses of refuge. Yet we see with how much reserve the functions of those must be exercised, who have the power of sending children there; if we consider that they have the right to withdraw a child from its parents in order to place it in the establishment, and that they must exercise this authority every time that the parents have to reproach themselves with the disorderly conduct of their child. The law has foreseen the possibility of abuse, and has endeavored to provide a remedy: the child has, according to the law, the right of protection by the ordinary judge against the decision of the functionary who sends it to the refuge. The parents have the same right, and it is not infrequently exercised.

For the rest, it is not persecution or tyranny which are to be dreaded in these establishments. However necessary it may be that a house of refuge should not present the severity and the discipline of a prison, it would be equally dangerous if it had the too indulgent and too intellectual discipline of a school. But if these establishments in America should deviate from their true end, it would be less from inclining too much to severity than leaning improperly to mildness.

The fundamental principles upon which the houses of refuge rest, are simple; in New York and Philadelphia, the children are separated during night in solitary cells; during the day they may communicate with each other. The separation during night seems to be indispensably necessary from a regard to good morals; it may be dispensed with during day; absolute isolation would be intolerable to children, and silence could not be maintained among them without punishments, the violence of which alone must make us repugnant to them. There would be, besides, the greatest disadvantages in depriving them of social relations, without which their intellectual progress would be checked.

In Boston they are separated neither night nor day. We have not remarked that in this house of refuge any disadvantage results from their sleeping together. But their danger is, in our opinion, not the less, and it is avoided in Boston only by a zeal and vigilance altogether extraordinary, which it would be a mistake to expect, in general, even from persons the most devoted to their duties.

The time of the children is divided between the instruction which they receive, and the various labors which they have to learn and to perform: they are taught that elementary knowledge which will be useful to them in the course of their lives, and a mechanical art, which, at some future period, may furnish them the means of subsistence. Their intellectual occupations give to the establishment the aspect of a primary school, and their manual labor in the workshop is the same with that in the prison. These two different traits are the characteristics of a house of refuge.

Their patrons do not limit themselves to a development of the minds of the children, and the skill of their hands. An effort is made above all to cultivate their hearts, and to inculcate the principles of religion and morals. Mr. Hart, superintendent of the house of refuge in New York, often told us, that he should consider any success attendant on his efforts altogether impossible without the aid of religion.

When a young delinquent arrives at the house of refuge, the superintendent acquaints him with the regulations of the establishment, and gives him, for the guidance of his conduct, two rules, remarkable for their simplicity: (1) never lie; (2) do the best you can. The superintendent inscribes his name in the great register of conduct. This register is destined to contain all the information relative to the children. It states, as accurately as possible, their previous life, their conduct during their stay in the house, and after they have left the establishment. The child is then placed in the class proper for its age, and its known morality. Mr. Hart, of New York, defines the first class as that composed of the children who never swear, never lie, never make use of obscene or indecorous expressions, and who are equally zealous in the school and in the workshop. According to Mr. Wells, of Boston, this same class is composed of those who make positive, regular, and constant efforts towards being good.

In Boston, the admission of a child into the house of refuge is accompanied by circumstances which have appeared to us worthy of being reported: the establishment forms a small society, upon the model of society at large. In order to be received in it, it is not only necessary to know its laws, and to submit to them freely, but also to be received as a member of the society by all those who compose it already. The reception takes place after the individual in question has gone through the fixed period of trial, if the candidate is not rejected by a majority of the votes of the little members composing this interesting society.

In every house of refuge the inmates are divided into good and bad classes. Their conduct makes the children pass from one into the other. The good classes enjoy privileges which the bad ones are denied, and the latter are subject to privations which the former have not to undergo.

Eight hours, at least, are assigned every day to labor in the workshops, where the children are occupied with useful arts, such as shoemaking, joiner's work, clothmaking, carpenter's work, etc. Four hours daily are spent in the school. After rising and before going to bed, prayers are offered. Three meals take half an hour each; in short, there are about fifteen hours of the day occupied with study, labor, etc., and nine hours with rest. Such is, with little difference, the order established in New York and Philadelphia. This order is the same every day, and only varies according to the change of the seasons, which has an influence upon the hour of rising and retiring. The house of refuge in Boston differs from the above mentioned; the intellectual part of education occupies here a more prominent place. Only five hours and a half are daily occupied by labor in the workshops; four hours are passed in the school, more than one hour is spent in religious instruction, and all the children have two hours and a quarter every day for recreation. These hours of recreation are not the least profitable ones to the children. Mr. Wells, the superintendent of the Boston house of refuge, takes part in their games, and while their bodies are developed by gymnastic exercises, their moral character forms itself under the influence of a superior man, who, we may say, becomes a child with them, and whose authority is never greater than at the moment when he does not make them feel it.

The children learn in the school, reading, writing, and

arithmetic; they also receive some instruction in history and
geography. The Lancasterian method of mutual instruction
has been adopted in all of them. The children in general show
great facility in learning. It has been often remarked in
America, that the houses of refuge are composed of a class
of children more intelligent than others; the nature of these
establishments itself explains this fact. In general, children
abandoned by their families, or who have escaped from their
homes, and for this reason have been early reduced to their
own resources, and constrained to find within themselves the
means of subsistence, are received here. It is therefore not
surprising that they should make rapid progress in their
learning. Most of them have, moreover, a restless, adven-
turous mind, anxious for knowledge. This disposition, which
first led them to ruin, becomes now, in the school, a powerful
cause of success. No useful books which they desire for their
information are withheld from them. In Philadelphia, there
are in the library of the establishment more than fifteen
hundred volumes, which are all for the use of the children.

The hours of labor are fixed invariably for all, and none
are absolved from them. Nevertheless, a task is given, after
the performance of which, the young inmate of the house of
refuge, who is more active than the others, may amuse
himself.

The superintendence of the children in the school and
workshops, does not cease in the hours of leisure. They play
freely with each other, but gambling of whatever kind is
strictly prohibited.

All things in their discipline are favorable to health. Every
day they are obliged to wash their feet and hands. They are
always dressed cleanly; and their food, though coarse, is
abundant and healthy. None are allowed to eat anything but
what is prescribed by the ordinary discipline; water is the
only beverage. There is no shop in which the children may
obtain food or drink, and great pains are taken that they
do not procure it by communications with persons out of
the establishment.

Food, clothing, and bedding, are furnished by the administration. The labor of the children alone is let out by contract,
and the restrictions which abound in the contract are such,

that the contractor can have no kind of influence in the establishment.

In New York and Philadelphia, eight hours a day are given to the contractor; in Boston, five hours and a half only. The contractor, or his agents, come into the establishment to teach the various arts. For the rest, they are not allowed to have any conversation with the children, nor can they retain them a minute longer than the fixed time. It will be easily understood, that, with such conditions, it is not possible to stipulate advantageously in a pecuniary respect with the contractors, but the children are not made to work in order to yield profit. The only object in view is to give them habits of industry, and to teach them a useful trade.[3]

It is therefore not surprising that the support of the houses of refuge costs more than other penitentiary establishments. On the one hand, the young inmates are better fed and clothed than convicts, and a greater expense is incurred for their instruction. But, on the other, their labor does not yield as much as that of criminals who are sent for a long time into the prisons. So also, as we shall soon see, the young pupil of the house of refuge leaves the establishment as soon as he can be placed anywhere else with advantage. Liberty is restored to him when he knows a trade; that is to say, at the moment when his labor would become productive to the establishment.

The administration of the American houses of refuge is almost entirely *en régie;* that is, it manages its own supplies without contract. It is justly believed that the system of contract, applied to all the branches of administration, would be irreconcilable with the moral management which the nature of the establishment requires.

Though, on the whole, the subsistence of the young prisoners is expensive, everything seems to be calculated to avoid unnecessary expense. The houses of refuge contain both boys and girls, who, though under the same roof, are perfectly separated from each other. But this circumstance permits some labor to be done by the girls, which, if it were performed by others, would be a charge to the house. Thus they do the washing, mend the clothes, and make the greater part of their own dresses, and those worn by the boys. They also do all business in the kitchen for the whole house; thus they are employed in a way useful for themselves, and for the house, while it would be difficult to give them any other productive work.

This order of things is established and maintained by disciplinary means which we ought to examine. Two principal means are employed: punishments and rewards; but we must make a distinction upon this point, between the houses of refuge of New York and Philadelphia, and that of Boston.

In the two first establishments the punishments inflicted for disobeying the discipline are: 1] privation of recreation, 2] solitary confinement in a cell, 3] reduction of food to bread and water, 4] in important cases, corporal punishment — that is to say stripes.

In New York, the house is expressly authorized to apply stripes. In Philadelphia, the regulations do not permit them expressly, but merely do not prohibit them. The distribution of punishments belongs to the superintendent, who has a discretionary power in the establishment.

While the refractory children are subjected to these various punishments, according to the character of their offense, distinctions of honor are accorded to the children whose conduct is good. Besides the honor of belonging to the first class, those who distinguish themselves in this, wear badges of honor; lastly, the superintendent designates among the best, a certain number of monitors, to whom he confides part of the surveillance with which he is charged himself, and this testimony of confidence is for those whom he has chosen — a distinction to which they attach great value.

In Boston, corporal chastisements are excluded from the house of refuge; the discipline of this establishment is entirely of a moral character, and rests on principles which belong to the highest philosophy.

Everything there tends to elevate the soul of the young prisoners, and to render them jealous of their own esteem and that of their comrades. To arrive at this end, they are treated as if they were men and members of a free society.

We treat of this theory with reference to discipline, because it has appeared to us, that the high opinion instilled into the child, of his own morality and social condition, is not only fit to effect his reformation, but also, the best means to obtain from him entire submission.

First, it is a principle well established in the house, that nobody can be punished for a fault, not provided for, either by the divine law, or those of the country or the establishment. Thus the first principle in criminal matters, is also established in the house of refuge. The regulations contain the following principle: "As man is not capable of punishing disrespect or irreverence to God; therefore, if a boy be irregular in his behavior at religious services, he shall not be allowed to attend them — leaving the punishment with a higher power, and for a future day." In the house of refuge in Boston, the child, withdrawn from religious service, incurs, in the opinion of his comrades and of himself, the severest of all punishments.

In another place it is expressed, that the children shall not be required to denounce the offenses of their comrades, and in the article which follows, it is added, that nobody should be punished for a fault sincerely avowed. We know in France, public establishments, in which this denunciation is encouraged, and where it is practiced by the better subjects of the house.[4]

A book of conduct exists, likewise, in Boston, where everyone has his account of good and bad marks; but that which distinguishes this register from those of other houses of refuge is, that in Boston, each child gives his own mark. Every evening the young inmates are successively asked; everyone is called upon to judge his own conduct during the day, and it is upon his declaration that the mark, indicating his conduct, is inscribed. Experience has shown that the children always judge themselves more severely than they would have been judged by others, and not unfrequently it is found necessary, to correct the severity and even the injustice of their own sentence.

If any difficulty arises in the classification of morality, or whenever an offense against the discipline has been committed, a judgment takes place. Twelve little jurymen, taken from among the children of the establishment, pronounce the condemnation or the acquittal of the accused.

Each time that it becomes necessary to elect among them an officer or monitor, the little community meets, proceeds to the election, and the candidate having most votes is proclaimed president. Nothing is more grave than the manner in which these electors and jurymen of tender years discharge their functions.

The reader will pardon us for having dwelt so long on this system, and for having pointed out its minutest details. We need not say that we do not consider this an infant republic in good earnest. But we believed ourselves obliged to analyze a system so remarkable for its originality. There is, however, more depth in these political plays, which agree so well with the institutions of the country, than we would suppose at first glance. The impressions of childhood and the early use of liberty, contribute, perhaps, at a later period, to make the young delinquents more obedient to the laws. And without considering this possible political result, it is certain, that such a system is powerful as a means of moral education.

In fact, it is easy to conceive the elasticity of which the youthful mind is capable, when all the sentiments proper to elevate it above itself are called into action.

The discipline is, however, fitted still more for those cases where the moral means which we have just indicated, prove insufficient.

Children, whose conduct is correct, enjoy great privileges.

They alone participate in the elections, and are alone eligible; the vote of those who belong to the first class, counts for two — a kind of double vote, of which the others cannot be jealous, because it depends upon themselves alone to obtain the same privilege. With the good are deposited the most important keys of the house; they go out freely, and have the right to leave their place, when the children are assembled, without needing a peculiar permission; they are believed on their word, on all occasions; and their birthday is celebrated. All the good do not enjoy these privileges, but whoever belongs to a good class, has a right to some of these prerogatives. The punishments, to which the bad children are subject, are the following:

Privation of the electoral right, and the right of being elected; they are not allowed to come into the room of the superintendent, nor to speak to him without permission, nor are they allowed to converse with their comrades; lastly, if it should be required, a physical punishment is applied. Some-

times "bracelets" are put on ; sometimes, the offender is blind-
folded ; or he is shut up in a solitary cell. Such is the system
of the house of refuge in Boston.

That of the establishments of New York and Philadelphia,
though infinitely less remarkable, is perhaps better. Not that
the Boston house of refuge does not appear to be admirably
conducted, and superior to both the others, but its success
seems to us less the effect of the system itself, than that of the
distinguished man who puts it into practice.

We have already said that the great defect of this house
of refuge is, that the children sleep together. The system,
moreover, which is established there, rests upon an elevated
theory, which could not be always perfectly understood ; and
its being put into practice would cause great difficulties, if
the superintendent should not find immense resources in his
own mind to triumph over them.

In New York and Philadelphia, on the contrary, the theory
is simple. The isolation during night, the classification during day, the labor, the instruction — everything, in such an
order of things, is easily understood. It neither requires a
profound genius to invent such a system, nor a continual
effort to maintain it. To sum up the whole, the Boston discipline belongs to a species of ideas much more elevated than
that established in New York and Philadelphia, but it is difficult in practice.

The system of these last establishments, founded upon a
theory much more simple, has the merit of being within reach
of all the world. It is possible to find superintendents who are
fit for the Philadelphia system, but we cannot hope to meet
often with such men as Mr. Wells.

In spite of the well-marked difference between the two systems, of which one can be practiced only by superior men,
while the other is on the level of ordinary minds, we must
acknowledge that, both in the one and the other case, the success of the houses of refuge essentially depends upon the
superintendent. It is he who puts the principles upon which
the system acts into action, and he must, in order to arrive at
a happy result, unite in his person a great number of qualities, the union of which is as necessary as rare.

If a model of a superintendent of a house of refuge were
required, a better one, perhaps, it would be impossible to find,

than that which is presented by Mr. Wells, and Mr. Hart. A constant zeal, an indefatigable vigilance, are their lesser qualities; to minds of great capacity, they join an equanimity of character, the firmness of which does not exclude mildness. They believe in the religious principles which they teach, and have confidence in their own efforts. Endowed with deep sensibility, they obtain still more from the children, by touching their hearts, than by addressing their understandings. Finally, they consider each young delinquent as their child. It is not a profession which they perform; it is a duty they are happy to fulfill.

We have seen how the youth enters the house of refuge, and what discipline he is subjected to. Let us at present examine by what means he may obtain the restoration of liberty, and let us follow him into the society which he re-enters.

The principle above laid down, that the inmate of a house of refuge does not undergo a punishment, finds here, again, its application. As he has been sent to the house for his own interest only, he is allowed to leave it as soon as his interest requires it.

Therefore, as soon as he has learned a trade, if, during one or several years, he has acquired moral and industrious habits, he is believed to be capable of becoming a useful member of society. Yet absolute and complete liberty is not restored to him, because, what would become of him in the world, alone, without support, unknown by anybody? He would find himself precisely in the same situation in which he was, before he entered the house. This great danger is avoided: the superintendent waits for a good opportunity to bind him out as apprentice with some mechanic, or to place him as a servant in some respectable family. He avoids sending him into a city, where he would relapse into his bad habits, and find again the companions of his disorderly life, and every time an opportunity offers, employment for him, with farmers, is preferred. At the moment he leaves the establishment, a writing is given to him, which, in kind words, contains advice for his future conduct; the present of a Bible is added.

In general, it has been found inconvenient to restore liberty to these juvenile offenders, before they have been in the house at least one year, in order to acquire habits of order.

Leaving the house of refuge, he does not cease to belong to

the establishment, which, binding him out as an apprentice, reserves all the rights of a guardian over him. If he leave the master with whom he has been placed, he is, according to the law, brought back to the house of refuge, where he must again remain until he has given a new proof that shows him worthy of liberty. In time he may be successively brought back to the establishment, and restored to liberty, as often as the managers think it necessary; and their power, in this respect, does not cease, until the individual in question has arrived at the age of eighteen, if a female; and of twenty, if a boy.

During his apprenticeship, the child is the object of continued attention, by the house of refuge. The superintendent corresponds with him, and endeavors to keep him in the path of virtue by his advice; and the youth writes on his part to the superintendent, and more than once the latter has received letters from young delinquents, full of touching expressions of gratitude.

Now, what results have been obtained? Is the system of these establishments conducive to reform and are we able to support the theory by statistical numbers?

If we consider merely the system itself, it seems difficult not to allow its efficiency. If it be possible to obtain moral reformation for any human being, it seems that we ought to expect it for these youths, whose misfortune was caused less by crime, than by inexperience, and in whom all the generous passions of youth may be excited. With a criminal, whose corruption is inveterate, and deeply rooted, the feeling of honesty is not awakened, because the sentiment is extinct. With a youth, this feeling exists, though it has not yet been called into action. It seems to us, therefore, that a system which corrects evil dispositions, and inculcates correct principles, which gives a protector and a profession to him who has none, habits of order and labor to the vagrant and beggar whom idleness had corrupted, elementary instruction and religious principles to the child whose education had been neglected; it seems to us, we say, that a similar system must be fertile of beneficial effects.

There are, however, cases in which it is almost impossible to obtain the reformation of juvenile offenders; thus experience has taught the superintendents, that the reformation of girls, who have contracted bad morals, is a chimera which it is useless to pursue. As to boys, the most difficult to be corrected are those who have contracted habits of theft and intemperance. Their regeneration, however, is not so desperate a task as that of girls who have been seduced, or have become prostitutes.

It is also generally thought in the United States, that it is necessary to avoid receiving, in the house of refuge, boys above sixteen, and girls over fourteen years. After this age, their reformation is rarely obtained by the discipline of these establishments, which is less fit for them than the austere discipline of the prisons.

In Philadelphia, it is believed, that more than half of the children who have left the refuge, have conducted themselves well.

Being desirous of ascertaining ourselves the effects produced by the house of refuge in New York, we made a complete analysis of the great register of conduct, and examining separately the page of each child, who had left the refuge, investigated what was its conduct since its return into society.

Of four hundred and twenty-seven male juvenile offenders, sent back into society, eighty-five have conducted themselves well, and the conduct of forty-one has been excellent. Of thirty-four, the information received is bad, and, of twenty-four, very bad. Of thirty-seven among them, the information is doubtful; of twenty-four, rather good than otherwise, and of fourteen, rather bad than good.

Of eighty-six girls who have returned into society from the house of refuge, thirty-seven have conducted themselves well, eleven in an excellent manner, twenty-two bad, and sixteen very bad. The information concerning ten is doubtful; three seem to have conducted themselves rather well, and three rather bad than otherwise.

Thus of five hundred and thirteen children who have returned from the house of refuge of New York into society, more than two hundred have been saved from infallible ruin, and have changed a life of disorder and crime for one of honesty and order.

CHAPTER EIGHT

ESTABLISHMENT OF

HOUSES OF REFUGE

IN FRANCE

IF FRANCE should borrow from the American houses of refuge some principles on which these establishments are erected, she would remedy one of the chief vices of her prisons.

According to our laws, the criminals, under the age of sixteen, are not to be confounded with convicts of maturer years, and the law gives the name of house of correction to the place where they are detained. Yet, with very rare exceptions, the young delinquents and the old criminals are placed together in our prisons. Nay more: it is well known that the child not yet sixteen years old, who has been acquitted on account of want of judgment, is nevertheless, according to circumstances, rendered to its parents, or conducted into a house of correction, in order to be *elvé et détenu* (educated and detained) during such a number of years as the judgment of the court shall determine, and which never exceeds the period of his arrival at his twentieth year.

Thus, if a child, accused of a crime, is acquitted, the courts have the right to send it back to its parents, or into a "house of correction." This alternative makes it easy to comprehend the intention of the law. The parents receive it, if they show a guaranty of morality, and the child is restored to them, that they may correct its evil dispositions and reform its bad habits. On the contrary, if the judges have good reason to believe, that the faults of the child are owing to the fatal example of its own family, they will take care not to restore the child to it, where it would only accomplish its corruption. They, therefore, send it into a house of correction, which will be less a prison than a school; it will be "educated and detained," says the law. Now, we ask, is the intention of the legislature fulfilled? Do the young prisoners receive the education which it was the intention of the law to procure for the unfortunate child?

It can be said that, in general, the prisons, in which with us the juvenile offenders are detained, are but schools of crime; so that all the judges who know the corrupting discipline of these prisons, are averse to condemn an arrested youth, whatever may be the evidence of his offense. They rather acquit him and restore him to liberty than contribute on their part further to corrupt him, by sending him into one of the prisons. But this indulgence, the motive of which is so easily understood, is not the less fatal to the guilty, who find in this impunity an encouragement to crime.

There is also a right sanctioned by our civil laws, and the operation of which is in some sort suspended by the defect of our prisons: we mean the power which belongs to the parents of causing those of their children, who are minors and whose conduct is reprehensible, to be detained in a prison.

What parents would use their authority, if they knew into what a den of corruption their children would be thrown?

There is then in this respect a void in the system of our prisons which it is important to fill. This would be obtained by establishing houses of refuge or correction founded upon the principles of those of which we have given a picture.

It would certainly be difficult to adopt entirely the American system: thus, the power given in the United States to all officers of the police to send children, whose conduct is suspicious, into the house of refuge, though no specific offense be imputed to them; and the extraordinary right which they have even of taking a child from his parents if they do not take sufficient care of its education. Would not all this be contrary to our customs and laws?

But the discipline of the American houses of refuge would have great advantages in France if only applied to young convicts, or to those who, without being declared guilty, are to be detained during a fixed time in consequence of a positive judgment.

If our houses of correction, the viciousness of which frightens the courts, should undergo a reform, the magistrates would send there without repugnance a number of young delinquents, vagrants, beggars, etc., who abound in all our cities, and whom an idle life leads infallibly to crime. This reform might be effected by building, in the houses of correction, solitary cells, which would prevent communication during night, and by the adoption of a system of instruction and labor, analogous to that which is practiced in New York and Philadelphia.

It would be necessary, however, to make an important change in our legislation, in order to insure success to the houses of correction in France.

The greater part of the happy results crowning the endeavors of the American houses of refuge, are principally owing to the discretionary power with which the managers of these establishments are invested, to retain or return to society according to their pleasure, the children of whom they have received the guardianship. They use this right for the interest of the young delinquent, for whom they endeavor to find an advantageous place, as an apprentice. And each time that a favorable opportunity offers itself, they can avail themselves of it, because they have unlimited authority over the children sent to the refuge.

According to our laws, the director of a house of correction could do nothing like it. He would be obliged, in order to restore liberty to a young delinquent, to wait for the expiration of the period fixed by the judgment. What would be the consequence? That, on leaving the house of correction, the child would find itself as embarrassed respecting its fate as previously to its being sent to the refuge. It would be full of good resolutions and principles, but incapable of putting them into practice.

It seems to us that a single modification of article sixty-six of the penal code, would greatly remedy this inconvenience.

The young delinquents, under the age of sixteen years, are of two kinds: those who, having acted with discretion, are declared guilty and convicted, and those who, having acted without discretion, have been acquitted but are detained for the sake of their education. Respecting the first, their fate is positively settled by the judgment and ought to be so. They have committed a crime, they must suffer the punishment. One is but a corollary to the other. This punishment and its duration can be pronounced only by the courts. If it is fixed, it must be suffered to its whole extent, according to the terms of the judgment: in this case, the special interest of the child is of little importance; it is not only for the purpose of correction, that it is imprisoned: it is particularly for the interest of society and the sake of example that the punishment is inflicted.

But the child acquitted in consideration of its want of discretion, stands in a different position. It is detained in a house of correction, not in order to secure its person, but because it is thought that it will be in a better place than in its own family. A good education is afforded, which it would not find elsewhere; it is looked upon as unfortunate only, and society takes upon itself to give that which fortune has denied. It is not for public vengeance, but for its personal interest, that it is placed in the house of correction: as it has committed no crime, no punishment is to be inflicted upon it.

In respect to the young prisoners who are in this position, it seems to us that the duration of their stay in the house of correction ought not to be fixed by the courts. We appreciate the position, that the judicial authority alone ought to retain the power of sending them there, according to the circumstances, of which it has the opportunity of judging. But why should they be burdened at the same time with determining the number of years during which the education of a child may be completed? As if it were possible to foresee, in each case, the time which may be requisite for the correction of the vices, and the reformation of the evil inclinations of a child!

Would it not be more judicious to invest the inspectors and directors of the house with the guardianship over children whose education is confided to them, and with all the rights which appertain to the guardianship?

If it were so, the directors of the establishment would study the dispositions of the children placed under their authority. They would be able to seize with much more advantage upon the favorable moment to restore them to liberty. The time during which a child would have to remain in the house of correction, would thus be determined in a much more judicious way. And if a good opportunity should offer itself for one among them to be indentured as an apprentice, or in any other way, the directors would make use of it.

Even if all the advantages should not result from this change which it promises, something would already be gained, by effacing from our laws the provision in question. This provision is in fact the source of the worst abuses: it will surprise us little if we consider that the law confers a power upon the courts, without furnishing, at the same time, a rule for its exercise. Thus it empowers the court to send to the house of correction, for a certain number of years, (at its discretion) children acquitted in consideration of want of judgment. But upon what principle do they adjudge the number of years which the child has to stay in the house of correction? The law is silent on this point: the courts themselves are ignorant respecting it. If a court pronounce a punishment, it is measured by the offense. But by what standard shall the stay in the house of refuge be measured by anticipation, if the education of a child is in question, whose intellectual state is unknown to the judges, and of whose future progress they can know nothing?

This impossibility of finding a basis for the sentence, produces a completely arbitrary execution of the law. The judges will condemn a child to be detained until his fifteenth or twentieth year, without having the least standard to go by. This badly defined authority causes often the most revolting decisions.

A child of a less age than sixteen appears before a court. The first question is as to its capacity: if it is adjudged to have acted with discretion, it is sentenced to be detained in the house of correction. As this is a punishment pronounced by the court, it is proportionate to the offense, which appears not very grave, considering the youth of the convicted prisoner. It will, therefore, receive a sentence of some months imprisonment only.

Let us suppose another youth of the same age indicated. His offense is light, and the court finds he has acted without sufficient discretion. This youth will be sent for several years to the house of correction, to be educated and detained indeed, but, in fact, to be locked up in the same prison with the first, with this difference only, that he remains there a long time, while the former, who has been declared guilty, passes but a short time in the same place.

Thus it may be justly said, that for offenders under sixteen years, it is better to be found guilty than to be acquitted. Whoever has any experience in the administration of criminal justice, will acknowledge the defect which we point out. It is a defect not to be imputed to the magistrate, but belongs altogether to the law and its operation. This evil would be remedied in a great degree, in all cases in which children are detained without being convicted, if the courts would merely decree their detention in the house of correction, without fixing irrevocably the period of detention. By the sentence, the directors of the house would be authorized to retain the child for a fixed period, but it would be lawful for them to restore him to liberty before the expiration of the term, if circumstances permitted. They would not retain the child longer than the fixed period, but they would be at liberty to retain him for a shorter period.

If seems, therefore, to us, that a great advantage would result from a change of the provision of the law in question. The houses of correction would then become, in the true meaning of the word, houses of refuge, and they would be able to exercise upon the mind of the young delinquent a salutary influence, which, in the actual state of our legislation, is unattainable.

We only indicate here the principal changes which would be requisite to arrive at this end. Many questions connected with this subject, ought to be discussed and investigated, if a reform is to be produced fertile of happy results. Thus it would first be necessary to examine which would be the best means of interesting public opinion in the success of the reform; to determine the elements which shall compose the houses of refuge; to fix the principles of their organization, and to discuss the question, "where and in what number ought they to be established?" etc. All these questions, and many others which we pass over in silence, must be submitted to the investigation of men enlightened and versed in the knowledge of our laws, our customs, and the actual state of our prisons.

If this discipline should be introduced among us, pains ought to be taken to remove every thing which is of a nature to impede its success in this country.

We have already spoken of the danger, which is the most difficult to be avoided in this matter, viz., the difficulty of keeping a house of refuge in the proper medium between a school and a prison. In the United States, the houses of refuge approach, perhaps, too much to the former, and this defect may become fatal to them, when children, instigated by their parents themselves, may wish to find advantages denied them in their family. It ought, therefore, to be kept in mind, that these establishments, to fulfil their true object, must preserve, though differing from a prison, part of its severity, and that the comfort as well as the moral instruction which the children are sure to find in the house of refuge, ought not to be such as to make their fate enviable by children whose life is irreproachable.

We may, on this occasion, remind our readers of a truth which cannot be neglected without danger, viz., that the abuse of philanthropic institutions is as fatal to society as the evil itself which they are intended to cure.

APPENDICES
NOTES
INDEX

CONVERSATION WITH

MR. ELAM LYNDS

I HAVE passed ten years of my life in the administration of prisons, he said to us; I have been for a long time a witness of the abuses which predominated in the old system; they were very great. Prisons then caused great expenses, and the prisoners lost all the morality which they yet had left. I believe that this system would have led us back to the barbarous laws of the ancient codes. The majority at least began to be disgusted with all philanthropic ideas, the impracticability of which seemed to be proved by experience. It was under these circumstances that I undertook the reform of Auburn. At first I met with great difficulties with the legislature, and even with public opinion: much noise was made about tyranny; nothing short of success was requisite for my justification.

Q. Do you believe that the discipline established by you might succeed in any other country than in the United States?

A. I am convinced that it would succeed wherever the method is adopted which I have followed. As far as I can judge, I even believe that in France there would be more chances of success than with us. I understand the prisons in France stand under the immediate direction of government, which is able to lend a solid and durable support to its agents: here we are the slaves of a public opinion which constantly changes. But, according to my experience, it is necessary that the director of a prison, particularly if he establish a new discipline, should be invested with an absolute and certain power; it is impossible to calculate on this in a democratic republic like ours. With us, he is obliged to labor at once to captivate public opinion, and to carry through his undertaking — two things which are often irreconcilable. My principle has always been, that in order to reform a prison, it is well to concentrate within the same individual, all power and all responsibility. When the inspectors wished to oblige me to act according to their views, I told them: you are at liberty to send me away; I am dependent upon you; but as long as you retain me, I shall follow my plan; it is for you to choose.

Q. We have heard it said to Americans, and we are inclined to believe it, that the success of the penitentiary system must be partly attributed to the habit, so general in this country, of obeying scrupulously the laws.

A. I do not believe it. In Sing Sing, the fourth part of the prisoners is composed of foreigners by birth. I have subdued them all, as well as the Americans. Those whom it was most difficult to curb, were the Spaniards of South America — a race which has more of the ferocious animal, and of the savage, than of the civilized man. The most easy to be governed were Frenchmen; they submitted the most readily, and with the best grace to their fate, as soon as they considered it inevitable. If I had the choice, I should prefer superintending a prison in France, to directing one in the United States.

Q. What is then the secret of this discipline so powerful, which you have established in Sing Sing, and of which we have admired the effects?

A. It would be pretty difficult to explain it entirely; it is the result of a series of efforts and daily cares, of which it would be necessary to be an eyewitness. General rules cannot be indicated. The point is, to maintain uninterrupted silence and uninterrupted labor; to obtain this, it is equally necessary to watch incessantly the keepers, as well as the prisoners; to be at once inflexible and just.

Q. Do you believe that bodily chastisement might be dispensed with?

A. I am convinced of the contrary. I consider the chastisement by the whip, the most efficient, and, at the same time, the most humane which exists; it never injures health, and obliges the prisoners to lead a life essentially healthy. Solitary confinement, on the contrary, is often insufficient, and always dangerous. I have seen many prisoners in my life, whom it was impossible to subdue in this manner, and who only left the solitary cell to go to the hospital. I consider it impossible to govern a large prison without a whip. Those who know human nature from books only, may say the contrary.

Q. Don't you believe it imprudent at Sing Sing, for the prisoners to work in an open field?

A. For my part, I should always prefer to direct a prison in which such a state of things existed, than the contrary. It is impossible to obtain the same vigilance, and continual care from the guardians, in a prison surrounded by walls. Moreover, if you have once completely curbed the prisoner under the yoke of discipline, you may, without danger, employ him in the labor which you think best. It is in this manner, that the state may make use of the criminals in a thousand ways, if it has once improved the discipline of its prisons.

Q. Do you believe it absolutely impossible to establish sound discipline in a prison, in which the system of cells does not exist?

A. I believe that it would be possible to maintain considerable order in such a prison, and to make labor productive: but it would be quite impossible to prevent a number of abuses, the consequences of which would be very serious.

Q. Do you believe that it would be possible to establish cells in an old prison?

A. This depends entirely upon the state of those prisons. I have no doubt, that, in many old prisons, the system of cells might be introduced without great difficulties. It is always easy, and not expensive, to erect wooden cells; but they have the inconvenience of retaining a bad smell, and consequently of becoming sometimes unhealthy.

Q. Do you really believe in the reform of a great number of prisoners?

A. We must understand each other; I do not believe in a *complete*, reform, except with young delinquents. Nothing, in my opinion, is rarer than to see a convict of mature age become a religious and virtuous man. I do not put great faith in the sanctity of those who leave the prison. I do not believe that the counsels of the chaplain, or the meditations of the prisoner, make a good Christian of him. But my opinion is, that a great number of old convicts do not commit new crimes, and that they even become useful citizens, having learned in prison a useful art, and contracted habits of constant labor. This is the only reform which I ever have expected to produce, and I believe it is the only one which society has a right to expect.

Q. What do you believe proves the conduct of the prisoner in the prison, as to his future reformation?

A. Nothing. If it were necessary to mention a prognostic, I would even say that the prisoner who conducts himself well, will probably return to his former habits, when set free. I have always observed, that the worst subjects made excellent prisoners. They have generally more skill and intelligence than the others; they perceive much more quickly, and much more thoroughly, that the only way to render their situation less oppressive, is to avoid painful and repeated punishments, which would be the infallible consequence of insubordination; they therefore behave well, without being the better for it. The result of this observation is, that a pardon never ought to be granted, merely on account of the good conduct of a prisoner. In that way, hypocrites only are made.

Q. The system, however, which you attack, is that of all theorists?

A. In this, as in many other points, they deceive themselves, because they have little knowledge of those of whom they speak. If Mr. Livingston, for instance, should be ordered to apply his theories of penitentiaries to people born like himself, in a class of society in which much intelligence and moral sensibility existed, I believe that he would arrive at excellent results; but prisons, on the contrary, are filled with coarse beings, who have had no education, and who perceive with difficulty ideas, and often even sensations. It is this point which he always forgets.

Q. What is your opinion of the system of contract?

A. I believe it is very useful to let the labor of prisoners by contract, provided that the chief officer of the prison remains perfect master of their persons and time. When I was at the head of the Auburn prison, I had made, with different contractors, contracts which even prohibited them from entering the penitentiary. Their presence in the workshop cannot be but very injurious to discipline.

Q. Wages for the labor of a prisoner, are very low in France.

A. It would rise in the same degree as discipline would improve. Experience has taught us this. Formerly, the prisons were a heavy charge to the state of New York; now they are a source of revenue. The well-disciplined prisoner works more; he works better, and never spoils the materials, as it sometimes happened in the ancient prisons.

Q. Which is, in your opinion, the quality most desirable in a person destined to be a director of prisons?

A. The practical art of conducting men. Above all, he must be thoroughly convinced, as I have always been, that a dishonest man is ever a coward. This conviction, which the prisoners will soon perceive, gives him an irresistible ascendency, and will make a number of things very easy, which, at first glance, may appear hazardous.[1]

During all this conversation, which lasted several hours, Mr. Elam Lynds constantly returned to this point — that it was necessary to begin with curbing the spirit of the prisoner, and convincing him of his weakness. This point attained, every thing becomes easy, whatever may be the construction of the prison, or the place of labor.

RULES AND REGULATIONS

FOR THE CONNECTICUT

STATE PRISON

Duties of the Warden

1] He shall reside at the prison, and shall visit every cell and apartment, and see every prisoner under his care, at least once every day.

2] He shall not absent himself from the prison for more than a night, without giving notice to one or more of the directors.

3] It shall be his duty to cause the books and accounts to be so kept as clearly to exhibit the state of the convicts, the number employed in each branch of business, and their earnings, the number in the hospital, the expenses of the prison, and all receipts and payments, purchases and sales; and to exhibit the same to the directors at their quarterly meetings, or at any time when required. The quarterly accounts of the warden shall be sworn to by him, and shall specify minutely the persons from whom or to whom moneys are received or paid, and for what purpose.

4] It shall be the duty of the warden to make all contracts, purchases, and sales, for and on account of the prison — to oversee and command all the inferior officers in all their various duties, and see that they conform to the law, and the rules and regulations perscribed by the directors. He shall see that the prisoners are treated with kindness and humanity, and that no unnecessary severity is practised by the inferior officers — but if the security of the prison shall be in danger, or personal violence should be offered to him or any of the officers or guards, then he or they shall use all lawful means to defend themselves, and secure the authors of such outrage. In executing the duties of his office, the warden should never lose sight of the reformation of the prisoners, and should carefully guard himself against personal and passionate resentment. All orders should be given with mildness and dignity, and enforced with promptitude and firmness.

5]   It shall be his duty to treat persons visiting the prison with uniform civility and politeness, and to see that they are so treated by the inferior officers.

6]   As it is by law the duty of the directors to see personally to the condition and treatment of the prisoners, no regulation or order shall be made to prevent prisoners having ready access to the director who shall be present, nor shall any punishment be inflicted upon them for speaking to a director. In discharging this part of their duty, the directors will deem it proper not to suffer a convict to hold any conversation with them in the hearing or presence of other prisoners.

7]   The warden may, with the advice and consent of the directors in writing, appoint one person to be a deputy warden, and may, with such consent and advice in writing, remove him.

Duties of the Deputy Warden

1]   He shall be present at the opening and closing of the prison, during the performance of religious services, and also at all other prison hours.

2]   He shall daily visit the hospital, cookery, cells, and see that every part of the institution is clean and in order.

3]   It shall be his duty to exercise, under the direction of the warden, a general inspection and superintendence over the whole establishment, and all its concerns, to see that every subordinate officer strictly performs his appropriate duties, to visit frequently the places of labor and yards without notice, and see that the convicts are diligent and industrious, and generally to see that the rules and regulations of the institution are enforced, and that every precaution is taken for the security of the prison, and the prisoners therein confined.

4]   He shall attend to the clothing of the convicts, and see that it is whole, properly changed, and in order.

Duties of the Overseers

1]   There shall be an overseer of each shop, to be appointed by the warden.

2]   Each overseer shall, on entering upon his duties, take an accurate account of the various implements and tools belonging to his department, with the value of the same in money, and shall lodge a copy of such account under his hand with the warden, and such account shall be corrected quarterly, by adding such new implements as may have been purchased, or such as may have been broken, damaged, or lost. He shall keep an account of the stock furnished his department, and of the articles manufactured there and taken therefrom, and also of the daily and weekly earnings of each convict. He shall see that all the property belonging to his department shall be carefully preserved, and that the work is well and faithfully done, and shall consult and promote the interest of the state, or the contractor who may employ the convicts. It is especially enjoined upon each overseer, to preserve in his department the most entire order.

No conversation between prisoners shall be allowed. Nor shall any overseer converse with a prisoner, except to direct him in his labor. If any prisoner is idle, careless, or refractory, he shall be forthwith reported to the warden or deputy warden for punishment. Each overseer shall enter upon his book the name of each sick or complaining prisoner, and shall, before nine o'clock in the morning, deliver to the warden or deputy a list of such names, with the date, which list shall be placed in the hospital.

3] Each overseer shall perform his regular tour of night duty, as he may be directed by the warden.

Duties of the Watchmen

1] It shall be the duty of the several watchmen to perform all such various duties and services, for the safety and security of the prison, as may be directed by the warden, both by day, and during the night; to be vigilant and active while on post, and to maintain, while off from duty, and in the guard room, both towards each other and all other persons, a gentlemanly deportment; to refrain from all those acts which are inconsistent with the strictest decorum — treating with an uniform politeness and civility, all persons who shall visit the prison; recollecting that the reputation, as well as the safety of the institution, depend essentially upon them, individually as well as collectively. They are cautioned that they are to be neat and clean in their own persons, and that the guard room shall at all times exhibit a specimen of neatness and order; and that their arms are always in repair, and ready for service. No watchman shall be allowed to hold any conversation with a prisoner, except to direct him in his labor. Nor shall he receive from, or deliver to a prisoner, any article or thing, without the knowledge of the warden or his deputy.

2] It shall be the duty of the warden to designate some person who shall be employed at the prison, to see, personally, that the various rations ordered by these rules are weighed or measured for the day, according to the number of prisoners, and delivered to the head cook; and he shall keep an exact account of all such rations, so by him delivered, and shall, under oath, render the same quarterly to the warden, under his hand, to be laid before the directors.

3] Each and every person who shall by the warden be

appointed to any office in or about said prison, shall be held as engaged to, and attached to the institution; and if in office at the time a vacancy shall happen in the office of warden, as bound to continue his services at the prison, for at least one month after the death, removal, or resignation of the warden, unless sooner discharged by his successsor; and in case any such officer shall refuse or neglect to perform his duty, he shall forfeit three months' wages, to be recovered by any succeeding warden, and this bylaw shall be considered as one of the terms on which each officer shall contract, and as assented to by him.

Cleanliness

1]   The hall and cells shall be swept daily, and the sweepings carried outside of the wall. The floor of the hall shall be washed once a fortnight through the year. The cells shall also be frequently washed and whitewashed.

2]   The beds and bedding shall be taken out of the prison and aired in the yard, once a week in the warm season, and once a fortnight during the rest of the year, when the weather will allow; and each prisoner is to take the utmost care that his cell be kept neat, and that his furniture be not injured: and in default of observing this rule, his bed, bedding, and bedstead, to be taken from him until he will conform.

3]   The utmost care is to be taken that the persons of the prisoners are kept clean. For this purpose they shall have suitable accommodations for washing.

4]   The night pails shall be kept carefully clean, and their contents carried without the walls, and covered in the manner now practiced.

5]   No filth, nuisance, or offensive matter, shall be suffered to remain in or about the prison, shops, or yard; but the whole establishment must be made to exhibit throughout, a specimen of neatness, good order, and cleanliness.

Hospital and Physician

1]   The warden, with the approbation of the directors, shall appoint some proper person to be the physician, who shall receive such compensation as shall be fixed and agreed upon by the directors.

2] The hospital shall be furnished with the necessary beds, bedding, bedsteads, tables, and all other necessary utensils, for the comfort and accommodation of the sick, and shall at all times be kept in a state of readiness to receive such patients as are ordered there by the physician.

3] The physician shall direct such supplies, stores, and furniture, as may be necessary in his department; and his order in writing shall authorize the warden to procure the same. He shall record in a book all the orders so given, designating the articles and the time when given. He shall also keep an account of the various articles belonging to his department. He shall also record in said book, his visits, the names of the patients reported as sick or complaining, the names of such as are ordered to the hospital, or as are ordered to their cells on sick diet, or are ordered to their shops. He shall visit the institution every other day through the year, and oftener if it shall be neccesary, or if sent for, and shall personally see every patient or prisoner, who may, by the respective overseers, be reported as sick or complaining. He shall also enter the names of such as shall be discharged from the hospital, or shall die, the nature of the complaint and the prescription, and shall subjoin such other remarks as he may deem expedient, respecting the nature of each case, and the treatment thereof, or in relation to the general health, diet, or employment of the prisoners, or cleanliness of the prison, which book shall remain at the prison, and shall be always open to the inspection of the warden and directors.

He may apply to the warden for the assistance of such convicts as may be necessary to nurse and attend upon the sick, and he, as well as the warden, shall endeavor to render the condition of the sick prisoner, in all respects, as comfortable as his situation will admit. Whenever any prisoner shall not be sufficiently ill, as to make it necessary that he be ordered to the hospital, the physician may direct such diet to be prepared for him, from the hospital or prison stores, as he may deem necessary.

4] If it shall so happen that the directions or prescriptions of the physician shall not be complied with, or duly observed, it shall be his duty to enter such failure or omission in his book, with the reason thereof, if he shall be acquainted with the same, to the end that proper measures may be taken to prevent future omissions.

General Regulations

1]   No officer or person connected with the institution, shall be permitted to buy from, or sell to any convict any article or thing whatever, or make with him any contract or engagement whatsoever, or cause or allow any convict to work for him or his benefit, or grant any favor or indulgence to a convict, except such as the laws allow. Nor shall he receive from any convict, or from any one in behalf of such convict, any emoluments, presents, or reward whatever, or the promise of any for services or supplies, or as a gratuity. Nor shall he take or receive to his own use and benefit or that of his family, any fee, gratuity, or emolument, from any person committed to his custody, nor, from any of their friends or acquaintances, or from any person whomsoever, and every officer offending herein, shall be forthwith dismissed.

2]   The compensation to each and every officer, shall be fixed and settled by the directors before he enters upon the duties of his office, and no officer shall be allowed or permitted to take or receive any other or greater compensation than the sum so fixed; nor shall he take or receive either from the public property or in the labor or services of the convicts, any perquisite whatever, without the consent of the directors in writing.

3]   Spirituous liquors shall in no case be furnished to the convicts, except on the prescription of the physician. And each and every officer is hereby required wholly to abstain from their use, during the period of his employment at this institution, on penalty of being dismissed.

4]   No officer except the warden, shall strike, beat, or punish corporeally any prisoner, except in self-defense.

5]   In case any officer shall be absent from the prison, except upon the public business of the same, the rateable compensation of such officer shall be stopped during the time of such absence.

6]   Each cell shall be furnished with a Bible, and the convicts may have such other religious books and attendance, as the warden, with the assent of the directors, may think suited to improve their morals and conduct.

7]   All sums which shall be received from persons visiting the prison, shall be accounted for to the state, and deemed a part of the income of the prison, and such sums shall be included in the quarterly accounts of the warden.

Duties of the Convicts

1]   Every convict shall be industrious, submissive, and obedient, and shall labor diligently and in silence.

2]   No convict shall secrete, hide, or carry about his person, any instrument or thing with intent to make his escape.

3]   No convict shall write or receive a letter to or from any person whatsoever, nor have intercourse with persons without the prison, except by leave of the warden.

4]   No convict shall burn, waste, injure, or destroy any raw materials or article of public property, nor deface or injure the prison building.

5]   Convicts shall always conduct themselves toward the officers with deference and respect; and cleanliness in their persons, dress, and bedding, is required. When they go to their meals or labor, they shall proceed in regular order and in silence, marching in the lock step.

6]   No convict shall converse with another prisoner, or leave his work without permission of an officer. He shall not speak to, or look at visitors, nor leave the hospital when ordered there, nor shall he make any unnecessary noise in his labor, or do any thing either in the shops or cells, which is subversive of the good order of the institution.

Rations and Bedding

1]   The rations for each convict per day, shall be one pound of beef, one pound of bread, to be made of rye flour

and corn meal unbolted. Five bushels of potatoes to each
hundred rations, and a porridge for supper, to be made of
twenty pounds of corn meal, and six quarts of peas, to each
hundred rations. Each convict to be furnished with pepper
and salt.

2]   Each convict shall have a straw mattress, three blankets in winter, and two in summer, and two coarse cotton
sheets of sufficient size — the whole to be kept carefully clean.
They shall not be permitted to sleep in their clothes, nor lie
down or rise until notice shall be given by the bell. Their
meals shall be taken in their cells.

A Letter addressed to us

By Judge Wells of Wethersfield,

former Commissioner and Director

of the State Prison of Connecticut,

October, 1831.

SINCE building the prison at Wethersfield, I have been of the opinion, that had we to build it a second time, we should be able to do it at much less expense. In the present structure many useless expenses were incurred; for example, we have a roof covered with slate, gutters of copper, and cornices. In a climate like ours, it is better that the eaves should drop directly upon the ground, otherwise the water is liable to freeze in the gutters.

It appears to me, that in constructing a prison, two great errors may easily be committed.

The first consists in the want of a proper proportion of strength in the different parts of the building. Thus it happens, that we often see walls of five or six feet in thickness, composed of enormous blocks of stone, bound together by cramp-irons; to these are joined doors and windows which in strength are not equal to a wall of one foot in thickness; and a massive and expensive door is sometimes mounted upon hinges, and secured by fastenings, proper only for much lighter ones.

The second error arises from the idea that the edifice must be so constructed as to endure through all coming ages. Public spirited and benevolent individuals are devoting much of their time and talents to devising improvements in the construction of prisons. One improvement suggests another, and it is not in the power of any man to foresee the result of these different efforts. By them public opinion is changed; and society at length looks with an unfavorable eye, upon an establishment which is not capable of admitting all the improvements suggested by experience. Within twenty years, an entire revolution of opinion often takes place; the old prisons do not any longer meet the wants of the community, and they are abandoned. Such is the history of the greater part of the prisons of the United States. It is, therefore, very important that these establishments should be built upon the least expensive plan, since otherwise they become obstacles to improvement; obstacles, the more difficult to be overcome, the greater the expense bestowed upon their construction.

The distinguishing feature in the modern system, consists in the substitution of vigilance in the place of strength of material. In the modern prisons, the eye and ear of the watchman are incessantly on the alert, and should never be withdrawn. Absolute silence should be maintained by day and by night.

This constant vigilance contributes to render the construction of our penitentiaries less expensive. Experience has shown that no greater strength of walls is necessary in a prison, than that requisite to withstand the elements, to secure stability to the structure, and to resist the sudden attempts of the prisoners to escape. It is unnecessary to give to them greater strength than to ordinary public buildings.

The prison at Wethersfield is built of sandstone in irregular blocks. The walls are three feet in thickness at the base, and two at the top. Two and a half at the base, and one and a half at the top, is sufficient, with external buttresses to strengthen the walls.

The top of the walls should be on a level with the ceiling of the upper tier of cells.

The walls cost ten cents per cubic foot; say four for the stone, four for the work, one for the mortar, and one for scaffolding and other incidental expenses.

The cells are of brick, and cost twenty cents per cubic

foot. Many of them are floored with a single stone. Each of these stones cost us four dollars. The floor of the others consists of plank three inches in thickness, covered with a layer of brick. The whole is covered with cement, and cost $2.00 for each cell. The doors of the cells are composed of oak plank, three inches thick, strengthened by four bolts, running through them transversely. Each door, deducting the iron work, cost $2.50. I have estimated the cost of each cell at $28.00, comprising the masonwork, hinges, locks, and grates.

It may be a question, whether, in building a prison, it is more advantageous to employ convicts or free laborers. I should say, that this would depend upon the manner in which they are already employed. If they are engaged in profitable labor in their workshops, it is better to leave them there. If, on the contrary, they are not so engaged, they may be put to a business which requires no great degree of intelligence, or with which they are already acquainted. They may do the iron work, prepare and carry the materials, make the mortar, etc. But the expense for additional guard, which is necessary if the convicts are thus employed, will be so great as nearly to counterbalance any advantage.

It has been asked, whether the avails of the labor of the convicts will probably be sufficient to cover the annual expenses of maintaining the prison? Upon this point I will make but a single remark, in addition to what I have already stated to you in conversation. If in France it has been thought questionable, whether the labor of the convicts would be sufficient for their support, I can say, that previously to the establishment of the new prison, we had in Connecticut as strong reasons for supposing that the labor of the convicts would be inadequate to this object, as the French themselves. Our former prison was a continual source of expense. During the last ten years of its existence, it received from the public treasury, over and above all that was earned, $8,400 per annum. Few individuals dared to hope that the new prison would support itself, and nothing but the highest evidence would have led us to believe, that adding the former annual loss to the present annual gain, the difference to the state treasury would be more than $16,000 per annum — but such is the fact.

It is said, that free laborers in France do not find employment as readily as in America, and, as a consequence, it is more difficult to render profitable the labor of convicts. But if the free laborer is able to support himself and family, although with great effort, the convict ought to do equally well, since his maintenance costs less; and if the edifices are favorable to inspection, they may be superintended by a small number of individuals, and consequently at small expense.

If the price of labor be less, than the expenses of support will also be less; these two things are correlative, and between them, there exists of necessity an exact proportion.

I remain, therefore, strong in the belief, that in a prison advantageously constructed, the labor of the convicts, if well directed, ought completely to indemnify the state.

AN ESTIMATE OF THE COSTS AND DIMENSIONS OF A PRISON BUILT TO CONTAIN FIVE HUNDRED CONVICTS

Length of main building	250 ft.
Width of main building	50 ft.
Thickness of building wall at base	2½ ft.
Thickness of building wall at top	1½ ft.
Average thickness of wall	2 ft.
Thickness of wall at foundation	3 ft.
Depth of foundation	3 ft.

The whole makes a total of 49,000 cubic feet of stone laid in mortar at ten cents per foot.

Length of secondary buildings	270 ft.
Width of secondary buildings	30 ft.
Height of external walls	18 ft.
Below surface of ground	3 ft.
Thickness at base	2 ft.
Thickness at top	1½ ft.

Secondary buildings would consist of two ranges of buildings — one on each side of the yard, fifteen feet from the external wall to contain shops, storerooms, kitchens, schools etc. and each being two stories high with a shingle roof.

Cost of stone and masonry for main building	$4980
Shingle roof	1250
500 cells arranged in 5 stories at $28.00 each	14,000
Plastering	600
Brick floor at 4½ bricks per foot	200
Cost of secondary buildings at $3000 each	6000
Cost of external wall	3150
Buttresses to support wall	200
A walk upon the top of wall	200
Bars for windows	500
House for warden	2500
Incidental expenses	6420
Total	$40,000

(Expense per prisoner, $80)

This estimate is made according to the actual cost of the raw material as follows:

Stone (sand or free-stone) — per foot	$ 0.04
Timber (1 inch in thickness) — per 1,000 feet	10.00
Day's work for ordinary laborers	1.00
Iron — per pound	0.04

In building the prison, it is not necessary that hewn stone should be used, except for the caps and sills of the windows and doors.

It should be observed, that nothing has been said in the above plan respecting windows and doors. In making the estimate for the walls, I have left out of account the apertures, and have considered the wall as forming a solid mass. The walls would therefore cost less than I have stated, and the excess would cover the expense of the doors and windows, together with a part of the grating.

At Wethersfield, the locks were made by the convicts, and cost about $2.25 each.

ESTIMATE OF THE EXPENSE OF GUARDING AND SUPPORTING FIVE HUNDRED PRISONERS, IN A PRISON SIMILAR TO THAT OF WHICH THE ABOVE IS A PLAN AND ESTIMATE.

(Food, clothing, and bedding of each prisoner per annum, $22)

Total expense of prisoners per annum	$11,000
1 warden	800
1 deputy warden	400
8 overseers of shops	2800
8 guards	2000
Medicine and hospital expenses	700
Chaplain	400
Lights, fuel, and other incidental expenses	1000
	$19,100

From the 500 prisoners, I have deducted fifty for those who are aged, sick, and engaged in unproductive labor. The remaining 450, ought to earn, one day with another, 25 cents each.

In computing the year at 300 days, the total gain should amount to

450 men, at 25 cents each	$33,750
Deducting the amount of expenses	19,100
There remains a net gain of	$14,650

This result will not appear exaggerated, if it is recollected, that, during the last year, the one hundred and sixty men confined in the prison at Wethersfield, earned for the state more than half the above named sum of $14,650 or $7,824.

I have no doubt, that, at Wethersfield, the entire annual expense of a prison containing five hundred convicts, would be covered by $19,100.

And I am of opinion, that I have estimated the income to be derived from such a prison, sufficiently low.

In estimating the expense, I have taken as a basis, the actual cost of supporting and guarding the prisoners at Wethersfield; and, when I have spoken of the profits, I have taken care, on the other hand, to estimate the labor of the convicts at less than its actual value, in the same prison.

The value of a day's work, on an average, in the above calculation, is put at 25 cents per man, although, at Wethersfield, no convict is now hired at less than 30 cents per day, and some of them have produced to the state $1.00 per day.

NOTES

Introduction [PP. 15–40]

1. René Rémond, *Les États-Unis devant l'opinion française 1815–1852* (2 vols. Paris: Armand Colin, 1962).

2. Alexis de Tocqueville, *Oeuvres complètes.* Tome V. *Voyages en Sicilie et aux États-Unis,* ed. J. P. Mayer (Paris: Gallimard, 1957). A part, translated by George Lawrence, was published by the Yale University Press in 1960 and entitled *Journey to America.* An indispensable source of information about the journey is George W. Pierson's exhaustive study of *Tocqueville and Beaumont in America* (New York: Oxford University Press, 1938).

3. George W. Pierson, "Le 'second voyage' de Tocqueville en Amérique," In *Alexis de Tocqueville. Livre du centenaire 1859– 1959* (Paris: Ed. du Centre National de la Recherche Scientifique, 1960), pp. 71–85.

4. G. de Beaumont et A. de Tocqueville, *Du système pénitentiaire aux États-Unis et de son application en France, suivi d'un appendice sur les colonies pénales et de notes statistiques* (Paris: Fournier, 1833). The appendix was also written by Tocqueville. A second edition of the work, with a very long preface, was published in 1836. The third edition appeared in 1845.

5. Gustave de Beaumont, *Marie ou l'esclavage aux États-Unis. Tableau de moeurs américaines* (5th ed; Paris: Gosselin, 1842). The first edition of 1835 was followed by one in 1836 and two in 1840. A translation by Barbara Chapman was published by the Stanford University Press in 1958. Beaumont presented his data in a different form in a monograph on the social and political condition of Negro slaves and colored persons in the United States, published in 1837 in the *Mémoires de l'Académie royale des sciences morales et politiques*, Séries 2, Vol. I.

6. Rémond, *op. cit.*, p. 736.

7. A. Rivière, "Mirabeau criminaliste." *Rev. britannique*, (1889), V, 5–24.

8. *Ibid.*, pp. 12–13.

9. Rivière believed that Mirabeau had drawn his inspiration from America, but this is unlikely. There was nothing in American penal institutions before 1790 to inspire anybody. Mirabeau was probably influenced by British ideas. During his stay in England in 1784 he and Samuel Romilly, the future penal reformer, became fast friends. In 1788, Romilly introduced Dumont to Mirabeau in Paris. Dumont, a friend of Bentham, soon afterwards began to edit Bentham's papers for publication in French. Since it is claimed that Dumont supplied Mirabeau with material for some of his finest speeches, Phillipson assumes that "part of these materials undoubtedly came from Bentham." See Coleman Phillipson, *Three Criminal Law Reformers. Beccaria, Bentham, Romilly* (London and Toronto: J. M. Dent, 1923), p. 125.

10. *Archives parlementaires de 1787 à 1860*, Sér. I (1787–1799), XXVI, p. 320.

11. *Ibid.*, p. 323.

12. Ferdinand Dreyfus, *Un philanthrope d'autrefois. La Rochefoucauled-Liancourt, 1747–1827* (Paris: Plon, 1903), p. 94.

13. *On the Prisons of Philadelphia*. By an European. 46 pp. Philadelphia: Moreau St. Mery, 1796. The French edition was entitled *Des prisons de Philadelphie*. Par un Européen. It was re-issued in Paris the same year. A third edition appeared there in 1800 and a fourth in 1819.

14. Thorsten Sellin, "Philadelphia prisons of the eighteenth century." *Transactions, American Philosophical Society*, New series Vol. XLIII, Part I, 330.

15. Dreyfus, *op. cit.*, p. 307.

16. *Ibid.*, pp. 463–468.

17. *Ibid.*, p. 494.

18. Armand Mossé, *Les prisons et les institutions d'éducation corrective* (Paris: Sirey, 1929), p. 102.

19. Charles Lucas, *Du systéme pénitentiaire en Europe et aux États-Unis* (2 vols.; Paris: 1828, 1830), 1–144; 157–257. Livingston was considered, especially in Europe, as the greatest

legal philosopher since Montesquieu. He served as Secretary of State in President Jackson's cabinet and later as ambassador to France. For his biography, see William B. Hatcher, *Edward Livingston* (Baton Rouge, Louisiana: Louisiana State University Press, 1940). His system of penal laws is found in *The Complete Works of Edward Livingston on Criminal Jurisprudence* (2 vols.; New York: National Prison Association, 1873).

20. In 1827, Lucas had published his book, *Du système pénal et du système répressif en général, de la peine de mort en particulier,* which had been judged the best of the works submitted in competitions opened by Count de Sellon of Geneva and the Society of Christian Morality, Paris, on the subject of the legitimacy and the efficacy of the death penalty.

21. Frédéric A. Demetz et Abel Blouet, *Rapports* . . . *sur les pénitenciers aux États-Unis,* One vol. of two parts, (Paris: Imprimerie Royale, 1837).

22. The project is reproduced in Moreau-Christophe's *Revue pénitentiaire et des institutions préventives* I (1843–1844), 81–104.

23. Loc. cit., pp. 104–54.

24. Loc. cit., pp. 218–34. The "exposé des motifs" is also found in *Annales du Parlement Français* . . . *Session de 1844 du 27 décembre 1843 au 5 août, 1844* (Tome VI, No. XVI, pp. 1–8).

25. Annales, loc. cit., pp. 8–36; also in Moreau-Christophe's *Revue* . . ., I, 234–78.

26. Annales, pp. 36–58; Text of law adopted, pp. 58–62; *Revue* . . . II (1845), 57–584.

27. Moreau-Christophe's *Revue* . . . , II (1845), 452.

28. By 1852, 45 local prisons had been constructed with a total of 4840 cells and 15 more were under construction. See Paul Cuche, *Traité de science et de législation pénitentiaire* (Paris: Libr. gén. de droit et de jurispr., 1905), p. 343.

29. An interesting review of American influence on French prison reform is found in John H. Cary's "France looks to Pennsylvania. The Eastern Penitentiary as a symbol of reform." *Pennsylvania Magazine of History and Biography,* LXXXII (April, 1958), 186–203.

30. L'Ancien Régime et la Révolution.

31. M. C. M. Simpson (ed.), *Correspondence and Conversations of Alexis de Tocqueville with Nassau William Senior from 1834 to 1859* (2 vols. 2d ed.; London: 1872), Vol. I, iv–v.

32. Ibid., p. 124.

33. Ibid., p. 125.

NOTES

Translator's Preface [pp. 6–33]

1. When, in 1807, stripes were abolished in the Prussian army, it was believed necessary to substitute the laths (in German *Latten*) for the punishment of running the gauntlet. They consisted of triangular prismatic laths, nailed on the floor of a low and small prison, in such a way that one of the sharp edges of each lath was turned up, and that these edges formed, with other small pieces of wood corresponding in form on the surface, a number of small squares of sharp edges, on which the prisoner was obliged to lie or sit, no kind of furniture being allowed, nor was the prison high enough for the prisoner to stand in an erect position. It was so severe a punishment, that the prisoner could endure it but for a few hours at a time after a proportionate rest he was reconducted to this place of torment. The severest punishment of this kind lasted three days. It was inflicted for heavy offenses, and in consequence of a sentence by a court-martial only. In 1832, the king issued an order declaring that the moral state of the army was of a kind no longer to require this hard disciplinary measure. In the Austrian and Russian armies, and probably in some of the Italian states, corporal punishment continues to be made use of in the old style, but the period we hope is not distant, when even Austria will be obliged to follow the general progress of improvement. My expression that the American penitentiary system is a new victory of mind over matter, requires, perhaps, some explanation. I do not except the Auburn system, applied in so remarkable a way, in Sing Sing, to nearly one thousand prisoners. The Auburn system, as is well known, is mainly founded on the principle of silence, which isolates the prisoner in a moral respect. This silence, however, it will be objected, is supported by the whip, which, it must be allowed, is not a very intellectual or moral means of discipline. But, without speaking of those penitentiaries on the Auburn plan, in which corporal punishment is resorted to but in cases of extremity or not at all, and considering for a moment the question whether the Auburn principles can be applied consistently and effectually without the whip, as decided in favor of the Sing Sing discipline, I yet maintain that the principle on which this system is founded, partakes much more of a moral than physical character. The whip is the physical means to enforce the principle of silence, and, besides, it is not so much the actual pain inflicted upon the convict, which induces him to keep silence, as the knowledge of an inevitable and immediate punishment for any contravention of the rule; it is the thorough conviction which the prisoner acquires of the necessity of complying with the order of the prison, which makes it possible that from thirty to thirty-five persons are actually capable of superintending, of guiding, and watching nearly a thousand convicts, and in a manner altogether unknown in any of the old prisons where galley-slaves in dresses of two contrasting colors — a repulsive uniform of fools and villains — drag their heavy chains in yards, surrounded by high and thick walls and fortifications, and nevertheless, continual escapes take place, while they are a thing nearly unknown in Sing Sing (two or three escapes only excepted, during the time of the cholera, which carried off a great number in that prison) though many convicts work in the open field. There are, at present, in actual service at a time, six guards near the prison, eight guards distributed in the quarries, and twenty keepers, who watch the prisoners, and superintend and direct at the same time their labor. Thirty-four individuals, therefore, keep in order from eight hundred to a thousand convicts, and enforce the laws of silence and constant labor. There were at one time, one thousand and eighteen prisoners at Sing Sing, and the above number of guards and keepers were found sufficient. The locality, I allow, favors somewhat the watching over their attempts to escape, yet the whole remains a surprising phenomenon which could not possibly be produced except by the aid of moral power. If the whip is mentioned as a disciplinary measure, we must also mention labor as such, and if I mistake not it contributed much more to maintain order than the whip. That labor has a powerful disciplinary effect with criminals (it is the same with all men) the reader will find asserted by a high authority in the course of this book; it has, as Mr. Dumont, the translator and editor of Jeremy Bentham's works, expresses it with a word derived from medicine, a sedative effect, it calms and assuages the mind of the irritated convict. To the authority, indicated above, I would add Mr. Vasselot's, who was for a long time director of a *maison-centrale,* in France. He was twice in great danger of losing his life by the revolted convicts under his charge. They were idle; all disturbances, plots, etc., ceased, as soon as they were employed. He adds, "In order to live in safety in the midst of many hundred prisoners, it is better to love than to fear them." It appears to me, in visiting the American penitentiaries, that the salutary effect of labor shows itself strongly also in the expression of the faces of the convicts. They do not only look healthy, but I could discover none of those features, expressive of brooding revenge or deep hatred subdued only for the moment by physical force — in short, none of those criminal faces with which you always will meet in any of the old prisons, containing a large number of convicts. To repeat it then, silence is the fundamental principle; and this, as well as order in general, is maintained on the one hand, by continual employment; on the other hand, by the convict's perfect conviction that he must comply with the rules of the establishment; he may infringe them, and sooner or later — and generally it is soon — he comes to the thorough conviction, that he must yield, that the order of the penitentiary will be maintained, and that he is the only sufferer if he tries to contravene it. This conviction, however, is very different from a mere physical prevention of escape by walls, fosses, chains, bars between the feet, balls, clogs, iron horns, collars, manacles, bells fastened to the head, etc. But how are the convicts brought to this perfect conviction? How is it that we see at Sing Sing criminals who have been in Botany Bay, have escaped from different prisons and never have been kept in obedience except by powerful physical means, patiently submit here to the established order (even in cases of the greatest excitement, such as at the time of the cholera) and obey so hard a law as that of constant silence must be to every human being? If we answer: "all this is effected by the whip," the assertion is liable to serious misunderstanding. It is true that the whip is used; it is true that the stripes inflicted with it smart acutely. Since this small instrument produces so great results, I was anxious to know its exact effect; I devised a means to obtain this personal knowledge in a way which satisfies me that I experienced the effects of this disciplinary instrument in as great a degree as the refractory convict does. I do not deny that the pain inflicted by this whip, made much like the scourge used in former times for flagellations, is very acute, and without causing injury seems in a peculiar way painfully to affect the nerves, owing no doubt to its consisting of six thin cords; yet criminals have defied punishments much more severe than this, have often braved cruel tortures, and, in my opinion, stripes alone as they are inflicted in Sing Sing, would not be sufficient to produce such results, particularly if we consider that there is, comparatively speaking, seldom occasion to resort to them. The principle, however, upon which this punishment produces effects so great, it this, active in all men, that the present evil is always the greatest, which remains true, though extended and modified, if we say, "the nearer evil or pain is feared more than the distant, though greater." Ten smart stripes, certain to be inflicted the very next moment after an infringement of order, are feared more than a hundred stripes to be suffered aften the lapse of a year; the certain drawing of a tooth is feared more for the moment, than even death, which every one considers distant. If, then, punishment is certain of falling immediately upon the offender, it has the greatest effect. This, and the otherwise humane treatment of the criminals which does not brutalize them as other prisons do, the calm deportment of the keepers, who probably find no inconsiderable means of safety in resorting to corporal punishment only, if there is ground for it, are the causes of so unique a phenomenon as that exhibited at Sing Sing. The criminals are prevented from plotting or from any combination of their strength or thoughts otherwise than in the prescribed way, by silence imposed upon them, and by a strict compliance with the rules of the establishment; silence and order are maintained by labor and the thorough conviction of the unavoidable necessity of obedience; conviction of necessary obedience is produced by the threat of corporal punishment; corporal punishment is rendered effectual by its certainty and instantaneousness. I admit, that so many criminals can be kept in perfect submission by so few officers and guards only in a country in which the government is considered by the people as entirely their own, acting solely for their interest, and to which they therefore give all their moral support, as in the case with us. The same cannot take place in countries in which government and people form two different bodies. Yet the principles of silence, labor, and immediate punishment, will produce proportionately the same effect everywhere. The Study of a diseased or disordered state of our body, of the mind, or of political society, has led to the most important knowledge respecting their healthy state, and the nature of their organization. We frequently see in such a state, one faculty, organ, power, etc., developed at the expense of the others, which causes the disease by disturbing the necessary equilibrium, but at the same time offers a peculiar opportunity for observation. The prison of Sing Sing affords in a similar way a variety of most interesting observations; and among other things the all-important principle that crimes and offenses are not checked by the severity of the law, but by the certainty and rapidity of punishment, is most strikingly exhibited. If it were possible to devise a system of administering justice which would infallibly punish immediately after the offense had been committed, many hideous crimes might be prevented by the threat of very trifling punishments. This is impossible; the necessity of protecting innocence, though suspected, brings with it the possibility of impunity, on which the criminal calculates when he commits a premeditated crime, as every man grasps at the most favorable hope; but the problem remains to arrive at least as near perfection as possible; and if we consider it already a necessary evil that many criminals escape punishment, how much more afflicting an evil must the abuse of the pardoning power appear to us, which has been carried to a degree that the criminal is perfectly right in counting it among the chances (sometimes the probabilities) of impunity. But we shall speak more on this subject. For the rest, I have on various occasions stated, that I consider the Pennsylvania penitentiary system much more philosophical in its principle, more radical and thorough in its operation, more practical and easy in its application, more charitable in its whole spirit than the Auburn system, wherever the means can be obtained to erect the necessary buildings, which often will be difficult, and in such cases the Auburn system remains, so far, the next preferable.

2. The House of Representatives of Massachusetts recently appointed Joseph Tuckerman and Louis Dwight, of Boston, and John W. Lincoln, of Worcester, commissioners to make personal inspection of all the jails and houses of correction in the state, with a view to devise or obtain plans and descriptions of such houses, better calculated to subserve the important design of their institution; to prepare a tabular form of annual returns; to examine the several statutes for the regulation of the existing institutions, and report thereupon at the next session, which such suggestions of change or modification, as in their judgement may conduce to their improvement in security, economy, health, or moral benefit.

3. The attention of the legislature has often been called to this subject, and the necessity of a separate prison for female convicts urged with great force. The inspectors of this prison repeat the recommendation to the legislature, to provide for this unfortunate and criminal class of the community, a different place of confinement; a place which, by the discipline established, shall tend to reform, and not, as in their present condition, lead to inevitable ruin.

No doubt is entertained, but the same discipline which now controls and subdues the male convict, may be made equally serviceable with the females. Under the charge of a judicious matron, we cannot believe but great moral reformation may be produced. This consideration alone calls with great force for a change in the mode of punishing female convicts. It is also worthy of consideration, to inquire whether the expense to the state would not be diminished by such change. The state now pays one hundred dollars a year for each female convict kept at Bellevue. They are not employed at anything except cooking, washing, making and mending clothes for themselves, and this occupies but a small part of their time. The law is imperative as to the place where these convicts must be confined, and such sum must be paid as the corporation of New York chooses to demand, whether that sum be a fair compensation, or beyond the value of the services rendered. (From the "Report of the Inspectors of the Mount Pleasant [Sing Sing] State Prison," January, 1833.)

4. A shocking contrast between her name, which means *Peace in God,* and her deeds!

5. See her Life described (in German) by her *Difensor,* (Legal Counsellor) Bremen, 1832; and Beckmann's *History of Inventions, etc.,* translated from the German by Johnston, Vol. I., Division *Secret Poison.*

6. Delicacy is one of the most active principles in female life — in respect to morals as well as manners, language, dress, taste, feelings, and thoughts. It is the same principle which causes women all over the globe to wear wider garments (if their tribe or nation dress at all) then men, induces the men to court the women, and not the women the men, and which, in short, makes coarseness, want of taste, deficiency in neatness, boldness, etc., in women so shocking and disagreeable to every feeling person, and — to repeat — on account of which, an indelicate woman has deviated much more from the character, destined for her by the Creator, than a man who offends against delicacy.

7. There are some crimes to which their dependant situation induces them, sooner than men, but they are comparatively few in number.

8. I have it from the best authority, that, in Sing Sing, the proportion of recommitted convicts, who had gone to live in the country, to those who had gone to the city of New York, is, in all probability, not more than one to twenty.

9. In writing this, I am well aware of the fact that some master workmen in the city of New York have taken, from their own accord, convicts of Sing Sing, whose term had expired, because they have great confidence in their new habits, their industry and skill. The law therefore might provide for those cases, and allow a convict to return to New York, provided the agent is satisfied that the master who wishes to have him is a worthy person. I should think it however preferable to exclude them from New York altogether.

10. After the work had gone to press, I became acquainted, through the reviews, with several passages of Mr. Guerry's *Essai sur la Statisque Morale de la France, avec Cartes;* I have not yet been able to procure the work itself. To judge from those passages, the author coincides with my views respecting the influence of civilization on crimes, as I have stated them in the notes.

11. Page 26 of Dumont's *Rapport sur le project de loi pour le regime interieur des prisons,* printed, together with his report relative to the establishment of a penitentiary (delivered 1822) in Geneva, 1825.

12. The translator received information from Paris on the day when this introduction went to press, that a second edition of the original was preparing.

After the whole of the present work, the above preface not excepted, was in type, I received the extracts from the information obtained by his Majesty's Commissioners, as to the *Administration and Operation of the Poor Laws,* published by Authority, London, 1833. It is a work of the highest interest, uncovering as it does, a dangerous evil, in the very vitals of the community, which nevertheless grew out of laws, enacted with the best intentions; and, as the frailty of human nature establishes but too near a connection between pauperism and crime, workhouses and prisons, the one being so often the cause of the other, I seize upon this opportunity to recommend its perusal to all interested in penal matters, and the administration of paupers. It is a work full of most instructive matter.

Authors' Preface [PP. 35–36]

1. M. Ernest de Blosseville, author of the *Histore des Colonies penales dans l'Australie,* Paris, 1831. The system of transportation, to which public opinion in France seems pretty generally favorable, appears to us surrounded with dangers and difficulties.

2. This report has been handed in to the Minister of Commerce and Public Works. Count d'Argout has received it with an interest which we ought to acknowledge with gratitude.

Chapter One [PP. 38–52]

1. These cells were or are still thirty in number, in the Walnut Street Prison.

2. See notices of the original and successive efforts to improve the discipline of the prison at Philadelphia, and to reform the Criminal Code of Pennsylvania by Roberts Vaux.

3. See *Des Prisons de Philadelphie par un Européen,* (*La Rochefoucauld-Liancourt*) *l'an* IV., *de la Republique,* Paris.

4. In 1804 the erection of the first penitentiary in Baltimore was decreed and in 1809 a general reform of the criminal laws, in accordance with a new system of imprisonment, took place. The system of absolute isolation in certain cases, was not adopted in the Charlestown (Massachusetts) prison until June 21, 1811. In New Jersey it has been put into practice since 1797. In 1820 a law was passed in New Jersey, which decreed solitary confinement, not exceeding a fourth part of the imprisonment, with labor, to which the convict would have been formerly sentenced, for arson, murder, rape, blasphemy, perjury, burglary, forgery, etc.

5. See "Report to the Legislature by the Comptroller of the State of New York, March 2, 1819." "Fifth Report of the Boston Prison Discipline Society," pp. 412, 423, 454. See also "Report on the Prisons of Connecticut and Massachusetts."

6. The Auburn Prison, i. e. the southern wing, built in 1816–1818 contained sixty-one cells, and twenty-eight rooms, each of which afforded room for from eight to twelve convicts.

7. Cherry Hill is the new penitentiary of Philadelphia, put into operation in 1829.

8. On April 2, 1821, the legislature of New York charged the director of Auburn to select a class of criminals, the most hardened, and to lock them up in solitary cells, night and day, without interruption and without labor. On December 25, 1821, a sufficient number of cells was completed, and eighty criminals were placed in them.

Judge Spencer of Canandaigua, one of the most distinguished criminal lawyers of the state of New York, was a member of a committee, which reported on this decree of the legislature. In its report, it is recommended that the convicts ought to be classed according to their morality; that the hardened villains should be subject to solitary and uninterrupted confinement; and those who follow next in the scale of crime, should be, part of the time, subject to the same punishment, and during the rest of their imprisonment, should have permission to work; the less depraved would have the right to work the whole day.

9. This was in the year 1822, which followed directly after experiments had been made respecting solitary confinement without labor. Judge Powers, agent and keeper of the state prison at Auburn, relates what happened in the following terms:

During the year preceding January 1823, there was an average of about 220 convicts in prison. From the physician's report of that year to the inspectors, it appears that the average number of sick in the hospital was between 7 and 8. That there were 10 deaths, 7 by consumption, 5 of which were from among the solitary convicts. The physician speaks of convicts coming into the hospital from the cells, with difficulty of respiration, pain in the breast, etc., and concludes his report as follows: "It is a generally received and acknowledged opinion, that sedentary life, no matter in what form, disposes to debility, and consequently to local disease. It may be produced in the study or the prison; in the nursery and the college; or in any other place where muscular exertion is restrained. If we review the mental cases of disease, we shall probably find, that sedentary life in the prison, as it calls into aid the debilitating passions of melancholy, grief, etc., rapidly hastens the progress of pulmonary disease." From the order and cleanliness of the prison, we have no reason to conclude that any atmospheric cause reigns within its walls, calculated to produce serious disease; but confinement operates upon the existing germ of diseases, and hastens the progress of all those that must have otherwise terminated in death.

10. Public opinion in the United States attributes almost universally to Mr. Elam Lynds the creation of the system finally adopted in the Auburn prison. This opinion is also that of Messrs. Hopkins and Tibbits, charged, in 1826, to inspect the Auburn prison, and of Mr. Livingston. See his "Introductory Report to the Code of Prison Discipline, Philadelphia Edition," 1827, p. 10. We have found this opinion contested only in a letter addressed by Mr. Powers to Mr. Livingston in 1829.

11. In 1823, there were in Auburn but 380 cells. On April 12, 1824, the legislature ordered the construction of 62 more cells.

12. The manner in which Mr. Elam Lynds has built Sing Sing, would undoubtedly meet with little credit, were it not a recent fact, known by everyone in the United States. In order to understand it, it is necessary to know all the resources which an energetic mind may find in the new discipline of American prisons. If the reader is desirous of forming an idea of the character of Mr. Elam Lynds, and of his opinion on the penitentiary system, he has only to read the Conversation which we had with him, and which we felt obliged to give at length.

13. I shall show, in a note further on, that houses of refuge were first established in Germany, at least in modern times. But the founders of the New York house of refuge, it is nevertheless true, were unacquainted with their existence in Germany, and were led to this re-invention by the imperious wants of their own community.

14. This prison is at present in a degree abandoned; the cells destined for solitary confinement, are open to all convicts, who are at liberty to communicate with each other; we found sixty-four in the prison; the only thing which was defective in the system — absence of labor — has been retained. The convicts, with the exception of a very few, are entirely idle, because there is no workshop for united labor. In spite of the material defects of the establishment, something better might be done, on our opinion; but the directors of the prison are disgusted with the bad disposition of the place, and as for the system, it not having had the expected success, public attention is not any longer directed towards it. In a government where power is nowhere exerted, only those things are undertaken which interest public opinion, and which, consequently, give fame or profit to those who take part in them. The penitentiary of Philadelphia is conducted by individuals of great merit; that of Pittsburgh, already forgotten, finds agents of but ordinary capacity for its direction.

15. Not only in the Auburn prison, solitary confinement without labor, produced fatal effects on the mind and body of the prisoners. The prisons of Maryland, Maine, Virginia, and New Jersey, did not obtain happier results. In the latter prison, ten individuals are mentioned as having been killed by solitary confinement. In Virginia, when the governor ceased to pardon convicts, it was never the case that any one of them survived an attack of disease.

16. The Boston Prison Discipline Society was established in 1826. From that time to the present, i. e. during six years, it has spent $17,498.19, of which $15,681 were given by charitable persons. Mr. L. Dwight is of the greatest importance to the society; for, with indefatigable zeal, he collects all possible documents for the purpose of enlightening public opinion; shunning no fatigue; visiting good and bad prisons; pointing out the defects of the one, and the advantages of the other; the ameliorations which have been effected or such as ought to be introduced. He labors without interruption for the reform of prisons.

The reports published by this society are like an authentic book, in which all abuses and mistakes of the penitentiary system are registered, while at the same time all happy results are stated.

This society, which is convinced that religious instructions is the basis of the whole system of reform of prisons, has supported, during six years, from its own funds, ministers in the prisons of

Auburn, Sing Sing, Wethersfield, Lamberton, (New Jersey) and Charlestown.

The sum spent already for this object is $4,272.29.

17. The law which orders labor in the solitary cells, is of the date of April 23, 1829.

It happens by no means infrequently in the United States, that the true character of the Philadelphia penitentiary is not understood. Some take it to be the same with the former Walnut street prison, so much extolled in spite of its defects, and praise or blame it accordingly; others believe still that no labor is introduced, and attack it violently on that account.

18. It is truly remarkable, that the penal law, and that which regulates the mode of its execution, i.e. the system of imprisonment, form but one whole. This way of proceeding is logical and wise. In fact, the sanction of a punishment is in its execution. The judgment which condemns a convict is but a principle, an idea, if its execution does not make it something material. The law, therefore, which regulates this execution, is as important as that which ordains the principle; this is the reason why all laws decreeing imprisonment, ought to state carefully how this punishment is to be inflicted. This the legislature of Pennsylvania has done.

19. The penitentiary of Massachusetts was organized in 1829: that of Maryland in January, 1830; those of Tennessee and Kentucky were erected at the same period. The prison of Vermont has not yet been entirely completed. As to Maine, we consider its prison as established on the Auburn system, though, in principle, it was intended for solitary confinement without labor.

20. Mr. Charles Lucas, who has published a much esteemed work on the penitentiary system, has fallen into the mistake here mentioned.

"Two systems," he says, "present themselves, one belonging exclusively to the old world, the other to the new. The former is the system of transportation pursued by Great Britain and Russia; the second is the penitentiary system established in all the states of the Union."

". . . The penitentiary system," he says, in another passage, "which Caleb Lownes created in 1791 in Pennsylvania, from where it extended almost simultaneously in all the states of the Union."

21. In Ohio, New Hampshire, and some other states, there is, indeed, a system of imprisonment; but it is a bad system, and not a penitentiary system.

22. The place for convicted criminals in New Orleans cannot be called a prison: it is a horrid sink, in which they are thronged together, and which is fit only for those dirty animals found here together with the prisoners. It must be observed that those who are detained here are not slaves: it is the prison for persons free in the ordinary course of life. It seems, however, that the necessity of a reform in the prisons is felt in Louisiana; the governor of that state said to us, that he would not cease to ask the legislature for funds for this object. It seems equally certain that the system of imprisonment in Ohio is about to be entirely changed.

23. In general the Southern states are in respect to prisons as well as to all other things, far behind those of the North. In some of them, the reform of prison discipline is by no means asked for by public opinion. Quite recently the penitentiary system has been abolished in Georgia, after having been established a year before.

24. As soon as the law of March 30, 1831, shall be executed in Pennsylvania, this state will have the most complete system of imprisonment which ever existed in the United States. This law orders the erection of a prison on the plan of solitary confinement, destined for indicted persons, debtors, witnesses, and prisoners, convicted for a short term of imprisonment.

25. The prison of Blackwell's Island near New York, recently erected, is the only one which has been built for prisoners convicted of small offenses.

26. Prisons were observed, which included persons convicted of the worst crimes; and a remedy has been applied where the greatest evil appeared; other prisons, where the same evil exists, but where it makes less fearful ravages, have been forgotten; yet to neglect the less vicious, in order to labor only for the reform of great and hardened criminals, is the same as if only the most infirm were attended to in a hospital; and, in order to take care of patients, perhaps incurable, those who might be easily restored to health, were left without any attention. The defect, which we mention here, is felt in America by some of her most distinguished men.

Mr. Edward Livingston attacks this defect with great force. "After condemnation, there can be no association but of the guilty with the guilty; but, in the preliminary imprisonment, guilt is associated with innocence."

In order to show, still more clearly, the bad effects of so defective a system of imprisonment, for individuals indicted, Mr.

Livingston presents a table of persons arrested, tried, acquitted, or convicted at New York, from 1822 to 1826, inclusive. It results from this table, that four-fifths of the persons arrested in New York, for supposed crimes or offenses, and thrown, as such, into a prison, expecting the session of the court, have been acknowledged as innocent, partly by the police magistrates, partly by the grand jury, or after trial. We have met with none, in the United States, who were more afflicted by the bad state of the houses of arrest, than Mr. Riker, recorder of the city of New York—a magistrate of rare merit and great virtue, who connects with much knowledge, great experience in criminal affffairs.

27. There are no prisons to shut up slaves: imprisonment would cost too much! Death, the whips, exile, cost nothing! Moreover, in order to exile slaves, they are sold, which yields profit.

28. We comprise in this number, the crimes against the federal government, that of treason against the union, piracy, and robbing the mail.

29. The laws of the latter state also pronounce imprisonment for life in seven different cases.

30. A law of Connecticut orders a mother's hiding the death of her infant, to be punished with public exhibition of the mother with a cord round her neck.

A law of Massachusetts punished fornication with a fine, and adds that if the convicted individual shall not pay the fine within twenty-four hours after conviction, ten stripes with the whip, shall be inflicted upon him. Blasphemy, according to the laws of the same state, is punished with pillory and stripes. Forgery in Rhode Island is punished with the pillory. During this exhibition, a piece of each ear of the convict is to be cut off, and he is to be branded with a *C* (counterfeiting). After all this, he undergoes an imprisonment not exceeding six years.

31. For instance, a law of the State of Delaware orders for a single crime the fine of $10,000.

32. The laws of Delaware pronounce death against six different crimes, (capital crimes against the United States not included). They punish forgery thus: the convict is sentenced to a fine, the pillory, and three months solitary confinement; at the expiration of this punishment he wears on his back, for not less than two, and not more than five years, the letter *F* (forgery) in scarlet color, on his dress; this letter must be six inches long, and two inches wide.

Poisoning is thus punished: The convict may be sentenced to a fine of $10,000, one hour's exhibition at the pillory, and to be publicly whipped; he must receive sixty stripes, "well laid on"; he then goes for four years into prison, after which, he is sold as a slave, for a time not exceeding fourteen years.

Another heavy punishment pronounced for an offense comparatively slight is, twenty-one stripes for a pretended sorcerer or magician. In New Jersey, every person reconvicted for murder, rape, arson, theft, forgery, and sodomy, is punished with death.

33. The brand is placed in the United States, generally on the forehead. In the month of June, 1829, prisoners, who had been recommitted, were yet marked on the arm, when their imprisonment expired; the words *Massachusetts State Prison* were tattooed on the arm. June 12, 1829, this custom was abolished.

34. We do not deny to society the right to punish with death. We believe even that this punishment is, in certain cases, indispensable to the support of social order. But we believe that as soon as the law punishes with death without absolute necessity, it becomes useless cruelty, and an obstacle to the penitentiary system, the object of which is, to reform those whose life society spares.

35. In the United States, the "heads of society" are always far advanced on the path of reform: the rest of the social body, composing the mass of the population, follows generally the movement, though at a distance; and, if it be intended to lead it too far, stops quite short. It is thus that the Quakers have not been able to procure the abolition of capital punishment in Pennsylvania; its abolition, in cases of willful murder, being repugnant to the opinions of the mass: the same would take place in other states, the most enlightened in the Union, if the attempt should be made to abolish it in cases for which public opinion considered it necessary. The legislatures of the various states do nothing but what seems right to the majority; and if, in advance of public opinion, they should attempt innovations, the want of which was not yet felt, they not only would expose themselves to the loss of public favor, but also to seeing their work destroyed the next year.

36. Among the philosophers of the United States, who call for the abolition of capital punishment, Mr. Edward Livingston must be distinguished. He does not dispute the right of society to take away the life of certain of its members; he only maintains that this fearful punishment, which, without remedy, may strike an innocent person, does in general not produce the expected effect, and that it can be efficiently supplanted by punishments less rigorous, which produce less violent, but more durable impressions. Put upon this ground, the question is not solved, but brought to its true point.

Chapter Two [PP. 55–78]

1. Kentucky, Tennessee, Maine, Vermont, have also adopted this system, but so recently, that they cannot yet afford useful information.

2. The substance of this note is, that some have reproached solitary confinement with injustice, because it affects an individual whose mind has been cultivated, much more than him, who, without any education, has remained in a kind of brutal condition, but this inequality is the effect of every punishment. All infamous punishments are more cruel to one of higher social standing, than to him who has lived obscurely. One with a lively imagination suffers more than another of dull fancy. Indians cannot long endure privation of liberty; yet would this be any reason for abolishing imprisonment in a society where some Indians happened to reside?

3. Without speaking of the monstrous intercourse of convicts during night, it suffices to say, that the conversation of criminals in a prison, is solely upon crimes they have committed or intend to commit, after the expiration of their punishment. In such conversations, each boasts of his misdeeds, and all dispute greater villains, and the blackest individual among them becomes a type of depravity for the others.

All who have visited the prisons of France will acknowledge the truth of this picture. Mr. Louis Dwight gives a multitude of facts, in the Report of the Boston Prison Discipline Society, which proves that we are yet below truth in this exposition.

For the rest, the contagion of prisons and the uselessness of classifications, are two points well established in the United States. Mr. Livingston expresses himself on this point in the following terms:

> and it became evident that no reform could be expected, while it was suffered to exist. Classification had been tried in England, and partially here, but it was found to be an incomplete remedy — that system could only be perfected by individual seculsion: because, even when the class was reduced to two, one of them would generally be found qualified to corrupt the other; and if the rare case should occur, of two persons who had arrived at the same precise point of depravity, and the

rarer circumstance of the keeper's discernment being successfully employed in associating them, their approximation would
increase the common stock of guilt.

4. The Baltimore system is that of Geneva. In the latter place,
silence has been considered a cruel pain, which man has not a
right to impose upon his fellow creature. In order to be humane
toward prisoners, they are allowed to corrupt each other.

The right of society is contested: why? Society has a right to
fetter the arm which has committed murder, and should it not
have a right to stifle the voice which makes itself heard merely
in order to corrupt? We also hear of the rights of men! But is
it time to speak of the rights of liberty after the individual has
been thrown into prison?

5. We have met with the greatest kindness in visiting this
penitentiary. Mr. Samuel Wood, warden of the prison, and a
gentleman of rare merit, had given orders that we should always
be admitted, whether he were present or not. All the subordinate
officers had been instructed to open any cell for us, and to allow
us to have free intercourse with its inmate. Mr. Wood often said:
"We have no other interest than that of truth. If there is anything defective in our prison, it is important that we should
know it."

6. All said to us that Sunday, the day of rest, was to them
much longer than the whole week together.

7. Mr. Elam Lynds expresses himself, in a note which he has
given us, thus, on this subject:

Obedience to the law of society is all that is asked from a
good citizen. It is this which the criminal ought to learn: and
you teach him much better by practice than by theory. If you
lock up in a cell, a person convicted of a crime, you have no
control over him: you act only upon his body. Instead of this,
set him to work, and oblige him to do everything he is ordered
to do; you thus teach him to obey, and give him the habits of
industry; now I ask, is there anything more powerful than the
force of habit? If you have succeeded in giving to a person the
habits of obedience and labor, there is little chance of his ever
becoming a thief.

Convicts in solitary cells, who ask for labor, do not so because they love labor, but because isolation is so tedious to
them.

8. See letter of E. Livingston to Roberts Vaux, 1828. There
are undoubtedly some instances which prove the infraction of
the rule of silence. This is so true that in each of the prisons

some convicts had been punished for it and a certain number of infractions always remain undiscovered. But the question is not whether there are some cases of contravention; the point to be examined is whether these infractions of silence are of a nature to destroy the order of the establishment and to prevent the reformation of the prisoners.

9. It is impossible to see the prison of Sing Sing, and the system of working established there, without being struck with surprise and fear. Though the order is perfectly kept, it is apparent that it rests upon a fragile basis: it is owing to a power always active, but which must be reproduced every day, if the whole discipline is not to be endangered. The safety of the keepers is incessantly menaced. In presence of such dangers, avoided so skillfully, but with so much difficulty, it seems to us impossible not to apprehend some future catastrophe. For the rest, the dangers, to which the officers of the prison are exposed, form, for the present, one of the surest guarantees of order; every one of them sees that the preservation of his life depends upon it.

10. He is indifferently called *warder, keeper, agent* or *superintendent.*

11. It is generally thought that it is advantageous that the inspectors should not change too often, and that they should not be all renewed at the same time. In Boston, they are appointed for four years. In Philadelphia, the inspectors of the penitentiary are exempt from the militia service, from being jurymen, and overseers of the poor. Until the year 1820, there were five inspectors of the Auburn prison: this number was found to be too large, and it was reduced from that time to three.

12. At Auburn, the security is $25,000. The same at Sing Sing.

13. Each inspector receives $100. In Baltimore, the committee of superintendence receive annually $1,144.

14. The report of the inspectors of Wethersfield states, that little reliance can be placed on any system of regulations, if there is not a committee who assures itself of the execution of the rules by frequent personal inspection.

15. Though the salaries of the officers of American prisons are rather high, they are much less than they at first appear. The various arts and occupations in that country are so profitable, that every individual endowed with some capacity, finds easily a more profitable career, than that offered by the administration of prisons. And men like Mr. Samuel Wood would not be found at the head of American penitentiaries, were they not influenced by a nobler sentiment than that of pecuniary interest.

16. Each cell is ventilated by a proper contrivance, and contains a *fosse d'aisance,* which by its construction is perfectly odorless. It is necessary to have seen these cells of the Philadelphia prison, and to have passed whole days in it, in order to form an exact idea of their cleanliness and the purity of the air which one breathes there.

17. The cells at Auburn are much smaller than those at Philadelphia; they are seven feet long and three and a half wide. A ventilator keeps the air pure.

18. For much stronger reasons, every game at hazard is prohibited: the regulations are uniform on this point and faithfully executed.

19. We only indicate here the most important points of which the order, discipline, and government of the penitentiaries are composed. In order to know the details of the established rules in the new prisons, the division of the day, the nature of the labor, the duties of the officers and of the prisoners, the nature of the authorized punishments, the obligations imposed upon the contractors, etc., we refer to the regulations of the Connecticut State Prison (Wethersfield) given in the Appendix.

20. The system of the American prisons, which is to make the labor of the prisoners as productive as possible, is perfectly correct in that country where the price of labor is so high.

No fear is entertained, that the establishment of manufactories in the prisons will injure the free working classes. In truth it is generally the interest of a nation, that the mass of production should constantly increase, because prices fall in proportion as quantity increases, and the consumer, paying less, grows rich by it. Nevertheless, in countries where the abundance of production has reduced the prise of manufactured articles to its lowest term, production cannot be increased without exposing the working class to injury. It may be said that production has its lowest price, when the gain of the workman allows him to provide for the merest necessaries of life. If wages have sunk to this point, manufactories in prisons are much more dangerous than the erection of manufactories in society. Indeed it is not a mere competition with which the establishments of free workmen have, in such case, to contend. The prison works, not in order to gain, but to diminish its expenses; it lowers the prices at pleasure, without endangering its existence. If the price of articles depreciate, the contractor pays less for the labor of the prisoners, and the government must pay more for their support. On the other hand, the ordinary workman can live only when he makes money; and if the price of the article becomes so depreciated that it yields no profit, either for the workman or for the owner of the manufactory, the establishment must cease.

If, therefore, manufactories are established in prisons, a competition against the industry of free men takes place, which becomes fatal, if the latter are reduced to the alternative of stopping their work or working at a loss. To resume, the work of free people must cease if it yield no profit; while manufactures in prison, supported by government, stand against all chances, whether they yield much or little; because their object is not to gain as much as possible, but to lose as little as possible. The capital of a free manufactory is limited, and cannot stand against all chances; the capital of a prison — the public treasury — is infinite.

They were, undoubtedly, these considerations, which have repeatedly induced the British government to stop the labor of prisoners, and to invent "treadmills" — machines which work without producing.

Looked upon merely as regards the interest of the prisoner, these machines fulfil but half the object for which the prisoner is made to work. They occupy and preserve him, indeed, against the dangers of idleness, but if he leaves the prison, of what use is it to him to know the art of turning the treadmill? The treadmill, therefore, is absolutely bad for the prisoner; but the interest of society is also to be taken into consideration. The difficulty for a government to decide on this point is very great. It is extremely arduous to determine the moment when manufactories, or any productive labor, may be established without detriment to free, industrious citizens. As it is also a delicate question of equity to decide to what point the interest of the state, and the moral situation of the criminal, may be taken into consideration, without oppressing the honest and free member of society. Absolute theories on these questions are useless; their solution depends entirely upon a perfect knowledge of the state of things in each separate country. In one case, however, the treadmill appears to us absolutely bad; that is, if it is used as a productive machine. It increases production, without teaching the convict any useful art.

However this may be, the special question on the treadmill is, that of labor in general, so grave for several countries of Europe, and presenting no difficulty to the United States. In that country the treadmill would be conducive to no good whatever.

On the contrary, as production is yet in the United States

below the wants of consumption, it is the interest of society to increase production, and to teach the prisoners a useful art, by which they may support themselves at some future period.

21. The arts pursued in the Philadelphia penitentiary, are weaving, shoemaking, tailoring, joiner's work, etc.

22. In the *maison centrale de detention* at Melun, a considerable library exists for the use of the convicts. It belongs to the contractor, who lets the books for a certain sum. The reader may judge from this fact, of the nature of the books.

23. It is probable, that if the prison of Sing Sing is finished, a great variety of professions will be taught in it. The beautiful marble quarries on the spot, and the neighborhood of the Hudson River which offer so convenient an opportunity of transportation, will furnish, for a long time to come, sufficient occupation to the prisoners; but will the danger of allowing a thousand criminals to work in the open field, never be cause of fear?

At Auburn and Baltimore, the work consists chiefly in weaving, shoemaking, joinery, cooperage, locksmith's work.

24. See Article 4 of Section I of the regulations of the Connecticut prison in Appendix.

25. The law of the State of New York does not permit the superintendent to give more than three dollars to the convict at the time of his leaving the prison, but he must give him clothes, which must not cost more than ten dollars. At Philadelphia the superintendent may give four dollars to the liberated criminal. At Boston he is authorized to give five dollars and a decent suit of clothes worth about twenty dollars. The inspectors of the Massachusetts prison seem to regret that so much is given to the convicts whose terms have expired.

26. Generally speaking, the most dangerous moment for a delivered convict, is that when he leaves the prison. Not unfrequently they spend their whole *pécule* within the first twenty-four hours of their liberty. In Geneva, to redress this evil, the whole *pécule* is not delivered to the convict when he leaves the jail. It is sent to him to the place of his new residence. The same is now done in France with the convicts who leave the bagnes and *maisons centrales*. This is a wise measure, which it is important to preserve.

27. The convict would be willing enough to work as much as is necessary in order to *désennuyer* himself, and to exercise his body, and to remain idle when he felt himself fatigued. But this is not allowed, and justly so; he must always work or not at all. If he refuses to work in a line he has begun, he is placed in a dark cell. He has therefore the choice between constant leisure in darkness, or uninterrupted labor in his cell. His choice is never long in suspense, and he always prefers labor.

28. No register is kept of disciplinary punishments. We have been told that about five or six whippings (among one thousand prisoners) take place every day at Sing Sing. At Auburn, though very frequent in the beginning, they are now very rare. One of the officers of this prison said to us: "I remember having seen, at the beginning, nineteen prisoners whipped in less than an hour. Since the discipline was well established, I once had no occasion to resort to the whip a single time for four months and a half."

29. In 1828, a revolt broke out in Newgate (New York) and could be subdued only by firing upon the rebel convicts. But, after their reduction, a hundred of them refused to work; they were put in solitary confinement without labor; these means, however, remained without effect for seventy days; thus two months' labor was lost. The superintendent of Newgate where solitary confinement with reduction of labor was the only disciplinary measure, said on this subject: "The actual way of punishing, whatever may be its duration, weakens the convict, without curbing him at all."

30. See our conversation with Mr. Elam Lynds in Appendix.

31. The law of the state of New York, allowed formerly the keepers to lay on thirty-nine stripes, and no more. The revised statutes say, "The officers of the prison shall use all suitable means to defend themselves, to enforce the observance of discipline, etc." The law of Connecticut allows stripes in positive terms: "Moderate whipping, not exceeding ten stripes for any one offense." Twenty stripes might therefore be inflicted, for two offenses, on the same individual. The law of Maryland also permits stripes explicitly, the maximum of which must be not more than thirteen.

In a trial of an assistant keeper at Auburn, accused of having whipped a convict, Judge Walworth said, in charging the jury at Cayuga, at the Court of Oyer and Terminer, September, 1826:

> That confinement with labor merely, had no terrors for the guilty. That the labor which the human body was capable of performing, without endangering its health, was but little more than many of the virtuous laboring class of the community daily and voluntarily performed for the support and maintenance of their families. That to produce reformation in the guilty, or to restrain the vicious from the prepetration of crime by the terrors of punishment, it was absolutely necessary that

the convict should feel his degraded situation, should feel that he was actually doing penance for his wilful violation of the laws of his country. That he must, in his own person, be made to feel the difference which should exist between the situation of the upright and honest freeman, who labors for his daily bread, and the vile and degraded convict, who, by fraud or robbery, has deprived that honest freeman, or his family, of the hard-earned rewards of his industry. That mistaken or misapplied sympathy for such offenders, was injustice to the virtuous part of the community. That the system of discipline adopted by the inspectors of the prison, under the sanction of the laws, was well calculated to have the desired effect of reforming the less vicious offenders, and of deterring others from the commission of crime, by the severity of punishment inflicted, and that, too, in the best possible way. A mode of punishment, where comparatively little bodily suffering is felt, and the greatest severity of the punishment is inflicted upon the culprit, through the medium of the mind. That it was, however, through terror of bodily suffering alone, that the proper effect upon the mind of the convict was produced; and therefore the necessity of a rigid enforcement of the prison discipline upon every convict, by the actual infliction of bodily suffering, if he would not otherwise submit to the rules.

32. We will mention here a remarkable fact, which proves the efficiency of this discipline. On 23 October a fire broke out in the Auburn prison. It consumed a part of the buildings belonging to the prison. As it became dangerous even to the lives of the prisoners, the latter were let out of their cells, but the order was not disturbed for a moment. All assisted zealously to extinguish the fire, and not one of them attempted to profit by this circumstance to escape.

33. Messrs. Allen, Hopkins, and Tibbets, inspectors of the Auburn prison, express themselves, on the necessity of investing the superintendent with discretionary powers, thus:

The men upon whom the responsibility of the safekeeping of the convicts rests, ought to possess the authority to punish them, if they neglect or refuse to obey the laws of the establishment.

For the proper exercise of this power, they are, and ought to be, amenable to the laws. But we understand it to be a principle of the common law of this state, as it certainly is of reason and common sense, that every keeper of a prison must have such power of personal correction.

The condition of a prisoner, is that of personal restraint. As the prisoners are always the most numerous, and have, therefore, the advantage of physical force, they must take the mastery whenever they think expedient, if there is no power of punishment; or when that power is fettered or imperfect, their submission will be proportionably incomplete.

Upon this method of governing, our opinions are entirely decided and unanimous, and we hesitate not to state to the legislature our settled conviction, that the government of felons in a prison must be absolute, and the control over them must be perfect. The principal keeper must be a man of firmness, discretion, and vigilance, and he ought to be the responsible person in all matters relative to the conduct and safe-keeping of the prisoners. Without this, there can be no discipline nor economy. Every consideration requires this; the safety of the lives of the officers, and of the prisoners themselves, requires it. It is indispensable to economy, and to profitable labor; and if there can be any hope of reformation, it must not be where the prisoner stands upon his rights, and exacts conditions; but where he is brought to a sense of his degradation, and feels the sadness incident to dependence and servitude, and becomes willing to receive any indulgence as a boon, and instruction, advice, and admonition, as a favor.

It is proper to remark, that we have been informed of complaints which had been made against the officers of the Auburn prison, and too great severity of discipline. Some of us took pains to investigate the grounds of those complaints, and sought interviews with some respectable persons who had supported them, and with some members of a grand jury of Cayuga county, before whom the subject had been brought. In one instance, a convict had called out to the prisoners in the mess-room to rise. He was instantly struck down by the keeper attending, and, we believe, struck after he was down. In no case have the grand jury thought proper to interfere, though the subject has been more than once before them; and we believe that the corporal punishment now inflicted at the Auburn prison, is not more than is requisite to preserve proper obedience.

It has been often discussed in the United States, whether underkeepers ought to refer to the superintendent, before they inflict corporal punishment, or whether they shall have the power to punish "on the spot." The inspectors of the Auburn prison have discussed this question in one of their reports, and it is their opinion, that the inferior officers ought to be invested with the power in question. "The danger of abuse, is an evil much less than the relaxation of discipline produced by want of authority." This opinion has prevailed.

34. In Boston the regulations are likewise in writing, and the duties of the officers are traced in it. However, these provisions are directory only: the superintendent and the sub-director are invested not the less with a discretionary power.

35. Mr. Elam Lynds, with whom we have had numerous conversations on this point, has often told us that when the prisoners at Auburn were in constant solitary confinement, a great number of them passed more than half their time in the hospital.

36. At Auburn the prisoners are treated much more severely: in Philadelphia they are much more unhappy. In Auburn, where they are whipped, they die less frequently than in Philadelphia, where, for humanity's sake, they are put in a solitary and sombre cell. The superintendent of Walnut Street Prison, where the disciplinary punishments are mild, told us that he had incessantly to punish the prisoners for infractions of discipline. So that the disciplinary punishments at Walnut Street, milder than those at Auburn, are also more often repeated and more often fatal to the prisoners than are the severe chastisements used in Auburn.

Chapter Three [PP. 80–102]

1. Among the number of estimable philanthropists, who, in our opinion, somewhat deceive themselves on this point, we will mention Mr. Tukerman, of Boston, who hopes that a day will appear, when, all the wicked having been regenerated, prisons will be no longer wanted. It is certain, that, if there were many individuals as ardently devoted to the cause of humanity, his hope would be no chimera. The name of Mr. Tukerman cannot be pronounced without veneration; he is the living personification of benevolence and virtue. A disciple of Howard, he spends his life in doing good, and strives to alleviate all human miseries; though of a feeble body, pale and almost lifeless, yet, if a good act is to be done, he becomes animated, and full of energy. Mr. Tukerman, as we said, perhaps deceives himself on some questions; yet he renders immense services to society. His charity towards the poor of Boston, has given him the authority of their guardian. And, if his kindness for them is extreme, it must not be believed that his severity, whenever just or necessary, is less manifested: the poor love him, because he is their benefactor, and they respect and fear him, because they know the austerity of his virtue. They know that his interest in them depends upon their good conduct. Mr. Tukerman does more for the good order and police of Boston, than all the aldermen and justices of the peace.

2. The inspectors of the Philadelphia prison, signalize in the following terms one of the advantages of solitary confinement:
"Personal vanity, which so often leads a prisoner to value himself upon being regarded by his fellows as a staunch man, there deserts him; for there is no one to applaud, admire, or see him."

3. Respecting the frightful contamination in prisons of the old kind, and the deplorable effects of the false shame of appearing less familiar with crime and immorality than others, we refer the reader to Vidocq's Memoirs.

4. "But from a closer and more intimate view of the subject, I have rather abandoned a hope I once entertained, of the general reformation of offenders through the penitentiary system. I now think that its chief good is in the prevention of crime by the confinement of criminals." (Mr. Niles, former commissioner of the Penitentiary of Maryland, December 22, 1829.)

5. In Boston all are admitted who present themselves.

6. There is no school regularly kept in the Philadelphia prison; but as soon as the inspectors or superintendent discover good dispositions in a prisoner, or, by whatever motive, feel interested in his favor, they bestow more care upon him than on others, and begin by imparting the first elements of instruction. One of the inspectors of the penitentiary, Mr. Bradford, spends much time in this good work.

7. See "Second Report on Penitentiary of Philadelphia," 1831.

8. All the prisoners of one wing of the penitentiary partake, in Philadelphia, of the same sermon: but as the penitentiary will have seven distinct parts, seven consecutive religious instructions would be requisite to be given by the same minister, or else seven ministers be occupied with the same subject at once.

9. The adversaries of Auburn say, that the system of reformation has met there with so little success, that it has been entirely abandoned. It must be admitted that the efforts to regenerate the criminals are not always crowned with success; but it would not be exact to say that reformation is given up at Auburn; we can attest, on the contrary, that the gentlemen who direct the establishment, pursue this end with ardor.

10. Mr. Barrett receives a salary of $200.

11. In the evening when they have returned to their cells, after the day's work is over.

12. We must say, that at Sing Sing the school, though held with care, appeared to us to be restrained to too small a number. The number of convicts admitted to the Sunday school varies from sixty to eighty, a small proportion to one thousand convicts. The direction of this establishment, seems to be too little of a mental character; a circumstance caused undoubtedly by the fact that the superintendent and his inferior officers are solely occupied with maintaining the external order, which is constantly in danger. We were witnesses of a fact which proves how great the effect of the school at Sing Sing might be, if more attention were paid to it. A poor Negro, who had learned to read in prison, recited by heart to us, two pages of the Bible, which he had studied during the leisure hours in the week, and committed not the least mistake in the recitation.

13. See Conversation with Mr. Elam Lynds in the Appendix.

14. Mr. Smith himself said to us, that he was very cautious as to external signs of repentance in the convicts; he added, that in his eyes the best proof of the sincerity of a convict was his not desiring to leave the prison.

15. It is an opinion pretty general in the United States, that the number of crimes increases more rapidly than the population, even in the states of the North. This is a mistake, which rests on a fact misunderstood — the constantly increasing crowd of prisoners. It is true, that, on January 30, 1832, there were 646 convicts, i. e. 96 more than cells at Auburn. At Sing Sing, during the same period, the cells a 1000 in number, were not sufficient. In each of these prisons, it was necessary to double [place two prisoners in] a certain number of cells. This is destructive to the whole penitentiary system. However quickly new prisons are erected, the number of convicts increases still faster. The increase of criminals is owing to three principal causes: (1) The population of the state of New York increases with unparalleled rapidity; (2) The revised statutes have increased the number of cases in which the prisoner is sent to the state prison (penitentiary); (3) infinitely less pardons are granted of late, than formerly. This last cause alone would be sufficient to explain the progressive accumulation of convicts in the prisons of Sing Sing and Auburn.

16. We have met, however, with extreme kindness, in the various authorities, and an extraordinary readiness to afford us all the information we wished for. Mr. Flagg, secretary of state at Albany, Mr. Riker, recorder at New York, Messrs. M'Ilvaine and Roberts Vaux in Philadelphia, Mr. Gray in Boston, and all the inspectors of the new prisons, have furnished it, with a great mass of valuable documents.

Mr. Riker has procured for us the general statement of crimes committed in the whole state of New York during the year 1830. This is a very interesting document, but we have returns for one year only.

17. We speak here of the old prisons of Pennsylvania and Maryland. The new penitentiaries of these states are yet too recently established to occupy us here with their effects.

18. The freed person commits more crimes than the slave, for a very simple reason; because, becoming emancipated, he has to provide for himself, which, during his bondage, he was not obliged to do. Brought up in ignorance and brutality, he has been accustomed to work like a machine, all the motions of which are caused by an external power. His mind has remained utterly undeveloped. His life has been passive, thoughtless, and unthinking. In this state of moral annihilation, he commits few crimes: why should he steal, since he cannot be a proprietor? The day when liberty is granted to him, he receives an instrument, which he does not know how to use, and with which he wounds, if not kills himself. His actions, involuntary when he was a slave, become now disorderly: judgment cannot guide him, for he has not exercised it: he is improvident, because he never has learned to think of futurity. His passions, not progressively developed, assail him with violence. He is the prey of wants, which he does not know how to provide for, and thus obliged to steal, or to die. Hence so many free Negroes in the prisons, and hence their greater mortality than that of slaves. Must we conclude that it is wrong to emancipate slaves? Certainly not; as little as we must preserve an evil forever, because it exists. Only it seems to us necessary to acknowledge, that the transition from slavery to liberty, produces a state more fatal than favorable to the freed generation, and of which posterity alone can reap the fruits.

19. In order to know all the advantages afforded by statistics and to the art of making use of them, it is necessary to read the excellent work which Mr. Guerry has just published under the title of *Statistique Morale de la France* — Paris, 1832.

20. With us, besides the number of convictions, the number of accusations and prosecutions, not followed by conviction, is ascertained; also the proportion of crimes committed, to the convictions, is very nearly known. In the United States, it would be very difficult to obtain a document of this nature; first, no officer is charged by government to draw it up; and, second, it may be said, that, to a certain point, the basis itself of such a document, does not exist.

Constituted as our judicial police is, it is customary to state the crime as soon as it is committed, and then to search for the author, who is condemned, though he may be absent. In the United States, another proceeding takes place; nobody is condemned, if not present at the trial; and, as long as the criminal is not apprehended, little attention is paid to the crime. With us, it would appear, that the crime is prosecuted; in the United States, the criminal. This explains why we know better the number of crimes committed, independently of convictions pronounced upon their authors.

21. This is one of the causes, to which the extraordinary increase of crimes in Connecticut is attributed. It appears to us, indeed, incontestable, that the merited reputation of the excellent penitentiary of Wethersfield, must have contributed to increase the number of convictions. But, it is evident, that this cause is not the only one, since the increase in question is progressive, and anterior by twenty years to the foundation of the penitentiary.

22. We say that in Massachusetts, where there are less convictions, the prisons are bad: *they were bad,* and are not any longer so: we are obliged to speak of the past, because the question here is to appreciate their effects.

23. Great efforts are made in the United States to correct a vice, which is very common — intemperance.

24. Mr. Livingston has expressed this truth more than once and does so with particular energy in his letter to Roberts Vaux, 1828.

25. See Edward Livingston's "Introductory Report to the Code of Prison Discipline," p. 7. See also "Notices of the Original and Successive Efforts to Improve the Discipline of the Prison at Philadelphia and to Reform the Criminal Code of Pennsylvania," by Roberts Vaux, pp. 53–54. See *Du Systeme Penitentiaire en Europe et aux États-Unis,* by Charles Lucas.

26. Those who maintain that the Walnut street prison has really produced the effects generally ascribed to it, answer our objection thus: that the rigors of solitary confinement, and all that accompanies the system of isolation, has a salutary effect not only on the prisoners, but also on all those who fear being sent there. This influence may undoubtedly exist; but it is not the influence of a penitentiary system which reforms the guilty; it is the effect of a punishment, which acts by way of terror; in this point of view, the punishment of death would be the best punishment; now, in the opinion of the enthusiastic partisans of the penitentiary system, the merit of this system is not in its cruelty and terror. It is necessary, therefore, in order to judge of the *penitentiary system*, properly so called, to consider merely the effect it has directly on the reformation of the prisoners. It is remarkable that the system of Walnut street is at present acknowledged as defective, by those even who attribute to it so happy an efficacy.

27. In 1826, it was for the first time attempted to obtain, by means of circulars directed to postmasters, sheriffs, attorney generals, etc. information respecting the morality and conduct of convicts, after the expiration of their imprisonment in Auburn. This correspondence lasted until 1829, when it was dropped; it was considered too expensive, and its results too uncertain.

28. There are more crimes of a grave nature committed in France, but the whole number of crimes is less than in America.

29. In using the term "first conviction" above, we mean as it respects this prison only; there are nearly twenty who have been in other prisons.

30. The superintendent of the prison at Columbus (Ohio) says in his report: "of sixty-five convicts, who are in the penitentiary of Ohio, fifteen are recommitted convicts. I know that fifteen or twenty individuals, formerly imprisoned in this prison, are at this moment in the prisons of Kentucky, Virginia, or Pennsylvania."

Chapter Four [PP. 103–111]

1. The outer wall of the Philadelphia prison alone cost $200,000; yet it is of all prisons that which requires least a high enclosing wall, because each prisoner is isolated in his cell, which he never leaves.

2. In comparing the Philadelphia penitentiary to a castle of the middle ages, we but reproduce a comparison used by the Philadelphia Prison Society, which speaks with praise of this building in the following terms:

This penitentiary is the only edifice in this country, which is calculated to convey to our citizens the external appearance of those magnificent and picturesque castles of the Middle Ages, which contribute so eminently to embellish the scenery of Europe.

3. See Letter of Judge Welles of Wetherfield (in the Appendix) in which the estimate of a prison for five hundred prisoners is to be found. This estimate is probably incomplete;

because even the most experienced architects always omit some items. But even if his estimate were doubled, the construction of the penitentiary would still be half as expensive only as our prisons.

4. Letter of Judge Welles in the Appendix.

5. See note twenty of chapter two.

6. We shall show that the penitentiary system in question is less expensive than the old system of prisons. Yet even if the new system should be more expensive for its establishment and support, it would be, perhaps, finally, less onerous to society, if it is true that it has the power of reforming the wicked. A prison system, however economical it may be in appearance, becomes very expensive if it does not correct the majority of the prisoners. Because, as Mr. Livingston has well said: "Discharging an unreformed thief, is tantamount to authorizing a tax of an unlimited amount to be raised on individuals."

7. These accidental causes explain why a day's labor in the prison yields on an average, in Baltimore, twenty-six cents, while at Auburn it produces but fourteen cents. The sale of manufactured articles also incurs sometimes difficulties in Connecticut. With us a day's labor of 17,500 convicts, in the *maisons centrales,* produces but four cents, on an average, a day.

8. The reasons of this difference are: (1) that the contractor is obliged, by his contract, to pay the ignorant and unskilled prisoner as well as him who works with skill and talent, (2) the contractor is not sure that he can sell the article which he causes to be made, and yet he never can interrupt the labor, (3) the day's labor in the prison is shorter than that of a free mechanic: the latter works in winter from six in the morning to eight in the evening, while the prisoner works only from eight in the morning to four in the afternoon, (4) it seems that, at this moment, the contractors, and particularly the one at Auburn, have obtained too favorable conditions. This is one of the reasons why Auburn yields less than Wethersfield and Baltimore. With us, the contractor pays for the prisoner who works for him, a little more than half the wages of a free workman. But this contractor has a general contract, and for a long term.

Chapter Five [PP. 112–114]

1. This number has been furnished to us in the office of the minister of public works, by the division, the chief officer of which is Mr. Labiche. All the documents which we possess relative to the prisons of France, are from the same source.

2. The defect of our *maisons centrales* is not in their government, but in the principle of their organization. Perhaps it would be impossible to turn the actual system to better account. We have seen of late a central prison (that of Melun) where we admired the order of the labor and the outward discipline. The direction of the central prisons is confided to the minister of the interior and to very capable persons. But whatever may be done, prisoners, who have free intercourse with each other, will not be made better, and their mutual corruption will not be prevented.

Chapter Six [PP. 115–131]

1. The prisons have for a long time deserved most of the reproaches made against their physical management. It was therefore not without reason that the abuses and vices, which infected them, were attacked. Consequently, we are far from blaming the efforts of those who have succeeded in correcting the evil; except that, by the side of a wise and moderate philanthrophy, there also exists a zeal which surpasses its end. There are in France prisons in which undoubtedly changes respecting their salubrity are desirable, but in general it may be said that in our prisons the prisoners are as well fed and clothed as they need to be. Every amelioration on this point would become an abuse in the other extreme, not less fatal than that which it was intended to remedy. The task of those who justly called for better clothes and better bread for the prisoners, seems at an end; at present the work of those must commence, who believe that there is in the discipline of prisons a moral part, which ought not to be neglected.

2. The Prison in the street *de la Roquette* near the cemetery *Père Lachaise.*

3. In France, the mean term of wages for a day's labor of all sorts of workmen, may be stated at two francs, fifty centimes; in the United States it is double. This price, which, in Paris, varies from three to four francs, is less by two-thirds in the other cities, except some of the largest, as Lyons, Marseilles, etc. Labor is, therefore, infinitely lower in France than in America.

4. See our Conversation with Mr. E. Lynds in the Appendix.

5. Though but one and the same system ought to be established for all convicts, we can very well conceive that there might be differences in the discipline according to the weight of punishments, whether distinguished by their name or duration: thus prisoners for police offenses might be allowed to save a *pécule,* greater than that granted to convicts sentenced for grave crimes, etc. If we ask for a uniform system, we only wish for the application of the fundamental principles of the penitentiary system to all prisoners — isolation during night and silence during day; and we assert, that these two principles once admitted, the variety of prisons becomes useless.

6. Article 16 of the law of October 6, 1791, decrees: "Every person sentenced to confinement, shall be locked up *alone* in a place, into which daylight shines, without iron or fetters; he shall not have any communication with other convicts or with persons without, as long as his imprisonment lasts." This is exactly the theory of solitary confinement: it is the system of Cherry Hill, (Philadelphia).

7. See Circular of the Minister of the Interior of March 22, 1816 and Ordinance of April 9, 1819.

8. "It must not be concealed that one great reason why crimes are so infrequent in the full employment the whole country offers to those who are willing to labor. At the same time the ordinary rate of wages for a healthy man is sufficient to support him and a family. This is a point which you will not lose sight of in comparing the institutions of America with those of Europe." (Letter of the Attorney General of Maryland, January 30, 1832.)

Chapter Seven [PP. 138–146]

1. We found, when visiting the house of refuge of New York, that more than half of the children, who had been received there up to that time, were in this establishment in consequence of some misfortune. Thus of 513 children, 135 had lost their fathers, 40 their mothers, 67 were orphans, 51 had been pushed on to crime by the notorious misconduct or want of care of their parents. There were 47 whose mothers had married again.

2. The various authorities which may send children to the house of refuge, are: (1) the courts of justice, (2) police officers, (3) commissioners or managers of the alms-house.

The revised statutes of the state of New York declare:

Whenever any person, under the age of sixteen years, shall be convicted of any felony, the court, instead of sentencing such person to imprisonment in a state prison, may order that he be removed to and confined in the house of refuge, established by the society for the reformation of juvenile delinquents in the city of New York; unless notice shall have been received from such society, that there is not room in such house for the reception of further delinquents.

3. The reader sees, that, in the United States, nothing similar exists to what is practiced with us. In the *Maison des Madelonettes,* destined in Paris for young prisoners, discipline is entirely invaded by the contractor. He considers every child as his property and if it is intended to give instruction to the juvenile prisoners, the contractor does not permit it. "I am robbed," he says, "of the time which belongs to me." He regards merely his own interest; that of the children does not concern him. Thus he only thinks how he can turn their labor to the greatest profit. As it requires time to learn a mechanical profession, he rarely takes the trouble to teach it to them; he prefers occupying them with certain manual labors, which require neither skill nor experience, such as making pasteboard, *agraferie*. These labors, productive for him, are of no use to the children, who know no mechanical art when they leave the house.

4. See in Vidocq to what frightful consequences this evil practice leads.

Appendix A [P. 165]

1. In saying this, Mr. Lynds probably alluded to a fact, of which we had been informed a few days before at Sing Sing.

An individual, imprisoned in that penitentiary, had said that he would kill Mr. Lynds, the superintendent of Sing Sing, upon the first opportunity. The latter, informed of the prisoner's resolution, sent for him, made him come into his bedroom, and, without appearing to perceive his agitation, made him shave him. He then dismissed him with these words: "I knew you intended to kill me, but I despise you too much to believe that you would ever be bold enough to execute your design. Single and unarmed, I am always stronger than you are."

INDEX